DATE DUE

DEMCO 38-296

THE EUROPEAN ECONOMY
BETWEEN THE WARS

This publication is based partly on international research carried out between 1989 and 1993 within a scientific network on the *Economic History of Europe Between the Wars*. The network was initiated and supported by the European Science Foundation.

THE EUROPEAN ECONOMY BETWEEN THE WARS

Charles H. Feinstein
Peter Temin
Gianni Toniolo

OXFORD UNIVERSITY PRESS
1997

Mexico City Nairobi Paris Singapore
Taipei Tokyo Toronto

and associated companies in
Berlin Ibadan

Oxford is a trade mark of Oxford University Press

Published in the United States
by Oxford University Press Inc., New York

British Library Cataloguing in Publication Data
Data available

Library of Congress Cataloging-in-Publication Data

Feinstein, C. H.
    The European economy between the wars / Charles H. Feinstein,
Peter Temin, Gianni Toniolo.
    Includes bibliographical references and index.
    1. Europe–Economic conditions—1918–1945. I. Temin, Peter.
II. Toniolo, Gianni, 1942– . III. Title.
    HC240.F418   1997   330.94'051—dc21   96-52312

ISBN 0–19–877480–X
ISBN 0–19–877481–8 (Pbk)

1 2 3 4 5 6 7 8 9 10

Typeset by Best-set Typesetter Ltd., Hong Kong
Printed in Great Britain
on acid-free paper by
Biddles Ltd,
Guildford & King's Lynn

For Anne, Charlotte, and Francesca

Contents

List of Figures, Map, and Tables

Figures

Map

Tables

Introduction

> There is now no possibility of reaching a normal level of production in the near future. Our efforts are directed towards the attainment of more limited hopes. Can we prevent an almost complete collapse of the financial structure of modern capitalism? With no financial leadership left in the world and profound intellectual error as to causes and cures prevailing in the responsible seats of power, one begins to wonder and to doubt.
>
> (Keynes 1932: 71)

Chaos, crisis, and catastrophe are terms which feature prominently in the economic history of inter-war Europe. They are applied to price and money supplies, foreign exchange rates, gold and capital movements, banking systems, and external trade. Early in the period there were several spectacular episodes of hyper-inflation in central and eastern Europe, and many other countries suffered severe though less drastic inflation, and corresponding depreciation of the external value of their currencies.

There was a short-lived post-war boom followed by a slump, and a number of countries experienced serious banking crises in 1920–1. These inflationary and financial problems were a direct consequence of the First World War. So too was the colossal burden of inter-Allied debts, and the attempt of the Allies, particularly France, to extract huge sums in reparations from Germany. The struggle to cope with these enormous obligations was one of the critical factors in the financial instability of the 1920s.

A further aspect of great significance was the widespread belief in financial and political circles that it was essential to return to the pre-war gold standard if the growth and prosperity of the pre-1914 era were to be re-established, whatever the sacrifices their countries would have to make in order to force down wages and prices so that the pre-war value of the currency could be restored. The attempt to achieve this reconstruction of the gold standard dominated the financial policies of Britain, France, Germany, Italy, Belgium, the

Scandinavian countries, Czechoslovakia, and many other central and eastern European nations.

An apparent measure of progress was achieved by the mid-1920s, and confidence and production revived. Improved economic understanding among the major powers was reflected in the acceptance in 1924 of the Dawes Plan for the future payment of reparations. A new measure of political agreement was achieved with the ending of the French occupation of the Ruhr and the signing of the Locarno Pact. A brief interlude of relative stability and economic growth followed, but could not be sustained. In the mid-1920s agricultural producers were hit by falling prices, especially for wheat and sugar, and signs of impending recession were evident in Germany from 1928. The following year saw the beginning of a series of damaging banking panics and failures in Europe, culminating in 1931 in the collapse of the largest Austrian bank, and serious bank crises in Germany and the United States.

The collapse in output and employment in both industrial and primary producing countries combined to create the 'Great Depression', a worldwide cyclical decline of unprecedented intensity and duration. In September 1931 Britain was no longer able to meet its obligations to supply gold to its international creditors, and was forced to abandon the gold standard. Numerous other countries followed her example, and the international economic system established at such high cost in the 1920s was completely shattered at the beginning of the 1930s.

With the disintegration of the gold standard, and the breakdown of international monetary co-operation, the world economy fragmented into hostile blocs, with mounting economic and political competition between the sterling area, the gold bloc, and the group of countries dominated by Nazi Germany. The period was marked by successive currency devaluations, the introduction of exchange controls, and the imposition of a wide variety of barriers to trade, all taking the major countries further away from the orthodox ideals of *laissez-faire*, free trade, and stable currencies.

Britain and the Scandinavian countries, freed by devaluation from the need to protect their currencies, were able to initiate expansionary monetary policies, and enjoyed five or six years of improving trade, rapid growth, and rising prosperity. For many other nations it was a time of deep distress and slow recovery. Although the United States began a rapid recovery after the suspension of gold payments in 1933 and the devaluation of the dollar in early 1934, unemployment and economic distress remained high throughout the 1930s. Conditions were even worse in those gold bloc countries which were determined to maintain their commitment to gold. As their competitive position deteriorated, the attempt to cling to their pre-1931 gold parities became increasingly untenable, and they were finally compelled to devalue. Belgium capitulated to the speculative pressures in 1935, France late in 1936, swiftly followed by Switzerland and the Netherlands. In many parts of central and eastern Europe growth was severely restricted by the collapse of farm prices and the contraction of multilateral trade.

The decline of the French franc, and a growing sense of the need for political solidarity on the part of the democracies, eventually pushed a reluctant France, Britain, and the United States to take some limited and tentative steps back towards a more co-operative international framework. This was given formal expression in the Tripartite Agreement, under which the three countries undertook to relax quotas and exchange controls, and to avoid competitive devaluations. Germany and Italy stood outside this framework, with Hitler and Mussolini forcing their economies progressively further in the direction of state control, militarism, and autarky, dragging with them many of the countries of central and south-east Europe in a web of exchange controls, tariffs, and special bilateral trading arrangements.

These successive developments had profound economic, social, and political effects on those who lived through these disturbed decades, and their recollection reverberated through the period of reconstruction of the post-war economic system. The aim of this book is to provide a brief description of these events, and to analyse the primary causes of the successive financial and economic developments, and of their interrelationship. The Great Depression of 1929–33 and the financial crisis of 1931 are placed at the centre of the narrative, and are presented both as the culmination of the policies and practices of the 1920s and as a powerful influence on the subsequent economic history of the 1930s. The unifying theme of the narrative is the impact of various forms and aspects of international economic organization on world economic stability.[1]

---

[1] Some of the material in this book draws on the chapter which we wrote for Feinstein (1995). That volume was based on a programme of research by a network on the *Economic History of Europe Between the Wars* sponsored by the European Science Foundation, and we should like to acknowledge the contribution to our work made by our colleagues in the network.

In order to place the events of the inter-war period in their historical context, we begin our account by looking briefly at the pattern of economic growth before and after our period. In the first chapter we also outline four key propositions or hypotheses, relating to the organization of international economic relations, which have been advanced by various writers to account for the failures of policy and performance in the years 1919–39. These propositions recur throughout our account of this period, though with differing emphases in different phases.

1

INTER-WAR GROWTH IN A SECULAR PERSPECTIVE

1.1 Europe's modern economic growth in a twentieth-century perspective

During the first part of the nineteenth century, and in some regions for long after that, the standard of living of European peasant families—their diet, clothing, housing, life expectancy, and literacy—had far more in common with that of their medieval ancestors serving on feudal manors than with their post-Second World War grandchildren. Industrial workers did not fare much better, packed as they were in filthy cities, and burdened from childhood with long working weeks in unhealthy working conditions.

An Italian working class family of four—whose average monthly consumption is now about 1,600 US dollars—had to survive in the 1890s on less than 180 comparable dollars, out of which they also had to cover health care and education expenses that are now provided free by the state. This represented bare subsistence on a diet which included meat only on rare festivities, and left little for tobacco and a glass of cheap wine in the local *osteria*, and that only for the head of the household (Rossi and Toniolo 1993).

The transformation in the daily life of ordinary European people that has taken place in little more than a century is the most revolutionary event, to date, in the history of the continent. And it has gone far beyond the wildest dreams of anybody attempting long-term predictions as late as 1914. For this far-reaching revolution, Simon Kuznets coined the term 'modern economic growth'. At its heart he saw an 'epochal innovation' consisting of the 'spreading application of science to processes of production and social organization' (Kuznets 1966: 487).

While modern economic growth is by no means a universal phenomenon, Kuznets showed that those countries in which it occurs experience a number of similar quantitative developments related to the long-run rates of growth of aggregate and sectoral production, to consumption and saving patterns, and to structural changes in the economy. Modern economic growth is typically characterized, and—some would say—defined by 'high rates of increase in per capita product, ranging from less than 15 to about 30 per cent per decade' (Kuznets 1966: 490). Its main features include an acceleration in the growth of population and consumption, and a rise in savings and investment ratios, as well as a shift in the composition of GDP away from agriculture. Aggregate product derives increasingly from the manufacturing and service sectors, with a similar change in the pattern of consumption.

For our purposes, it is worth noting that a tremendous increase in the international movements of goods, services, and factors of production was also a prominent feature of 'modern economic growth' in the late nineteenth century. After the outbreak of World War I, while other structural changes continued, the opening up of the world economy was reversed until 1945, when it resumed, albeit at a slower pace.

To put the topic of this book in the perspective of the European economic history of the twentieth century, we may start by observing that, by the last quarter of the nineteenth century, 'modern economic growth' was well under way in most areas of the old Continent. In the early part of the century it had spread from its cradle, in England, to Belgium, France, Switzerland, and the Rhineland. Some decades later, it reached Prussia and the Scandinavian countries in the North, and eventually it spread to some parts of Russia in the East, and to selected regions in central Europe, and the Italian and Iberian peninsulas in the South. Kuznets points to this sequential diffusion as yet another feature of 'modern economic growth'.

The unsettling consequences of this phenomenon on the equilibria of the old continent began to be felt in the process of political unification of two 'latecomers': Germany and Italy. The creation of two large and developing nation states was seen as a threat by the existing powers. At the same time, the newcomers somehow found that their ambition for growth and expansion was frustrated by the very presence of the established economic and financial giants. Soon, Europe found German troops marching into France and occupying Paris; it is not irrelevant to our story about the inter-war economy to recall that the First Reich was proclaimed in Versailles, when the Commune was still under siege. From then onward, Europe enjoyed some four decades of peace and growth; however, the consequences of 'sequential' and uneven development continued to be felt through the so-called 'Second Industrial Revolution', feeding on both ambitions and fears.

Table 1.1 puts the years encompassed by the two world wars in the perspective of European 'modern economic growth' during the twentieth century. For a period of just over one hundred years, from 1890 to the present day, the average annual rate of increase in the real GDP of the advanced countries of Europe was some 2.4 per cent per annum. The corresponding population growth rate was 0.6 per cent, so that real GDP per head in Europe as a whole increased at about 1.8 per cent per annum. These rates are broadly in line with those prescribed by Kuznets.

However, they were not consistently maintained in each of the main sub-periods into which it has become customary to divide the twentieth century. As shown in Table 1.1, during the first (1890–1913) and the last (1973–94) periods, i.e. for about two-fifths of the century, Europe's real GDP, in total and per capita, grew at about the average secular rate. In contrast, the two other sub-periods deviate sharply from this trend.

At one extreme, for over a quarter of a century after the Second World War, the economies of Europe grew at a rate twice as high as the secular trend. More remarkable still, this tremendous increase in

Table 1.1. Economic growth in Europe, 1980–1994 (average annual rates of growth)

	GDP	Population	GDP per capita
1890–1994	2.4	0.6	1.8
1890–1913	2.2	0.7	1.4
1913–1950	1.4	0.5	0.9
1950–1973	4.8	0.8	4.0
1973–1994	2.1	0.4	1.7

Note: The growth rates are weighted averages for 15 countries (Austria, Belgium, Czechoslovakia, Denmark, Finland, France, Germany, Ireland, Italy, the Netherlands, Norway, Spain, Sweden, Switzerland, and the United Kingdom), all adjusted for boundary changes.

Source: Maddison (1995: 104–11 and 180–7).

production, and the full employment which accompanied it, turned out to be compatible with low inflation and overall external stability, at least until the mid-1960s. At the other extreme, in the years from 1913 to 1950, economic growth slowed down to about one-half its long-run pace. The period that is the subject of this volume thus stands out as by far the least successful in the economic history of modern Europe.

1.2 Some quantitative features of the inter-war years

This marked slowdown in real per capita growth between 1913 and 1950 provides the background to the present history. Before proceeding to analyse the various aspects of the European economy during the inter-war years, however, it is useful to discuss briefly several 'stylized facts' that are prominent features of the aggregate quantitative changes between 1913 and 1950 (or between 1913 and 1938). They may be summarized as follows: (1) the slowdown in economic activity, while a worldwide phenomenon, was more pronounced in Europe than in North America; (2) far from keeping pace with output trends, international trade declined in real terms; (3) high and structural unemployment was the shocking new phenomenon of these years; and (4) the rate of growth of labour productivity increased more rapidly than in 1890–1913, and the pace achieved in the 1920s was particularly good.

Slower growth

As can be seen from Table 1.2, the reduction in the growth of real per capita GDP between 1913 and 1950 was steeper in Europe than in North America, its main competitor and trading partner. While the New World's secular growth rate was roughly comparable to that of the Old World, the latter displayed milder deviations from the trend. In the United States, the inter-war slowdown was moderate relative both to the previous period and to the secular trend, while the post-Second World War boom was much less sparkling than in Europe. Canada's growth pattern falls between those of the United States and of Europe. Japan, Europe's other major competitor, also suffered a sharp decline in economic growth between 1913 and 1950, but then accelerated to an exceptional 8 per cent per annum after the war, a brilliant performance which helped to raise its trend rate of growth over the century well above that in Europe and North America.

There is one dominant explanation for the severity of the European slowdown between 1913 and 1950 (and thus, paradoxically, in part also for the 'golden age' of the 1950s and 1960s): war. Our brief period includes two global military conflicts, both fought with unprecedented destructive strength on European soil. This is why, in what follows, special emphasis will be placed on the immediate and long-run effects of the Great War (including, among the latter, the second global conflagration of 1939–45). The whole period stands out as one of major divisions and lack of co-operation, with devastating results on the pace of economic progress. This is shown, among other things, by the above-average performance in 1913–50 of countries which remained consistently neutral, such as Sweden and Switzerland (Table 1.6).

The disruption of international trade

Lack of international co-operation and poor economic policies are reflected in the second of the quantitative 'stylized facts' outlined above: the disruption of international trade. Before 1913, the income elasticity of exports in the main European countries was considerably greater than 1. In the subsequent quarter of a century, export trade actually declined while production grew at only a slow pace (Table 1.3). Here again, the experience of the main European countries stands out as particularly disappointing when compared to that of North America. The contrast with the case of Japan is even

Table 1.2. Growth of real GDP per capita in Europe, the United States, Canada, and Japan, 1890–1994 (average annual rates of growth)

	Europe	United States of America	Canada	Japan
1890–1994	1.8	1.8	2.0	2.9
1890–1913	1.4	2.0	2.8	1.4
1913–1950	0.9	1.4	1.4	0.9
1950–1973	4.0	2.9	2.9	8.0
1973–1994	1.7	1.4	1.4	2.8

Source: Maddison (1995: 104–11 and 180–7).

Table 1.3. Growth of volume of exports, selected countries, 1890–1938 (average annual rate of growth)

	1890–1913	1913–38
France	2.8	−0.4
Germany	5.3	−2.2
Italy	3.7	−1.5
United Kingdom	2.6	−2.3
Canada	6.3	2.6
Japan	8.9	7.1
USA	3.9	0.8

Source: Maddison (1982: 248–51).

more striking. It shows that the dramatic fall in international trade during the Great War and the inter-war years was to a large extent concentrated on, or derived from, Europe. It had heavy repercussions on the Atlantic routes, both North and South, but little impact on the rapidly developing Japanese exports.

The rise in unemployment between the wars

High unemployment rates, particularly but not exclusively in the 1930s, still stand out in the collective memories of Europeans as the most deeply felt feature of their economies during the inter-war period. Visual artists and novelists, as well as a widely diffused oral tradition, have passed on to future generations stories of homeless people, of long queues for a free meal, of workers sitting idle outside their humble dwellings, of truly desperate families. The fact that quite similar photographs, paintings, and novels describe the Great Depression in North America means that, as far as unemployment in the 1930s is concerned, the contrast between the two sides of the Atlantic was not very pronounced. However, in most European countries the number of people out of work was higher than in the United States in the aftermath of the Great War and during the 1920s.

Comparing unemployment over time and across countries is a daunting task. The very noun 'unemployment' appeared for the first time only in 1888; the compilation of official statistics began much later. Moreover, since such statistics often derived from the records either of those receiving some sort of benefit, or of those registering with labour exchange offices, they depend heavily on specific institutional arrangements in individual countries. It is thus impossible to make an accurate comparison of the levels of inter-war unemployment with those prevailing in the quarter of a century before 1914. However, it seems likely that unemployment before the First World War was of shorter average duration than that experienced after the war.

More can be said about the relative magnitude of the phenomenon in the inter-war period and in the years after the Second World War. Table 1.4 may not be very precise as far as the absolute levels of unemployment rates are concerned, but it probably provides a broadly correct indication of relative variations across time (Eichengreen and Hatton 1988: 7). Exceptionally high unemployment rates stand out as a feature of the 1930s, while unemployment in the 1960s was exceptionally low. At the same time, the relative number of those out of work in the troubled decade of the 1920s looks, on average, to be broadly comparable with that of the 1980s and early 1990s, an aspect we shall return to in the concluding chapter.

Productivity continues to improve

While the number of unemployed rose, product per hour worked by those who retained their jobs continued to increase, and from 1913 to 1929 the pace was markedly more rapid than in the pre-1914 decades (see Table 1.5). The period under review was rich in technological innovations—some of them stimulated by the wars—while the accumulation of human capital benefited from the extension of education to larger groups in the population, and from higher university enrolment.

The observed trend in productivity growth is interesting and important for at least two reasons. First, it reinforces one of the

Table 1.4. Average unemployment rates, 1921–1993 (%)

1921–9	1930–8	1950–9	1960–73	1974–81	1982–9	1990–3
8.3	15.8	4.2	2.5	5.2	8.8	9.2

Note: Arithmetic average of average annual unemployment rates. 1921–38 covers France, Germany, and the United Kingdom; for 1950–93 Italy is also included.

Sources: For 1921–38, Galenson and Zellner (1957: 455); for 1950–93, Maddison (1991: 262) and OECD data from Crafts and Toniolo (1996: 7).

Table 1.5. Growth of productivity in Europe, 1890–1992 (average annual rate of growth)

	Output per hour worked
1890–1992	2.5
1890–1913	1.7
1913–1929	2.2
1929–1950	1.5
1950–1973	4.6
1973–1992	2.1

Note: Productivity is defined as real GDP per hour worked. The growth rates are weighted averages for 12 of the countries listed in Table 1.1, excluding Czechoslovakia, Ireland, and Spain.

Source: Maddison (1991: 274–5; 1995: 249).

main contentions of this book, namely that slow growth and depression were man-made rather than 'natural' phenomena. Secondly, it explains, at least in part, the extraordinary growth rates of the years after the Second World War: once man-made obstacles were removed, the European economies could exploit a vast backlog of accumulated technical knowledge and human capital.

Patterns in the growth of output

In this brief quantitative survey we have so far considered Europe as an aggregate. But nation states remained the protagonists. They received full international endorsement at the Versailles Peace Conference that dismembered the old Continental empires. Moreover, in retaining or gaining full economic sovereignty, it was nation states which were responsible for the policies that resulted in higher or lower growth rates for their individual economies, as well as for the disruption of the international economy. Table 1.6 shows the growth rates of nine European countries, the USA, and Japan during 1913–50 and two relevant sub-periods.

The first column in Table 1.6 covers the full period 1913–50. European countries are ranked by growth order, starting from the slowest. No simple organizing principle is possible here: given the length and complexity of the period, growth rates were the result of the participation or neutrality in one or both of the world wars, the speed of the respective recoveries, monetary and exchange rate policies, semi-planned fascist economies, and many other factors. The only possible *prima facie* observation here is the most obvious

Table 1.6. Growth in real GDP, selected European countries, the United States, Canada, and Japan, 1913–1950 (average annual rate of growth)

1913–50		1913–29		1929–38	
		WWI neutrals		*Off gold in 1931*	
Austria	0.2	Sweden	1.9	United Kingdom	1.9
Belgium	1.0	Finland	2.4	Denmark	2.2
Germany	1.1	Denmark	2.7	Sweden	2.6
France	1.2	Switzerland	2.8	Norway	3.1
United Kingdom	1.3	Norway	2.9	Finland	3.9
Italy	1.5	Netherlands	3.6		
Netherlands	2.4			*Gold bloc*	
Denmark	2.5	*WWI winners*		France	−0.4
Switzerland	2.6	United Kingdom	0.7	Belgium	0.0
Finland	2.7	Belgium	1.4	Netherlands	0.3
Sweden	2.7	Italy	1.7	Switzerland	0.6
Norway	2.9	France	1.9	Italy	1.6
		WWI losers		*Other*	
		Austria	0.3	Austria	−0.3
		Germany	1.2	Germany	2.5
Non-European nations					
Japan	2.2	Canada	2.5	USA	−0.6
USA	2.8	USA	3.1	Canada	0.0
Canada	2.9	Japan	3.7	Japan	3.6

Source: Maddison (1995: 180–3).

one: two of the fastest-growing countries, Sweden and Switzerland, remained neutral during both the First and the Second World War, and two others, Finland and Norway, were neutral in the first conflict.

The second column covers the years from 1913 to 1929. Here, European countries are classified according to their participation in the Great War, the most important single factor to affect individual performances, at least during the first half of the decade. The results are quite indicative: neutrals outperform all winners, while the latter (with the possible exception of the United Kingdom) do better than the cores of the two central empires, which were defeated in the war and lost a significant part of their territory. The third column takes into account the most important item in the economic policies of the 1930s: the adherence to the gold standard until 1935–6, or its abandonment in 1931. Here too the results are quite suggestive. Thos: who left gold definitely outperform the members of the gold bloc and Switzerland. Germany is listed under 'Other' since its currency remained only formally anchored to gold, while in practice policy makers were quite successful in 'insulating' the country from the deflationary effects of the gold standard rules.

It goes without saying that the associations in Table 1.6 cannot be taken as proofs of causal links: at best, they may be suggestive of research hypotheses. If so, they indicate again that in order to try to understand the slowdown in the process of 'modern economic growth' experienced in the period of our study, it is appropriate to explore first and foremost the effects of the war, and of ill-advised economic policies. In this vein, we have selected four relevant propositions among the large number of explanations provided by scholars for the poor performance of the European economy during the inter-war years.

1.3. Four propositions about international economic organization

Structural imbalances

The traditional explanation for the depth and persistence of the widespread post-war difficulties is the problem of structural imbalance within and between countries. The origins of this dislocation are found in the changes in the composition of production and demand resulting from the wartime disruption of international trade, from the geopolitical effects of the Peace Treaty, and from post-war changes in technology and in patterns of demand.

Although the effects of these changes are not always clearly spelled out, they may be taken to relate particularly to a misallocation of resources which was responsible for the high rate of unemployment in Europe in the 1920s, and which also made the adjustment process longer and more costly. The effects of these structural changes were felt in both labour and in product markets, in each of which, it is argued, there was appreciably less flexibility after 1918 (Svennilson 1954).

Lack of leadership

The next explanation which has been given prominence in relation to the late 1920s, notably by Brown (1940) and Kindleberger (1973), is the lack of central bank leadership in the operation of the restored gold standard: the proposition summed up in the phrase 'no longer London, not yet Washington'. The diminished financial status of the United Kingdom meant that London was unable to act as sole conductor of the international orchestra, or—in more modern terminology—to operate as the 'hegemon', while the United States was not yet willing to take over this role, despite the enormous improvement in its international economic standing.

The ability of London to perform its traditional role as the dominant economic power was further undermined by the enhanced strength of France's relative financial position after the stabilization of the franc in 1926, and the large accumulation of gold by the Bank of France. The specific economic connotation of this lack of leadership was that there was no country able and willing to stabilize the global financial environment by acting as international lender-of-last-resort.

Absence of international co-operation

A third factor which has been put forward as the primary explanation for the problems of the inter-war period is the absence of international co-operation between the United States, Britain, France, and Germany, and the failure of the major nations to co-ordinate international economic policy. Clarke (1967) argued this specifically in relation to the period from mid-1928 to the collapse of the gold standard in 1931, claiming that after the death of Benjamin Strong, governor of the Federal Reserve Bank of New York, the central bankers failed to achieve the necessary co-ordination of policy.

More generally, Eichengreen (1985, 1992a) suggested this as a central feature of the entire period, manifest particularly in the attempt of each of the main powers to secure for itself a disproportionate share of the world's limited stocks of monetary gold. Prior to the collapse of the gold standard in 1931, their unco-operative behaviour involved the imposition of tight monetary policies, not only by countries in deficit, but also by those—notably the United States and France—which were in surplus. This added to the deflationary pressures on the world economy, and also increased the vulnerability of the weak currencies, such as sterling and the mark, to speculative attack.

In other variants of this theme, the shortcomings of the inter-war adjustment mechanism are explained by the unwillingness of central banks to operate the gold standard according to the 'rules of the game', under which all movements in gold should have been fully reflected in compensating changes in domestic money supplies. The main reason for this tendency to neutralize changes in gold and foreign exchange reserves, rather than allow them to influence internal monetary conditions, was that post-war governments were no longer willing to give unconditional support to external equilibrium and the defence of the reserves.

Democratic electorates increasingly required that governments should attach greater weight to internal stability of prices and incomes. 'When the precepts of the gold standard ran counter to the requirements of domestic monetary stability, it was the latter that usually prevailed' (Nurkse 1944: 105). But the new position was not entirely symmetrical: there was always greater pressure to neutralize an outflow of gold than an inflow, and this imparted a deflationary bias to the whole system.

The inability of the powers to co-operate was dramatically symbolized at the World Monetary Conference in the summer of 1933, meeting in London shortly after the United States had abandoned the gold standard and allowed the dollar to depreciate. The gathering had been specifically convened to promote the co-ordinated stabilization of exchange rates, but in the middle of the proceedings Roosevelt announced that he was not willing to stabilize the dollar. He brusquely dismissed 'the specious fallacy of achieving a temporary and probably an artificial stability in foreign exchanges on the part of a few large countries only' (Hodson 1938: 194). This disastrous meeting starkly exposed the total lack of any common ground between countries, and hastened the further disintegration of the international monetary system. With global political relations also deteriorating rapidly the decade witnessed an epidemic of competitive currency depreciation; extended resort to exchange controls; the rise of protectionism, bilateralism, import quotas, and other barriers to trade; and the development of hostile, non-co-operating trade and currency blocs.

Old-fashioned political and financial ideologies

The final factor emphasized in the literature is the hold on policy makers of old-fashioned political and financial ideologies. The

former is seen as responsible for the insistence on substantial reparations. This produced a new pattern of international settlements that
made the smooth functioning of international payments dependent
upon the capability and willingness of the United States to continue
lending indefinitely to Europe. The destabilizing potential of this
'arrangement' is self-evident. Still more important was the financial
ideology reflected in the priority attached to the reintroduction of
the gold standard, even where this could only be achieved by sub-
jecting the economy to a severe programme of deflation, and ob-
structing future trade by the imposition of an overvalued currency.

Under the discipline which this doctrine enjoined—or the values
it projected—country after country surrendered its 'monetary sovereignty' and restricted its ability to accommodate balance of payments disturbances by any means other than retrenchment. The
consequences of this became apparent in the early 1930s, when the
constraints of the gold standard prevented countries from initiating
policies to alleviate economic distress—and even induced some
countries to pursue policies that intensified the economic decline
(Temin 1989).

Elements of these four problems of international economic organization can be found throughout the inter-war period, but the
first has dominated explanations of the early 1920s; the lack of
central bank leadership has been particularly invoked to account for
the developments of 1925–30; the inability of the major nations to
co-operate in the co-ordination of international economic policy is
given as a crucial factor underlying both the disintegration of the
attempt to reconstruct the pre-1914 gold standard and the emergence of rival trade and currency blocs; and the role of financial
ideology and the acceptance of the gold standard is seen as specially
important in accounting for the Great Depression and the propaga-
tion of the financial crises of 1930–5.

We shall return to these four propositions, and discuss their
validity and applicability, at appropriate points in the subsequent
narrative.

2

THE LEGACY OF THE
FIRST WORLD WAR

2.1 The economics of 'total war'

It is impossible to understand the economic history of inter-war Europe and, more specifically, that of its international economic organization without considering the long-lasting effects of the First World War. It was a war which was first bitterly fought, both on the battlefield and on what came to be known as the economic front, and then continued, more subtly, in post-war political and economic policies.

The First World War marked the true watershed between the nineteenth and twentieth centuries. This is particularly relevant when we consider our central theme of international economic organization. The late nineteenth century was characterized by a relatively well-functioning international payment system, based on the gold standard. London played a pivotal and stabilizing role, and the leading central banks co-operated as necessary. In addition, there was almost perfect mobility of factors of production, reflected in large-scale movements of labour and capital from Europe to the New World. This was the nineteenth-century international economic order.

The war itself was a major economic revolution. In pre-1914 peacetime economies the role of the state was extremely limited. Governments provided for defence, foreign policy, domestic security, and, in some cases, for free universal elementary education; they subsidized railways and built national roads. Total revenue, and expenses, seldom exceeded 15 per cent of GDP in the final years of peace. This pattern was so firmly established in everybody's expectations that a 'short-war theorem' had developed among governments and chiefs of staff. It held that, given the limited resources available and the disruption wrought on economic and social life, any 'modern' war was bound to be brief.

As it turned out, the theorem was based on very shaky foundations. It disregarded both the flexibility of a modern economy and the exceptional adaptability of mankind to almost any situation. The revolutionary aspect of the war economy consisted mainly in the rapid shift of resources from consumption to arms production, and in the attendant reorganization of the entire economic life of the belligerent nations. In a relatively short period of time, nineteenth-century thrifty governments were turned into twentieth-century big spenders. In the United Kingdom, military expenditure rose from about 4 per cent of GDP in 1913 to 38 per cent in 1916–17, bringing total government expenditure close to half of national income. In Germany, military spending alone rose to 53 per cent of GDP by 1917 (see further Table 10.1 below). A colossal amount of labour had to be swiftly diverted from peacetime production to military service, and to rapidly expanding armament factories, chemical industries, shipyards, and the like. Female labour was widely used in the countryside. The capital needs for this enormous resource reallocation were met chiefly by borrowing or simply printing large quantities of bank notes.

As soon as the illusion of a short war had vanished, all the contenders organized for 'total war'. In Germany, the brilliant head of the AEG electrical combine—Rathenau—was put in charge of an agency set up to exercise control from above over military supplies. In Italy, capable industrialists and top generals were given similar jobs. Germany's central planning of the supply of raw materials, and their distribution to companies working for the government, turned out to be particularly effective. It was accompanied by an industrial reorganization that more often than not entailed compulsory cartelization. Small industry was sacrificed to the needs of industrial giants.

In Britain, the Ministry of Munitions was created in 1915 under Lloyd George. It slowly acquired most of the features of Germany's War Raw Material Office, supervising private business and, when necessary, supplementing their efforts with direct investment. At the end of the war, Britain had some 200 government-owned plants. In many areas this colossal productive effort was coupled with an acceleration of technical progress both in products and in production processes. Internal-combustion engine vehicles, surface ships, submarines, aeroplanes, and several other products were drastically improved during the war, most of them subsequently enjoying peacetime development. At the same time, plants became larger and more efficient; the workforce—subject to military discipline—was 'scientifically' organized.

With hindsight, one may say that perhaps the most revolutionary aspect of 'total war' was general conscription. Society, particularly in the countryside, was deeply changed by the departure of almost all acceptable men, and their replacement by women, children, and older workers. While serving in the trenches, men were exposed to mass propaganda of various kinds as never before. And some of them learned ways of organizing large numbers of people for political purposes. After the war, it was almost impossible for the ruling classes to ignore the reality of mass movements and revert to the old cosy ways of élite politics.

In the international economy—the matter that interests us here—the war brought about two major developments. First, the displacement of the agricultural sector in the belligerent countries led to the lifting of import duties in order to gain access to the cheapest overseas supplies. The production of grains and meat in the fertile regions of the United States, Canada, Argentina, and Australia expanded to exploit their comparative advantage in supplying European markets.

Secondly, financial co-operation was undertaken by the Entente powers in the form of inter-Allied loans. At first, Britain lent to its financially weaker allies: France, Italy, and Belgium. Later on, the United States provided war loans to all the European countries fighting against the central empires. As a result of this co-operation, exchange rates of the Allies could be pegged at politically acceptable levels, and hard currency was made available to buy overseas supplies, mostly in the home markets of the creditor countries themselves.

2.2 The economic consequences of the war

The most enduring legacy of the war was social and political instability, both domestic and international. It is not our aim here to discuss this issue. Suffice it to say that, on the various domestic fronts, its ultimate results took the names of Mussolini in Italy, Primo de Rivera in Spain, and Hitler in Germany. And, of course, it was the war that opened the way to the October Revolution in Russia. More stable democracies, such as France and Britain, suffered from immediate post-war instability and for a moment even they feared revolution.

In the international arena, the period between the Armistice of 11 November 1918, and the crisis of 1923–4 that led to some kind of 'stabilization', was one of great upheaval. The war left a permanent scar on international relations that made co-operation much more difficult for many years to come. In the Balkans, and in parts of the former Russian Empire, active fighting remained endemic for a long time after the official end of the war, often dragging European powers into costly and useless interventions. Even more damaging, in the long run, was the way in which the peace treaties, particularly the one with Germany, were drafted. The unnecessarily punitive nature of reparations, the military occupation of the Rhineland, and, eventually, the direct intervention in the Ruhr all carried momentous consequences, some of which are related in the coming chapters.

Though we are convinced that unsettled domestic and international conditions played a major role in generating an unstable international economic environment, we confine our attention to those consequences of the First World War which directly affected the post-war organization and activity of the Continental economies, individually and collectively. Some of these were an immediate effect of the war; others followed from the way in which the great powers dealt with the issues which had still to be resolved when the armies finally called a halt to the slaughter and destruction. We look first at four direct effects of the war.

The two exogenous shocks

As we have seen, the war caused a major disruption of the real economy, on both the demand and supply sides. In every belligerent country there were swift changes of great magnitude in production and consumption patterns, such as those briefly outlined above. In particular, heroic efforts were made to increase productive capacity in war-related industries such as engineering, iron and steel, and shipbuilding.

The second exogenous shock occurred when much of this capacity became superfluous once the war was over. It proved exceptionally difficult to adjust to the required patterns of peacetime production as swiftly as required by sudden changes in demand created by unfulfilled wartime needs. This was, to a certain extent, the consequence of the devastation of transport networks and of fields, houses, factories, and mines during the fighting. The destruction was worst in France, Belgium, Italy, and Poland, but many other countries had also endured considerable loss of fixed assets. Much more important proved to be the difficulties connected with the relocation of physical assets and of labour to peacetime production. For instance, huge investments were made in shipbuilding, a particularly asset-specific industry that found itself perennially saddled with excess capacity. We shall say more about these problems in Chapter 4.

Another difficulty in returning to pre-war patterns was created by the changes that had occurred in world markets. Competitors whose economic circumstances were relatively little affected by the war, notably the United States and Japan, had seized the opportunity created by the inability of European manufacturers to maintain their normal trading activity, and had successfully invaded their markets. Japan, in particular, rapidly increased her sales to many Asian countries which had previously looked mainly to Britain for their imports. Moreover, huge export capacity had been built by cheap primary producers. The war also stimulated domestic production in non-European countries in order to substitute for imports from Europe. This is what happened, for example, to cotton textiles and other light manufactures in India and Latin America, thereby reducing the markets on which the pre-war output of the exporting nations had depended.

A more rigid economic environment

Once the war was over, the greatest possible degree of flexibility in prices and practices would be required in order to adjust to these devastating domestic and external shocks, but in fact the prevailing trend was towards greater rigidity. A long-run tendency for the flexibility of price and wage structures to decrease is likely to be a feature of all advanced democratic economies which give high priority to the stability of incomes, prices, and employment, but the war considerably hastened this process. In the post-war labour market, wage flexibility was diminished as many more decisions were centrally negotiated in a greatly extended process of collective bargaining. Behind this change lay the growth of working-class militancy, and the dramatic rise in the membership and strength of the trade union movement.

In the goods market there was similarly a tendency to reduced flexibility of property incomes and of prices. The war contributed to this by an increase in government intervention in economic life, the formation or strengthening of trade associations and cartels, and the imposition of numerous controls; each of these features survived in varying degrees into the post-war period.

More fundamentally, the war accelerated the trend towards larger business units, and in the extremely difficult circumstances of the 1920s many firms looked to collusion, to cartels, and to the exercise of monopoly powers to escape the consequences of increasing competition for shrinking markets. In Germany, cartels and other forms of industrial combination were already well established before the war; the increase in their scope and strength during the 1920s enabled them to resist falling prices by restricting production. In Britain, a similar trend was strongly fostered by the government, which deliberately promoted legislation and other measures to reduce competition in industries such as cotton, shipbuilding, and coal mining.

A weaker financial structure

The financial sector was also greatly affected by the war, and by the extensive interference in the peacetime patterns of both domestic and international markets which it stimulated. Most obviously, the war and its aftermath gave rise to unprecedented needs for revenue: it is estimated that the direct cost of the war in constant pre-war prices was the equivalent of five times the worldwide national debt in 1914 (Woytinski and Woytinski 1955, quoted in Aldcroft 1977: 30).

In all countries note issues and bank credits were expanded by immense amounts. Little or no attempt was made either to raise taxes or to borrow from the public on the scale needed to offset the additional demand on resources generated by the enormous military expenditures. The United Kingdom did more than any other nation to impose additional taxes, but even this was sufficient to cover only one-third of its expenditure (Morgan 1952: 104). In France and Germany the proportion financed in this way was very much lower, although the precise figure for the latter is complicated by the role of local taxes.

After the war finance ministers faced the need to service these swollen internal public debts. Many of them were short-term, and threatened monetary stability. There were also external demands for payment of war debts and reparations, while at the same time, international financial co-operation had entirely vanished. The reduction of budget deficits was made more difficult by the need to provide for reconstruction, and by new demands from active trade unions for higher expenditure on social security and unemployment benefits.

A large body of literature exists on some aspects of international financial dislocation, especially on reparations, on inter-Allied debts (more generally on Europe becoming a net debtor) and on the new pattern of international lending. Less is known about changes in the web of international banking that provided the grass-roots connection for the international transfer of short- and long-term capital, as well as for the actual day-by-day functioning of an international payment system.

A fragile international monetary system

The classic gold standard was an early casualty of the conflict. Within a few months of the declaration of war, almost all European central banks, including those in countries that were to remain neutral, had unilaterally suspended gold payments. During the war, the powers of the Entente developed their own payment system, backed by the inter-Allied loans, as noted above. This co-operation was designed to allow the belligerent countries to sustain the level of imports required to achieve the maximum military contribution to the common cause.

Once the war was over, co-operation ceased almost overnight. Inter-Allied financial assistance was suspended, and creditor countries immediately made it clear that they expected reimbursement of their war loans. At the same time, the victorious powers insisted on extracting an unrealistic amount of reparations from those they had defeated. French retaliation for the terms which Germany had imposed on her after victory in 1870 was the dominant factor in preventing a more realistic settlement. A typical inter-war British view of the overall financial outcome is given in the following scathing comment by Lionel Robbins (1934: 6):

> The inordinate claims of the victors, the crass financial incapacity of the vanquished, the utter budgetary disorder which everywhere in the belligerent countries was the legacy of the policies pursued during the war, led to a further period of monetary chaos.

We turn next to the developments which followed from the end of the war, including the shock to the domestic economies of the former belligerents, the signing of the peace treaties which settled relations between the former enemies, and the changes in the relations between the Allies. All these had further profound consequences for the financial and economic developments of the 1920s and beyond.

2.3 The economic consequences of the post-war settlements

The shock of economic restructuring and social unrest

During the war, as much as 30–40 per cent of the belligerents' GDP was directly or indirectly controlled by the state. While supplies to the army came to be the direct responsibility of governments, the rest of the economy was to a great extent subject to various forms of state supervision. Thus, forms of administrative controls were more often than not introduced on prices, wages, capital, and foreign exchange markets. The return to peacetime economic organization and production entailed a huge process of resource reallocation that, contrary to what is assumed in economics textbooks, not only required a long period of time, but also met with the resistance of the vested interests that had been created by the war.

Businessmen and industrialists were almost everywhere divided between those who favoured an immediate return to a *laissez-faire* economy and those—usually the suppliers to the army—who argued in favour of a slow 'return to normality', with strong state help in the process. While most proponents of the latter view only wanted the state to provide forms of financial support to ailing industries, and to guarantee the social peace, a militant minority in France, Germany, and Italy came to herald the birth of a 'technocrat' and 'corporatist' state that would actively support economic growth, particularly in the technologically more advanced sectors.

Whatever the pace was to be, industrial restructuring implied the closing of a number of plants (the case of shipyards is of particular relevance because of the magnitude of the supply cuts that were needed). Capital for the creation of factories that would meet consumers' demand was scarce at home and unlikely to come from foreign sources (see below). The result was unemployment. At the same time households were frustrated by the fall in the real value of the wartime savings they wanted to use to satisfy their pent-up demand for consumer goods. In several countries, the combination of these two conditions produced a short but deep recession between 1920 and 1921.

Social unrest was, however, the main post-war problem. Its discussion would lead us away from the particular economic focus of the present text, but the economic implications of the political developments must not be underrated. The almost universal explosion of working-class struggles and protests after the war can be primarily attributed to two factors.

The first was the powerful growth of their organization, strength, and solidarity. Workers had already formed increasingly successful unions in the years before the war, not only in Britain, where they dated back many decades, but on the Continent as well. The war provided a tremendous boost to these organizations. Maintaining the discipline and the morale of huge armies raised through compulsory conscription entailed both pressures and concessions, and the latter included promises of a better life for the masses as soon as hostilities were over. Life in the trenches also proved to be a tremendous catalyst for the emerging 'mass society': workers from various areas and occupations got to know each other's needs and local strengths while, at the same time, socialist propaganda could be much more effective in such huge concentrations of working-class people.

In addition, at home, the urgent need to increase production of military supplies, and overcome traditional restrictive practices, required recognition of, and concessions to, the trade unions. From 1916 onward, trade union membership increased steeply in the United Kingdom, Germany, and France.

Secondly, the Russian Revolution exercised considerable influence on working-class movements, even though this influence was ambiguous: a model for a militant minority, but at the same time a highly divisive factor for those who did not share this ideology.

The economic impact of social developments differed according to the relative weakness of the economies and of the governments that emerged from the war. Thus, in Germany, the social democratic government undertook a number of social reforms, certainly out of its own political conviction, but also to undermine working-class support for the revolutionary movement. Mines and metal-making were 'socialized', trade unions fully recognized, the eight-hour week introduced. Deficit spending by the state followed, partly feeding into the price spiral. As a result, however, social unrest diminished considerably; by early 1920, hours lost in strikes were already half the number one year earlier.

Other defeated countries saw more dramatic developments that undoubtedly contributed to economic destabilization in central and eastern Europe. Thus, Bulgaria was swept by quasi-revolutionary winds, while Hungary was actually briefly governed in 1919 by the Communists in the so-called 'Councils' Republic'.

In Italy—socially and economically the weakest amongst the large countries on the winning side—workers took over the management of a number of companies during the so-called 'red biennium' (1920–1). The working-class movement was eventually weakened by the division resulting from the creation of a Communist Party in 1921, while reactionary forces gained sufficient strength to enable them to seize power violently by the March on Rome (1922) that inaugurated twenty years of fascist dictatorship. The latter, however, was mostly the result of the failure of the old 'liberal' politicians to provide viable solutions to the post-war problems, particularly the social issues.

In France and Britain too, the enormous number of strikes during 1919 affected both industrial output and investors' expectations. In both countries governments regained control of the situation during 1920, often by the adoption of rather harsh repressive measures. However, while in France the trade union movement suffered a serious set-back, in Britain the circumstances and the results of the social conflict were different, because the trade unions had already developed strong roots, and because the victory of Lloyd George in the 1918 elections brought in a relatively sympathetic government.

The economic consequences of the peace treaties

The war finally ended, and after much wrangling, peace treaties were signed in 1919 with Germany (at Versailles), Austria (at St-Germaine-en-Laye), and Bulgaria (at Neuilly), and in 1920 with Hungary (at the Trianon) and Turkey (at Sèvres). Various aspects of these treaties were to be a cause of severe disturbance to post-war trade and production. First, the way in which the political map of central and eastern Europe was redrawn disrupted long-standing economic relations and created new barriers to trade. Secondly, the attempt to hold Germany responsible for the war by imposing huge demands for reparations for the losses suffered by the victorious powers became a major cause of political antagonism and economic discord.

Pre-1914 trading patterns, communications, and financial relations had long been adjusted to the existing political boundaries. In the large central empires these had evolved to coincide with customs and monetary unions. These well-established arrangements were all disrupted when the formation of new nation states led to the creation of numerous smaller political units in the territories of the former Russian, German, Austro-Hungarian, and Ottoman empires.

The most extensive territorial changes came from the breaking up of the Habsburg Empire, leading to the loss of territory to Italy and the creation of six small nation states (Czechoslovakia, Poland, Romania, Yugoslavia, and a much-diminished Austria and Hungary) in place of a single large multi-ethnic geopolitical entity (see Map 2.1). Germany lost all her overseas colonies and some of her best industrial and agricultural land, including Alsace-Lorraine and the Saar coal-mines, to France; Upper Silesia and other territory to Poland; and smaller areas or towns to Denmark, Belgium, Lithuania, and Czechoslovakia. The Russian Empire also suffered major territorial losses, including four areas which became independent states (Finland, Estonia, Latvia, and Lithuania); Bulgaria was forced to cede territory to Greece; and there were substantial changes in the former Ottoman Empire, though the areas which Turkey lost

Legend:

- New states established by 1920 with the encouragement of the Allied powers
- The remnant of Austria-Hungary, two independent and separate states established by the Allied powers
- Austro-Hungarian territory added to Romania and Serbia by the Allied powers. The enlarged Serbia became the Serb-Croat-Slovene kingdom, later known as Yugoslavia
- Former Russian territory joined to Romania

Populations in 1920

Poland	27,000,000
Romania	17,400,000
Czechoslavakia	14,600,000
Yugoslavia	12,000,000
Hungary	8,700,000
Austria	6,500,000
Finland	3,600,000
Lithuania	2,400,000
Latvia	1,800,000
Estonia	1,000,000
Danzig	400,000
Fiume	50,000

Danzig (Free city)

Fiume (Free city)

FINLAND · ESTONIA · LATVIA · LITHUANIA · RUSSIA · EAST PRUSSIA · POLAND · GERMANY · CZECHOSLOVAKIA · AUSTRIA · HUNGARY · BESSARABIA · ROMANIA · ITALY · YUGOSLAVIA · BULGARIA · ALBANIA · GREECE · TURKEY · Baltic Sea · Adriatic Sea · Black Sea

| 0 | 100 | 200 | 300 miles |
| 0 | 200 | | 400 km |

Map 2.1. The new states of central Europe after the First World War

Source: Martin Gilbert (1970), *First World War Atlas*. London: Weidenfeld and Nicolson. Reprinted by permission.

were outside Europe. The final outcome was that there were 38 independent nations in Europe in 1919, 12 more than in 1914.

In deciding on these changes to the map of central and eastern Europe, the victorious powers were primarily guided by the principle of national self-determination, not by economic considerations. This led to the creation of nation states: political entities encompassing people of the same language, culture, and tradition. This principle was perhaps consistent with the political needs and ideology of the time, but it did not necessarily respond to those of the economy. Foreign trade, in particular, was affected by the new frontiers, with significant consequences, both for the development of the region and for the overall performance of the international economy.

Furthermore, this huge process of border adjustments and state formation inevitably failed to reconcile and satisfy all the conflicting interests and aspirations involved, and so left behind a permanent residue of social and national resentments. In the view of one historian the territorial realignments may have created more problems than they removed (Thomson 1966: 633). The potential for further conflicts translated into the expectations of economic agents, particularly investors. In some cases endemic fighting continued well into the 1920s, increasing the overall sense of instability.

Each new state created its own currency, erected trade barriers to protect domestic industry, inaugurated independent fiscal and monetary policies. In particular, the imposition of tariffs (whether as a source of urgently needed revenue or as a means of protection), the loss of gold and exchange reserves, and the diminished possibilities for foreign borrowing by countries already over-burdened by debts and/or claims for reparations all helped further to restrict the scope for foreign trade. Even from a narrowly defined economic point of view—that is, without taking into account the adverse impact of political uncertainty on the expectations of economic agents— these developments had a deep effect on the international economy by distorting trade and capital flows relative to the pre-1914 situation.

By the last decade of the nineteenth century, the Habsburg Empire had become a well-functioning customs union; it was also a rather efficient, if not optimum, currency area. Each region within the empire tended to specialize in those industrial and agricultural products for which it enjoyed a comparative advantage. Vienna, and to a lesser extent Budapest, had developed into effective money and capital markets providing for the financial capital needs of the whole Dual Monarchy.

In the Danube region, where industrialization had hardly begun by 1914, the establishment of independent policy-maker regimes implied the encouragement of industrial development. Thus Romania, Yugoslavia, and Bulgaria tended to favour high-cost native firms by erecting tall tariff walls around them at a considerable cost to the consumer and to the large agricultural sector. In Hungary, a more industrially advanced country, this policy was less extreme but had none the less a negative impact on trade and growth.

The case of Czechoslovakia was different, in that the new state included the most highly industrialized parts of the former empire. Here the problem was that Czech industry was highly dependent on export markets which were severely affected by the new wave of protectionism. At the same time, the moderately protective agricultural policy of the Prague governments had serious effects on the export outlets of other former members of the empire, given the high income of Czech consumers.

Although less industrialized than Czechoslovakia, Poland had a similar problem. While it was not heavily dependent on the Danubian markets for its agricultural exports, its natural outlets for industrial trade were disturbed by the new frontiers. In the previous four decades the manufacturers of central Poland had developed 'as part of the wider Russian market in which, in certain branches, they had taken the technical lead . . . In the inter-war years this market vanished, and Polish trade was virtually nil' (Radice 1985: 34).

The international economy was also affected by the Bolshevik Revolution and by the civil war, which continued until the early 1920s. In the last part of the nineteenth century, the Russian Empire had been increasingly integrated into European trade and capital flows. After signing a separate peace treaty with Germany, the Bolsheviks effectively severed most of the country's pre-war links with the rest of the world. Trade was reduced to a fraction of its pre-1914 level, and western European capital was scared off by the repudiation of the Tsarist regime's foreign debt. True, new countries—Finland, Latvia, Estonia, and Lithuania—emerged at the edge of the former empire, but these were economically too small to compensate for the loss of trade with Russia.

To sum up: the dismemberment of the Dual Monarchy, the splitting off of parts of the German and Russian empires, and the latter's autarkic evolution all represented a major shock to the international economy. It was a cause of widespread resource mis-allocation, resulting in lower output and higher prices, particularly in central and eastern Europe. In the decades immediately preceding the war, this large area had made significant progress along the road of 'modern economic growth', and was thus becoming ever more important to Europe's overall trade and production. In due time, of course, markets adjusted trade and capital flows to the new situation, but this structure was less conducive to economic efficiency than the one which had prevailed before the war. Moreover, such adjustments were slow to come about—the market process always takes far longer than economists are ready to admit.

In the aftermath of the war, the adjustment was made even slower by uncertainty as to the stability of the new regimes, by fear of revolution, by the persistence of endemic conflicts, by lack of information in western capitals about the new leaders, and by the incompetence of some among the latter. It took, for instance, long years of diplomatic effort and a number of international conferences to re-establish more appropriate levels of trade with the Soviet Union. And it was not until the mid-1920s that German exports resumed their pre-war importance in the Reich's traditional central European markets.

The end of financial solidarity among the Allies

The abrupt end to the system of inter-Allied loans which had been put in place during the war delivered yet another shock to the international economy. The system had implied a flow of financial capital from the United Kingdom to the European members of the Entente, and from the United States to the latter, as well as to Britain. At the same time, part of this flow of capital was used to stabilize the belligerents' exchange rates for both political and economic reasons. If the downward trend in the currencies were too steep, it might be interpreted as the expression of a pessimistic assessment of the outcome of the war by the markets. And if the fluctuations around the trend were too wide and erratic, this would increase the cost of supplies in neutral markets.

Inevitably, however, the support for the European exchange rates served to weaken the dollar on the Japanese and neutral markets. While maintaining the domestic convertibility of the dollar,

Washington had to impose an embargo on the export of gold. All this was politically acceptable as long as it could be presented to American public opinion as part of an overall set of measures—military, economic, and diplomatic—aimed at maximizing a co-ordinated effort that would produce swift victory. Once the latter was achieved—in November 1918—few saw the necessity or even the possibility for a continuation of the wartime financial policy.

The war had been tremendously demanding on Europe's resources, both human and economic. In various parts of the Continent, particularly in the defeated countries, food emergencies developed which could be met only with considerable difficulty, given the lack of foreign exchange to pay for agricultural imports. In other areas, particularly of France, Belgium, and, to a lesser extent, Italy, reconstruction required considerable amounts of capital. Finance was needed all over Europe to carry on the reallocation of resources from war-related to peacetime production. In these circumstances, the European countries, especially Britain and France, argued in favour of a 'soft landing'. This would have meant a continuation of the financial assistance from the United States, and a slow relaxation of the wartime controls on exchange rates and, more generally, on the international economy.

At the same time, however, France invoked the imposition of very harsh conditions on the defeated powers, particularly on Germany. These required the payment of huge reparations to fund not only France's reconstruction and war pensions, but also her foreign debt. Indeed, the French insisted that the reimbursement of their debts to the United States and Great Britain must be linked to the actual receipt of reparations from Germany. The two sets of requests were not mutually consistent. If the aim was international solidarity to rebuild the European economy, then everyone should have been required to pay a price for the success of the co-operative effort; above all, those European countries that stood to benefit most from the Continent's swift recovery. If, on the other hand, the aim was justice—with everyone paying for the obligations incurred during the war—then there was no reason to establish a link between debts and reparations.

While individual European countries, particularly those on the Continent, proved to be short-sighted in their narrow focus on their own immediate interests, it was the attitude of the United States which had by far the largest impact on subsequent developments. Its political weight was considerable, since it had to be reckoned that its intervention in the war had been decisive in tipping the scale in favour of the Entente; and, what mattered most, it was now the world's dominant financial power. However, America did not respond adequately to its newly acquired responsibility as world leader.

There were good political reasons—both domestic and international—for this attitude, but in retrospect it is evident that there was a cultural gap as well. The then leaders of the United States lacked the necessary insight to understand where the long-term interests of the country actually lay. The Victory Loan Act passed by Congress in March 1919 authorized the government to open credit to foreign countries only for the purchase of goods directly or indirectly belonging to the government, and of grains the price of which was guaranteed by the United States. Europe was thereby provided with a safety net against a fall in food consumption below subsistence levels, but it was denied US credit for reconstruction and for postwar industrial conversion to peacetime production. The pace of both was thus slower, and the economic and political impact of the post-war shock to the world economy more substantial, than they would otherwise have been.

One of the features—both cause and effect—of the post-war shock was immense turmoil in the world markets for foreign exchange. Before 1914 the most severe financial crises resulted in currency devaluations of only a few percentage points, even for those European countries that were forced out of gold. Nevertheless, they were considered a national disaster. With the end of the wartime financial support from the United States to Europe, and of the attendant pegging of the Entente currencies to the dollar, exchange rates were left to their own fate. The United States resumed gold payments in 1919. By 1920, the pound had lost about 25 per cent relative to its pre-war parity. The exchange rates of the other members of the Entente soon lost over 50 per cent of their 1914 value and continued to fall. As an average for 1920, the French franc stood at 36 per cent of its pre-war gold parity, the Italian lira at 25 per cent. In the defeated countries of central Europe colossal exchange rate devaluations ended up feeding into hyper-inflation (see Chapter 3.1). By 1920, the German mark was worth only 7 per cent of its 1914 value: in the following two years it disappeared as an international currency.

Of course, the blame for this cannot all be laid at the door of the United States. Wartime currency pegging was obviously untenable after the end of hostilities, and it was necessary for the exchange rate of each individual currency to adjust to changes in purchasing power parity driven by their respective rates of inflation. In so far as markets reacted to uncertainty, it must also be recognized that domestic circumstances were of paramount importance.

Nevertheless, errors of judgement and policy by the international leaders were an important additional factor. The retreat from wartime financial solidarity was too abrupt. The lack of international credit for reconstruction and industrial restructuring magnified the markets' unfavourable expectations about the pace of recovery in France, Belgium, and Britain. Uncertainty about the amount of reparations and the settlement of inter-Allied debt was also a major source of volatility in international markets. Finally, the idea of re-creating an international monetary system based on gold was not only highly ill-advised—as we shall see—but was also left to the initiative of central bankers, rather than being part of a larger political design springing from the world's leaders.

Reparations

In discussing the economic consequences of the war and the peace treaties we have several times mentioned reparations without actually discussing them. In fact they deserve specific treatment: they were by far the most controversial issue in the peace treaty with Germany, and are widely regarded as one of the critical elements underlying the political and economic failures of the inter-war period.

Article 231 of the Versailles Treaty held Germany responsible for the war, therefore establishing the legal ground for reparations. These were supposed to cover war-related material damages. To start with, the definition was ambiguous: while the cost of reconstruction was undoubtedly included, a controversy soon developed as to the inclusion of compensation for personal losses (mainly pensions to widows and disabled men).

Keynes was the first to condemn reparations on the scale proposed at Versailles as economically irrational and politically unwise. In a famous polemic (Keynes 1919) he argued that it was not sensible, indeed was ultimately against the best interests of the victorious powers, to cripple Germany economically, since much of Europe's pre-1914 welfare had depended on German economic growth.

Moreover, Keynes envisaged difficulties in transferring real resources across borders, given the uncertainty as to how the post-war international capital market would work. His overall view was thus that reparations were 'vindictive', 'insane', and ultimately 'unworkable'.

Many modern historians regard Keynes's castigation of European leaders on this issue as excessively harsh. Negotiators at Versailles were aware that 'if the Weimar Republic was unduly hampered in employing its skilled population and material resources productively, the continent as a whole would not easily recover its prosperity' (Schuker 1988: 14). However, they faced enormous budgetary problems themselves as a result of the war, and public opinion could not possibly be convinced to bear all the burden after the huge sacrifices made during the conflict itself. 'La Boche payera' (The Hun will pay) was a powerful political slogan in early post-war France. Whatever the ultimate awareness by European leaders of the intricate web of problems bequecthed by the war, the fact remains that the reparation issue injected a considerable additional amount of uncertainty and acrimony into the volatile post-war economy.

A crucial feature of the Versailles Treaty was that no sum was fixed by the treaty itself. Soon after the Armistice, Germany was stripped of its gold reserves, most of its merchant navy, and whatever equipment (such as rolling stock) might have been of use to the victors. Deliveries of coal were also required. In the following months, preliminary reparation payments were required, pending a final settlement. In March 1921 the German failure to fulfil part of those preliminary requests prompted the occupation by Allied troops of the towns of Dusseldorf, Duisberg, and Ruhrhort on the east side of the River Rhine. Needless to say, this move did not contribute to a stable international environment. Only one month later, the so-called London Schedule of Payments for the first time formally established Germany's reparation obligations. Germany, however, dragged its feet so that the Allies again entered its territory in 1923, this time occupying the mining district of the Ruhr.

It was not until 1924 that an agreement was reached, the Dawes Loan, which created the pre-condition for a reasonably stable system of international payments which allowed private capital to flow into Germany. This made it possible for reparations to be smoothly transferred to France, which was due to receive the bulk of them (52 per cent), to the British Empire (22 per cent), to Italy (10 per cent), to Belgium (8 per cent), and to the other minor Allies.

The mechanism by which the post-war international payment system was allowed to work will be the subject of further discussion in the next chapter. Here we wanted to stress the immediate adverse repercussions of the post-war settlement on the world economy. While the sum finally agreed upon, and the schedule of payments, might not have been significantly above what Germany could reasonably have paid without crippling its economy, the manner in which the whole problem was dealt with between 1918 and 1924 added an enormous further element of uncertainty to an already volatile post-war international economy. At the same time, it made international relations difficult, acrimonious, and, eventually, full of damaging potential for revenge.

3

THE CRISES OF THE 1920s

W E have now set the scene by placing the inter-war economic performance of the European economy in its historical perspective, and discussing in some detail the economic and political consequences of the First World War and the post-war settlements. To begin our study of the period itself we look first at some of the critical financial developments in the 1920s. These include the problems of inflation and hyper-inflation which afflicted almost all the European economies, and the related instability of many of their banking systems. We then focus on the issue of exchange rates, and analyse the different routes followed by the main countries in their attempts to stabilize their currencies and to return to the gold standard. Our final theme in this chapter is then the operation of the gold standard during this decade, and the reasons why it failed to provide the benefits in international trade and growth its advocates had anticipated.

3.1 Accelerating prices and hyper-inflation

During the war years prices rose rapidly in all the belligerent countries as demand increased and supplies were disrupted. Neutral countries could not remain immune from this process. The extent to which prices surged upwards between 1914 and 1918 is shown for a selection of countries in the first column of Table 3.1. There was a brief respite immediately after the Armistice, when commodity prices fell, but from the spring of 1919 inflation resumed its course during a boom which lasted until the spring or summer of 1920. The boom was especially strong in the United Kingdom and some of the neutral countries, and in the United States. As can be seen from column (2) of Table 3.1 the extent of the inflation in 1920 varied widely, but the experience of rising prices was common to all countries.

From the middle of 1920 the boom gave way to a worldwide slump which continued until 1921 or, in some cases, a year later. The depression was particularly severe in the United Kingdom and the United States, but few countries escaped. During this downturn and in the subsequent years experience diverged sharply. Three distinct trends can be identified. In one group of countries, represented in the upper part of Table 3.1 by Germany and Austria, the decline in activity had no effect and inflation gave way to hyperinflation. In a second group, represented by Belgium, Finland, Italy, and France in the middle, inflation continued but was not allowed to get completely out of control. The third group, consisting of the Scandinavian countries, Switzerland, Britain, and the Netherlands, imposed strict deflationary policies of dear money and fiscal

Table 3.1. Consumer price indices, 1918–1926 (1914 = 100)

	1918	1920	1922	1924	1926
	(1)	(2)	(3)	(4)	(5)
Countries with hyper-inflation until 1922 or 1923					
Austria	1,163	5,115	263,938	86[a]	103
Germany	304	990	14,602	128[a]	141
Countries in which inflation continued after 1920					
Belgium	1,434	—	340	469	604
Finland	633	889	1,033	1,055	1,078
Italy	289	467	467	481	618
France	213	371	315	395	560
Countries in which inflation was controlled after 1920					
Norway	253	300	231	239	206
Sweden	219	269	198	174	173
Switzerland	204	224	164	169	162
United Kingdom	200	248	181	176	171
Denmark	182	261	200	216	184
Netherlands	162	194	149	145	138

[a] Linked to base year via gold price. For Austria the index for 1923 on this basis was 76. For Germany the hyper-inflation continued until late in 1923 and the price index for that year (1914 = 100) was 15,437,000,000,000.

Source: Maddison (1991: 300–3).

restraint, and by this means succeeded in actually reducing prices and wages until 1922 or 1923. Thereafter prices in this group of countries were broadly stable or falling.

Five countries proved totally unable to contain the war and post-war pressures and were ravaged by hyper-inflation. These were Austria, Hungary, Poland, Russia, and Germany. The last was by far the most remarkable case, culminating in wholesale prices rising at the astronomical rate of 335 per cent per month from August 1922 to November 1923 (Holtfrerich 1986: 17). Even as the inflationary spiral was gathering momentum there was heated controversy about its causes. Within Germany, almost all officials, bankers, and industrialists and a great many economists adopted the balance of payments theory, according to which the root cause of the inflation was to be found in the burden of reparations and occupation costs imposed on a defeated Germany. It was claimed that it was this which was primarily responsible for the magnitude of the deficit on the balance of payments, and that this deficit in turn caused the extraordinary depreciation in the external value of the mark, and forced up import prices. As the accelerating costs and prices spread through the economy, the authorities were compelled to expand the issue of paper money, thus fuelling the inflation. This analysis was supported by some foreign scholars, notably Williams (1922) and Graham (1930).

Opponents of this view reversed the causal chain and advocated a quantity theory explanation. They argued that it was the excessive issue of paper money which initiated the vicious circle, and traced this back to the size of the massive budget deficit. An authoritative inter-war exposition of the quantity theory explanation was given by Bresciani-Turroni (1937). Although some German economists had blamed the deficit on the Treaty of Versailles and the reparation payments, he argued that the crux of the problem was not to be found there but in the enormous increase in state spending, arising both from the heavy reliance on borrowing during the war and from the huge outlays required by post-war economic and social programmes.

The political parties were too weak to resist the pressure for this expenditure; the vested interests on either side were too bitterly divided to reach any agreement on how the necessary taxes should be allocated between labour and capital. The printing of paper money thus provided the only acceptable way out of the dilemma, and at least initially it could be argued by many of the contending social groups that the resulting inflation brought more benefits than costs.

The headlong expansion of the money supply in turn reduced the external value of the currency and so added further to the inflationary pressures. To make matters worse, the unexpectedly rapid pace of the inflation itself undermined attempts to balance the budget, since the real value of any revenue received was always less than had been anticipated when the taxes were imposed. Assessment of many taxes was also made more difficult in conditions of rapid inflation.

The effect of the expanded note issue was then intensified by a steep rise in the velocity of circulation. From the outbreak of war until the summer of 1921 the currency in circulation and the internal price level had increased broadly in line (apart from a brief 'flight from the mark' in 1919), so that there was virtually no change in the real value of the paper money in circulation. But then the signing of the London Ultimatum and the imposition of what were seen to be excessive demands for reparations changed expectations. From the summer of 1921 the flight from the mark became continually quicker, as first Germans and then foreigners lost confidence in the value of the mark. By the second half of 1922 the demand for real money balances was falling steeply (i.e. there was an abrupt rise in the velocity of circulation), and the acceleration in the rate of price increase outpaced even the exceptionally rapid growth of the money supply (Bresciani-Turroni 1937: 162–75; Holtfrerich 1986: 184–93).

The inability of post-war governments to cope with the abnormal fiscal problems created by the First World War, and with the socio-economic conditions which followed the Armistice, were responsible for the inflationary trends, not only in Germany and the other hyper-inflation countries, but also in many of the other countries in the second and third groups mentioned above. Apart from the enormous costs of the war and the post-war restoration, the years of conflict had transformed social and political attitudes, weakening the old order and accelerating the rise in influence of the working classes. In the tense and difficult situation created by defeat, devastation, and financial disorder the political parties in countries such as Austria, France, Belgium, and Italy could not agree on how the burden of taxation should be shared between the different social classes. As in Germany, distributional conflicts over taxes and incomes stand out as a principal source of financial instability in the post-war years.

3.2 Stability and crisis in the European banking systems

As noted above, the boom which followed the Armistice came to an end in the middle of 1920, and output, employment, and incomes began to fall in almost all countries; in a number of cases the recession proved to be fairly severe. Of the large countries of Europe, only Germany escaped a post-war slump due to the temporarily beneficial effects of hyper-inflation: exports were stimulated as long as the value of the mark depreciated more rapidly than the relative rise in German prices, and investment was stimulated by the fall in real interest rates. A number of countries also experienced a banking crisis in this period.

Whether or not such a crisis developed, and the extent of its severity, depended on several factors: the extent to which inflation after 1913 had eroded the value of their assets, the severity of the post-war depression in the real economy, the policy stance of the central bank, and the organization of the banking system. Banks were more likely to fail in countries where inflation had been more rapid, where the real slump was more severe and accompanied by a price deflation, where the central bank was unwilling or unable to act as a swift lender of last resort, and where banks established close financial links with their industrial clients, on the German model of 'universal banking'. Where such crises occurred this, in turn, produced feedback effects on the real side of the economy.

Thus in Britain, where there had been no panic or financial crisis since 1860, one would expect to find the highest degree of stability in the banking system, and 1920–1 was no exception. The separation between bank and industry was, by then, quite securely established, so that banks did well in terms of profitability and currency–deposit ratios during the post-war depression; the depression itself was rather mild; and the Bank of England had developed such a reputation as lender of last resort that it could defuse the possibility of banking panics by its very presence. The Irish system also remained stable, both because of factors similar to those in Great Britain and because of the close links between the two financial systems.

The French case is perhaps less clear-cut, but the reasons for the overall stability of its banking system may nevertheless be traced back to the factors mentioned above. During and after the war, most French enterprises continued in their time-honoured tradition of self-financing from retained profits. Universal banking existed in

France but was normally confined to small provincial banks. The crisis of 1921 made some enterprises less reluctant than before to resort to long-term bank credit, but it was, on average, a rather limited phenomenon. Deposits fell in real terms during the first part of the 1920s as a response to inflation and to the high yields of state bonds, but the reaction of banks was prudent: they increased the liquidity of their portfolio. The Bank of France favoured this process by encouraging the placement of government securities with banks. The real recession was rather mild and, what mattered greatly, was not coupled with price deflation.

The stability of the post-war German financial system is particularly interesting, and contrasts sharply with the collapse of 1931. From this particular point of view, inflation was a 'blessing' since it resulted in growth rather than a slump in the real sector, and in the economy being oversupplied with liquidity. Given the fact that central bank credit financed most of the government's expenditure, there could be no question about lending of last resort to financial institutions, which obviously proved to be unnecessary. Inflation also ensured the post-war stability of the Austrian and Polish banking systems. In Austria, however, the stabilization of the currency, with the necessary deflationary pressure, produced a stock exchange crash in 1924, and the resulting crisis in the real and financial sector of the economy caused widespread failures among small and medium-sized banks.

Elsewhere bank failures were more common; they characterized the post-war economies of Italy, Spain, Portugal, and Norway. In Italy the third and fourth largest universal banks in the country became insolvent between 1921 and 1923, partly as a result of overtrading during and soon after the war, and the difficulties were exacerbated by the cyclical downturn of 1920–1. One of these banks was declared bankrupt at the end of 1921, but deposits were to a large extent guaranteed by the central bank, which also saved a metal-making and engineering concern—probably the most important in the country—owned by the bank. In the following year, fearing a run on deposits if another large bank went under, the central bank staged a large lending-of-last-resort operation in favour of the fourth largest bank in the country. Thus, a pseudo-financial crisis characterized post-war Italy, due to the active policy stance of the central bank, which privileged bank stability over other policy goals such as currency stabilization.

The Spanish central bank was not as ready as its Italian sister to accommodate the liquidity needs of credit institutions in serious difficulty. It, therefore, remained on the sidelines in 1920 when an early recession in manufacturing made a number of Catalan universal banks insolvent. The crisis hit the most developed region in the country, with the eventual failure of the oldest and most prominent Spanish credit institutions. The crisis was very severe in Barcelona, but its effect on Madrid and Bilbao, the two other financial centres in the country, was relatively mild.

However, a new wave of runs on bank deposits unfolded in the second half of 1924; after years of persistently falling prices, both of goods and of financial assets (industrial shares), during which industrial companies required continuous assistance from credit institutions, a number of banks were dragged to insolvency. Again, the central bank remained passive: only in the case of the Banco Central, one of the largest in Spain, was it forced to yield to pressure from the government of Primo de Rivera, and provide enough assistance so that the Banco could actually overcome its problems.

In the Netherlands and in Scandinavia, bank failures followed the slump of 1920. In Denmark the central bank took a fairly active stance and was able to avoid a major confidence shock. The Bank of the Netherlands seems to have been less successful in this respect, and the failure of one of the largest commercial banks shook public confidence. The Norwegian case stands out for the length of its banking troubles, which lasted from 1923 to 1928. As the wartime boom in the real sector was particularly buoyant, the slump was relatively more serious than elsewhere, particularly given the strong deflationary policy imposed to stabilize the currency and return to gold. Given the links between manufacturing firms and banks, and the unwillingness of the central bank to let lending of last resort jeopardize its monetary stance, it is not surprising that bank failures followed one after the other for a longer period than anywhere else. It is likely that institutional innovation embodied in the Bank Administration Act made things worse rather than better.

To sum up: the post-war slump in the real economy resulted in financial panics and runs on banks whenever (1) the central bank decided to refrain from providing the necessary liquidity, either for policy reasons or from sheer prejudice, and (2) the banks had established close long-term relationships with their client firms of the kind that characterized the so-called universal banks. The story repeated itself on a larger scale ten years later. The lesson was not better learned because the gold standard prevented central banks from responding to the needs of banks—and economies—in the early 1930s.

3.3 Stabilization and the return to gold

As long as the post-war fiscal problems persisted, prices continued to increase and currencies to depreciate. Eventually, however, even those social groups who found some benefit in inflation began to fear its continuation, and the compromises necessary to reduce spending, raise taxes, and restrict the creation of credit were agreed. In many cases the process was assisted by foreign stabilization or reconstruction loans and by temporary credits, both mainly from London and New York, but in some cases arranged through the League of Nations.

The issue of domestic loans to fund the excessive short-term debt was also important, notably in the French and Belgian stabilizations. At various dates between 1922 and 1927 the major countries in the first and second groups of Table 3.1 achieved the necessary degree of financial stabilization to restore the gold standard, with its commitment to sound money and fixed exchange rates. By the end of the decade only the Spanish peseta remained to be stabilized.

The dates at which this was achieved *de facto* (legal restoration was sometimes delayed for various reasons) are given in Table 3.2, together with a measure of the extent to which the foreign exchange value of each currency had depreciated as compared with its pre-war parity. The countries are again arranged in three groups which correspond to those in Table 3.1. The extreme cases of inflation and hyper-inflation, leading to currency depreciation to 10 per cent of the pre-war parity or less, are shown in the upper group. In the middle group are examples of countries which allowed serious inflation to continue after 1920, and experienced depreciation of their currencies to between 10 per cent and 30 per cent of the pre-war rate. The six countries which imposed deflationary policies after 1920 and were able to return to gold at the pre-war parity are covered in the lower group.

The First World War had imposed heavy costs on Britain, but she had been less adversely affected than the Continental belligerents by physical destruction and financial disruption and, despite Keynes's

Table 3.2. Post-war stabilization of currencies, 1922–1929

	Year of *de facto* restoration of gold standard	New parity as percentage of pre-war
Currency depreciation to less than 10% of pre-war parities		
Germany	1923	0.0000000001
Poland	1926	0.000026
Austria	1922	0.00007
Hungary	1924	0.0069
Romania	1927	3.1
Bulgaria	1924	3.8
Portugal	1929	4.1
Greece	1927	6.7
Yugoslavia	1925	8.9
Currency depreciation to between 10% and 30% of pre-war parities		
Finland	1924	13.0
Belgium	1926	14.5
Czechoslovakia	1923	14.6
France	1926	20.3
Italy	1926	27.3
Return at pre-war parity		
Sweden	1922	100
Netherlands	1924	100
Switzerland	1924	100
United Kingdom	1925	100
Denmark	1926	100
Norway	1928	100

Sources: Brown (1940: i. 393–402, ii. 919 and 1028); Nurkse (1944: 116); Nötel (1986: 181–3).

forceful dissent, prevailing opinion strongly favoured a return to gold at the pre-war parity. The objective, the method, and the price to be paid were clearly set out early in 1920 in a memorandum by the Bank of England to the Chancellor of the Exchequer (quoted in Howson 1975: 18):

The first and most urgent task before the Country is to get back to the gold standard by getting rid of this specific depreciation of the currency. This end can only be achieved by a reversal of the process by which the specific depreciation was produced, the artificial creation of currency and credit, and for this the appropriate instrument is the rate of interest. The process of deflation of prices which may be expected to follow on the check to the expansion of credit must necessarily be a painful one to some classes of the community, but this is unavoidable.

None of the other belligerents shared this determination, but among the neutrals the Scandinavian countries, Switzerland, and the Netherlands were similarly committed to the restoration of the pre-war parity of their currencies. In Denmark voices were raised among politicians, businessmen, and economists recommending stabilization at about 75 per cent of the old parity, but they were unable to win the struggle for public opinion against the slogans of the deflationists, who demanded return to 'our old, honest krone'; there was a parallel debate in Norway, where an even greater appreciation of the currency was required.

In the event, a very high price had to be paid for this belief in the virtues of the return to gold at the old parity. In Britain the collapse of the export industries, and the sustained downward pressure on wages, employment, and working-class living standards, have frequently been seen as the sacrifice which the financial interests of the City imposed on industry in order to preserve the gold standard. In 1928 Keynes (1971–89 edn.: vol. 9, 85) commented on the contrasting fortunes of Great Britain, which had been financially conservative and responsible, and France, which had 'offended so grossly against all sound principles of finance' and was 'avoiding the sacrifices of deflation'. He noted that despite this the Bank of France had emerged much stronger than the Bank of England, and concluded with asperity: 'Assuredly it does not pay to be good.'

In Denmark and Norway the return to the gold standard caused a depression from 1925 to 1928 which was almost as severe as that in 1929–33, with sharply falling production and prices, an increased number of business failures, and very high unemployment. Sweden similarly experienced considerable difficulties at the beginning of the 1920s, in contrast with Finland, which chose not to follow the deflationary path.

Italy, together with the two other 'late stabilizers', France and Belgium, initially enjoyed a brief period when their exports benefited from exchange rates more favourable than those of the countries which followed orthodox deflationary policies. However, once Mussolini had decided that the lira should be stabilized at the *quota novanta*, representing a substantial upward revaluation of the prevailing rate, it became necessary to impose painful deflationary measures, resulting in slower growth of output and exports, and higher unemployment.

Once stabilization was achieved, further problems were created by the extent of the relative over- and undervaluation of currencies resulting from the independent and unco-ordinated process by which each country selected its parity. Some currencies, notably those of Britain, Italy, Denmark, and Norway, were probably over-valued; in other cases, including France, Belgium, and Poland, the rate selected provided a degree of undervaluation. These disparities had important consequences for competitiveness in foreign trade. In addition, other powerful forces were also at work, and these too contributed to the highly varied pattern of export performance in the 1920s. The data are given in Table 3.3, listed in the order indicated by the level achieved by 1929 relative to 1913.

In the case of Britain it has been generally accepted that the decision to return to gold at the pre-war parity of $4.86 resulted in an overvaluation of the currency by about 10 per cent. It would, however, be wrong to see this as the primary reason for the decline of the export sector shown in Table 3.3. Coal, textiles, shipbuilding, and other major export industries were already confronted by an extremely difficult structural problem created by technological change, the growth of substitute products, and the opportunity which the war had created for import substitution and for foreign competitors outside Europe, notably the United States and Japan, to capture a large share of Britain's traditional markets. Nevertheless, the overvaluation of sterling undoubtedly added significantly to the fundamental structural weakness, as did the high interest rates necessary to sustain the currency.

As Table 3.3 indicates, the 1929 volume of British exports was still 19 per cent below its level in 1913. Of the other European countries

Table 3.3. Volume of merchandise exports, 1924–1929 (1913 = 100)

	1924	1925	1926	1927	1928	1929
Denmark	142	138	147	170	179	181
Netherlands	125	135	140	161	166	171
Norway	111	122	130	141	143	167
Finland	125	139	142	160	156	161
Sweden	96	106	114	136	131	156
France	119	124	134	146	148	147
Italy	117	127	123	116	118	123
Belgium	—	73	76	96	108	107
Switzerland	87	90	87	98	101	101
Germany	51	65	72	73	82	92
Austria	76	82	77	87	92	86
United Kingdom	76	75	67	77	80	81

Source: Maddison (1991: 316–19).

which re-established their currencies at the pre-war parity against gold only Switzerland was unable to expand her exports above the pre-war level. The Scandinavian countries and the Netherlands all increased the volume of their exports very substantially relative to 1913, despite the probable overvaluation of their currencies. However, these increases consisted largely of specialized foods and raw materials which were less subject to competitive pressures than manufactured goods and coal. Some of these factors underlying the differential movements in exports in the 1920s are discussed in Chapter 4.2.

3.4 The 'rules of the game'

One consequence of the sequence of post-war financial developments and policies which was heavily emphasized in contemporary accounts of the period was the destabilizing effect of the massive flows of capital, both short-term and long-term. The process gained its initial momentum early in the 1920s, with the flight from currencies such as the German mark, the French franc, and the Italian lira, as those who could do so transferred their assets to what they perceived to be safer currencies. With the high interest rates necessary to defend the pound, London was a favoured haven.

Once confidence in the stability of the French and other Continental currencies—and in their underlying public finances—was restored, the speculative funds flowed back again in eager anticipation of capital gains when the new parities were legally established. For example, Italy was the recipient of a considerable capital inflow of this nature during the 18 months preceding the *de jure* stabilization of the lira in December 1927. There was a similar burst of speculation in 1925 and 1926 when the Danish and Norwegian krone appreciated sharply in anticipation of the *de jure* restoration of these currencies in January 1927 and May 1928 respectively.

The flow of gold to France

From a British perspective the loss of gold as flight capital rushed back to France after the success of the Poincaré stabilization at the end of 1926 was always mentioned and often resented as a major cause of the weakening in Britain's external financial position. In the first place France had elected to stabilize the franc at one-fifth of its pre-war value, whereas Britain had accepted the discipline necessary to restore sterling at the pre-war parity, and this was seen as a major source of balance of payments disequilibrium. Secondly, there was a dramatic increase in French reserves, accumulated at first in foreign exchange and later in gold, but the authorities did not respond to this by inducing a corresponding increase in the money supply. If they had done so this should have stimulated the rise in prices, which might have restored equilibrium.

In June 1928 French gold reserves were only 29 billion francs; by the end of 1932 they had increased by 53 billion francs but the increase in the note circulation over the same period was only 26 billion francs (Mouré 1991: 55–6). Instead, the returning French capital was mainly used for the purchase of government securities, either directly by the private sector or by the commercial banks as their deposits increased. The government in turn was able to repay a substantial part of its debts to the Bank of France. As a result, the large increase in the central bank's holdings of gold and foreign currency was to a considerable extent neutralized.

As seen from London, the gold standard was thus not operated according to the rules in France, and the necessary adjustment process was frustrated. The position was exacerbated by the very low level of French foreign investment. With their pre-1913 assets largely wiped out by the war and the Russian Revolution, French *rentiers* had become extremely reluctant to trust any more of their capital to foreign governments and enterprises.

Treasury and central bank officials in Paris and London argued bitterly in public and private over the reasons for the movement of gold to France, over what action should or could be taken in order for the flow to be reversed, and over whose responsibility it was to take the corrective measures. Even when it was recognized that the final outcome was not the result of a French policy wilfully designed to sterilize the inflow of gold, it was still regarded as a failing in the system leading to a serious maldistribution in international holdings of gold.

Eichengreen (1986) emphasized that the Bank of France could, in theory, have reduced its high reserve ratio by means of expansionary open market operations, but it was effectively precluded from doing so by statutory restrictions. These had been imposed by the 1928 stabilization law specifically to prevent a recurrence of the lax

monetary policies which were held responsible for the searing inflation of 1922–6. The British thought these restrictions should be
relaxed in the interests of international monetary co-operation; the
French were determined to protect their currency from any possibility of renewed inflation.

The United States gives priority to internal policy

Similar issues were debated with respect to the United States, the
other country to show a substantial increase in its gold holdings
during the 1920s. In the early part of the decade the American
banking authorities considered that this inflow was the result of the
abnormal post-war conditions in Europe, and that most of the gold
would in due course return to Europe and, therefore, should not be
used as the basis for domestic credit creation in the United States.
Neutralization was thus a deliberate policy, for which there were
'sound and compelling reasons' (Nurkse 1944: 73–5).

In the subsequent period, 1925–9, the United States continued to
neutralize any changes in the stock of gold, though on a less extensive scale. In 1928 and 1929 the Federal Reserve Board actually
initiated a progressive increase in interest rates in order to prevent
what it saw as an alarming rise in speculation on the stock exchange,
regardless of its implications for the requirements of international
stability. Countries such as Britain, which were running balance of
payments deficits at this time, might well have asked, with the
author of an official history of the United States in the world
economy (Lary 1943: 166):

whether a more aggressive policy of credit expansion could have been
safely followed with a view to supporting a higher level of prices and
money incomes in the United States, thus helping to meet the foreign
demand for dollars and relieving the strain on foreign exchanges and the
general world deflationary pressure that developed in the latter part of the
twenties.

Lary's answer was that, as was so often the case in the inter-war
period, considerations of internal policy were given far higher priority, and 'the threat to international stability, although not over-
looked, was regarded as a regrettable but necessary risk to be run in
rectifying an unsound domestic situation'.

Did the gold standard help to restore equilibrium?

These controversies over the policies of the two surplus countries, France and the United States, are a special case of the more general debate about the degree to which the recurrent crises in the international monetary system in the inter-war period could be attributed to the alleged failure of countries to operate the gold standard according to the rules followed in the pre-1914 era, thus depriving the system of its fundamental equilibrating mechanism. On a strict interpretation, the traditional policy required not merely that changes in holdings of gold should be automatically reflected in corresponding changes in the domestic currency, but that further purchases or sales of domestic assets should be made by the monetary authorities so that the impact of movements in gold was magnified in proportion to the central bank's reserve ratio.

In his League of Nations study of the behaviour of 26 countries during the years 1922–38, Nurkse (1944: 68) found that 'from year to year, central banks' international and domestic assets, during most of the period under review, moved far more often in the opposite than in the same direction'. The extent of the inverse correlation was even greater in the five-year period of fixed exchange rates when the restored gold standard was in operation: for 1927–31 international and domestic assets changed in the same direction in only 25 per cent of the possible cases, compared to 32 per cent for the inter-war period as a whole.

Various qualifications need to be made to this finding, such as the possibility that the response to the flows of gold might have been delayed, or that movements of private short-term capital might have distorted the pattern, and it must also be recognized that even the classical gold standard was not quite as simple and automatic as the textbook models suggested. Nevertheless, the broad conclusion was that there was an increasing tendency in the inter-war years to use gold reserves as a buffer to protect countries from the transmission of external shocks, rather than as the means by which fluctuations originating abroad were automatically transmitted to the domestic credit base.

In terms of the four factors noted in Chapter 1.3, it was the dislocation caused by the war and the post-war settlements that produced the capital and currency flows that put the gold standard under strain. The continuing controversies over the gold standard during the 1920s gave evidence both of a failure of leadership and the absence of international co-operation. All these discussions, of course, were undertaken within the framework of the gold standard, the presumed anchor of economic stability.

4

OUTPUT, PRODUCTIVITY, AND TECHNICAL PROGRESS IN THE 1920s

In this chapter the focus moves away from the financial policies and flows which were the dominant themes of Chapter 3 and to which we will have to return in subsequent chapters. Our aim here is to concentrate on developments in the 'real' economy; in particular to examine what was happening to output and output per worker during the 1920s.

After the massive economic problems caused by the First World War, some countries achieved relatively rapid improvements in industrial production; others struggled to regain their pre-war levels of output and advanced only a little beyond this in the late 1920s. Despite the difficulties, a number of factors helped to promote more rapid growth in productivity (output per hour worked), and this acceleration was a highly significant feature of the decade. In agriculture conditions were generally much less satisfactory than in industry, and what little progress was made at the beginning of the decade was soon interrupted; for most countries the second half of the 1920s was an acutely difficult period of falling farm prices and stagnant output.

We begin with an overview of the structure and stage of development of the various economies, and then analyse the movements in output in industry and agriculture. The final two sections examine the developments in productivity and the underlying sources of technical progress. We emphasize this feature of the 1920s as support for our fundamental proposition that the depression which overwhelmed the Continent at the end of the decade was the result of the policies which had been adopted during and after the war; it was not the uncontrollable outcome of a slowdown in technical progress or some other natural phenomenon.

4.1 The structure of the European economy

In 1913 the three most advanced countries, the United Kingdom, Germany, and France, had less than half of Europe's population, but accounted for 72 per cent of the Continent's output of manufactures, and a slightly higher proportion of its manufactured exports. As a result of the combination of the big three's own economic and political misfortunes, and the more successful performance of the Netherlands, Czechoslovakia, Spain, Italy, and the Scandinavian economies, this superiority had been slightly eroded by the end of the 1920s, but they were still the overwhelmingly dominant economic powers.

The best guide to the economic structure of the European economies in the inter-war period is given by the distribution of the labour force. The size and composition of the working population in the main European countries c. 1930 is analysed in Table 4.1. The number and proportion of occupied workers are classified in three sectors: (1) agriculture; (2) industry, including mining, manufacturing, and building; and (3) transport, finance, distribution, and other services. The 22 countries are listed in diminishing degree of industrialization, as indicated by the share of the working population in agriculture in column (2).

This ranking is also very strongly inversely correlated with economic prosperity as indicated by levels of per capita income. As can be seen in Figure 4.1, the lower a country's share of agricultural labour, the higher its per capita income. There were, however, a few countries (notably Switzerland, Denmark, and the Netherlands) with unusually high agricultural productivity, and they enjoyed a better standard of living than would be expected given the proportion of their labour force engaged in farming.[1]

---

[1] In some other cases (for example, Portugal) income is below the expected level. The probable reason for this is the classification of female farm servants as working in services, with a corresponding understatement of the proportion in agriculture relative to other countries.

Table 4.1. Occupational distribution of the working population, 1930

	Working Population (millions)	Percentage in		
		Agriculture	Industry	Services
	(1)	(2)	(3)	(4)
1. Less than 30% in agriculture, more than 40% in industry				
United Kingdom	21.65	6	46	48
Belgium	3.74	17	48	35
Switzerland	1.94	21	45	34
Netherlands	3.18	21	36	43
Germany	32.30	29	40	31
Total	62.80	20	43	37
2. About 35% in agriculture and in industry				
Austria	3.17	32	33	35
Denmark	1.59	35	27	38
Norway	1.17	35	27	38
France	21.61	36	33	31
Sweden	2.89	36	32	32
Czechoslovakia	6.72	37	37	26
Total	37.15	36	33	31
3. About 50% in agriculture and 20–30% in industry				
Italy	17.26	47	31	22
Portugal	3.95	48	18	34
Ireland	1.34	48	15	37
Hungary	3.83	53	24	23
Greece	2.75	54	16	30
Spain	8.10	56	21	23
Total	37.22	50	25	25
4. Over 65% in agriculture and less than 20% in industry				
Poland	15.00	65	17	18
Finland	1.72	65	15	21
Yugoslavia	6.48	79	11	10
Romania	10.46	79	7	14
Bulgaria	3.43	80	8	12
Total	37.09	73	12	15
Total Europe	174.26	41	30	29

Source: Bairoch *et al.* (1968).

The European economies fall broadly into four groups. In the top group were five highly industrialized countries. In the United Kingdom, Belgium, Switzerland, and Germany, at least 40 per cent of the labour force was working in industry; in the Netherlands the proportion was slightly lower than this, reflecting the larger size of the service sector. All these countries had less than 30 per cent of their working population still on the land; the proportion was exceptionally low in Britain and Belgium, and relatively high in Germany.

The second group of countries, including France, Czechoslovakia, Austria, and three Scandinavian countries, had also made considerable progress in the development from primary to secondary and tertiary activity, and by 1930 the working population was distributed in roughly equal proportions between the three sectors. Together the eleven countries in these top two tiers accounted for over 70 per cent of all the workers in industry and services in Europe.

The third group comprised the southern European countries of Italy, Portugal, Greece, and Spain, together with Ireland and Hungary. The share of the labour force in agriculture was still around half, and—except for Italy—the share in industry was still less than 25 per cent. The five countries in central and eastern Europe comprising the final group were still overwhelmingly agricultural and rural. They had 65–80 per cent of their labour force in farming and less than 20 per cent in industry. Together these two lower tiers accounted for almost two-thirds of all the workers in agriculture in Europe, and only a quarter of the workers in industry.

A very similar picture of the contrasts between industrial and non-industrial Europe can be drawn from data on the composition

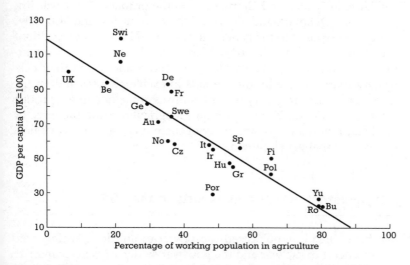

Fig. 4.1. GDP per capita and share of the labour force in agriculture, 1929

of merchandise exports (Table 4.2). Two-thirds of the exports of the industrial countries consisted of manufactured goods, with an even higher proportion for Switzerland, the United Kingdom, Austria, Germany, and Czechoslovakia. However, for two of the developed countries, the Netherlands and Sweden, the share of manufactures was only about 40 per cent, reflecting the extensive exports of meat, dairy products, fruit, and vegetables by the former, and of timber, wood pulp, and iron ore by the latter.

At the other end of the development ladder, the composition changes abruptly. For the twelve non-industrial countries exports consisted predominantly of foodstuffs and raw materials; manufactures accounted for only 15 per cent of the total. The differences between the two groups of countries in the scale of their export revenues is also very striking (see column (1) of Table 4.2). Exports of all kinds from the United Kingdom, Germany, and France comfortably exceeded those from all the remaining European countries combined. For many of the countries of eastern and southern Europe the extent of their participation in foreign trade was very limited.

There was thus very considerable diversity in the structure of economic activity and in vulnerability to changes in external conditions. The economic experience of the countries in the two upper groups of Table 4.1 was primarily dependent on developments in industry, though the absolute numbers occupied in farming were still large in France and Germany, and the primary sector was important for Denmark and Norway. These countries, and also Italy, were very exposed to the general state of world trade. The health of their economies could be strongly influenced by trends in competition from abroad, by changes in economic conditions in their customary markets, and by movements in exchange rates and tariffs. Conversely, the prosperity of the countries in the two lower groups rested almost entirely on conditions in agriculture and the price of food and raw materials, and most of them were much less vulnerable to external developments.

4.2 Industrial output and exports in the 1920s

We have already emphasized the powerful and long-lasting economic effects of the war and the post-war settlements in Chapter 2.

Table 4.2. Value and composition of merchandise exports in 1929

		Percentage of Total		
	Total Value (million $, f.o.b.)	Live animals, food, and drink	Materials, raw or partly manufactured	Manu-factures
	(1)	(2)	(3)	(4)
United Kingdom	3,542	7	16	77
Germany	3,210	5	22	73
France	1,965	13	21	66
Belgium	883	8	32	60
Netherlands	799	44	19	37
Italy	779	25	12	63
Czechoslovakia	606	11	17	72
Sweden	485	9	50	41
Switzerland	400	11	9	80
Austria	308	3	23	74
Industrial Europe	12,977	13	22	65
Denmark	430	82	6	12
Spain	410	57	21	22
Poland	315	33	47	20
Ireland	230	86	5	9
Norway	200	29	49	22
Hungary	180	67	13	20
Romania	170	41	58	1
Finland	160	9	74	17
Yugoslavia	140	47	44	9
Greece	90	34	64	2
Portugal	50	58	30	12
Bulgaria	45	29	63	8
Non-Industrial Europe	2,418	53	32	15
Total Europe	15,396	18	22	60

Source: League of Nations (1932) with conversion from national currencies based on annual average exchange rates given in Svennilson (1954: 318–19). The composition in columns (2) to (4) is based on the Brussels 1913 international classification. Re-exports, and exports of gold and silver, are excluded.

When we come to examine the detailed changes in production in the main industrial economies (see Table 4.3), a striking variety of different patterns of growth can be discerned, even over the relatively short period from 1913 to 1929. The fourteen countries divide into three distinct groups.

Table 4.3. Industrial production, 1913–1929

	1913–29 Growth rate (% p. a.)	Index numbers (1913 = 100)		
		1920	1924	1929
	(1)	(2)	(3)	(4)
Growth of at least 2.5 per cent per annum				
Finland	4.3	87	127	197
Netherlands	4.0	127	136	187
Czechoslovakia	3.9	87	124	186
Spain	3.2	103	130	166
Italy	2.9	104	128	158
Denmark	2.6	128	136	150
Growth of between 1.5 and 2.5 per cent per annum				
Sweden	2.3	96	109	143
France	2.2	62	110	142
Belgium	2.1	84	114	140
Norway	1.7	102	107	131
United Kingdom	1.6	100	111	128
Growth of 1 per cent per annum or less				
Germany	1.1	64	82	120
Austria	1.0	47	80	118
Hungary	0.2	48	67	103
Poland	−0.8	35	57	87
Total Europe	1.9	78	102	134

Note: Industrial production consists of manufacturing, mining, construction, and utilities, but for some countries only manufacturing is covered.

Sources: Mitchell (1978: 180–1) spliced where necessary to League of Nations (1945: 134–7) except for the following:

Belgium: Carbonnelle (1959: 358);

Czechoslovakia: Pryor *et al.* (1971), quoted in Kaser and Radice (1985: 542);

Finland: Hjerppe (1996: 128);

Germany: 1913 and 1925–9 from Mitchell (1978: 180) with interpolation for 1920–4 on basis of Wagenfuhr index quoted in Holtfrerich (1986: 204);

Hungary: 1913 and 1925–9 from Eckstein (1955: 171) with interpolation for 1920–4 on basis of League of Nations (1945: 137);

Poland: 1913 and 1920–7 from League of Nations (1945: 136) with 1928–31 spliced to Tomaszewski's compromise index for 1928–38 quoted in Kaser and Radice (1985: 565);

Spain: Prados de la Escosura (1995: 95);

Total Europe: Above indices combined with 1925–9 weights from League of Nations (1945: 128).

In the first, shown in the upper block, are six countries which increased their pre-war level of industrial output by at least 50 per cent. For the three most successful of these economies, Finland, the Netherlands, and Czechoslovakia, the overall increase was even better, over 85 per cent. In the second group, which includes France, Belgium, and the United Kingdom, are those which achieved only modest growth, raising pre-war output by 30–40 per cent by 1929. For the countries in the third group, including Germany and Austria, this was a most dismal period, with additions to industrial output of 20 per cent or less.

A substantial part of these marked contrasts can be explained by the two factors which were stressed in the previous chapters: the very great variations in the impact of the First World War and its immediate aftermath on economic and political conditions in the different regions, and differences in the nature and timing of the exchange rate policies adopted in the post-war period.

The direct and indirect consequences of the 1914–18 war affected economic activity in numerous different ways in individual countries (see Chapter 2). The divergent impact of its immediate effects is vividly demonstrated by the contrasts in column (2) of Table 4.3. By 1920 those nations which had remained neutral (the Netherlands, Spain, and the Scandinavian countries) and those which avoided occupation (Italy and the United Kingdom) were able to produce at least as much as they had in 1913; in the Netherlands and Denmark considerably more. In stark contrast, the devastation and disorganization in the belligerent countries which were defeated or occupied caused tremendous losses and a deep decline in production. In France and Germany output in 1920 was roughly one-third below the pre-war level; in Austria, Hungary, and Poland it plunged to less than half.

Some industries—notably steel, electricity and electrical engineering, motor vehicles, and chemicals—were strongly stimulated by wartime military requirements or by shortages caused by the interruption of pre-war trade flows. Not all of this increased production could find a market once the fighting ended, and certain industries were left with considerable excess capacity. In other sectors, as in the Swedish case discussed below, the spur created by the war continued to have very positive effects.

The direct effects of the war continued to be felt long after hostilities ceased in November 1918. As a rule, a natural catch-up process operated, so that once recovery began growth was most rapid in those countries which had suffered most in the war years. France, Austria, Poland, Czechoslovakia, Hungary, and Belgium all achieved a very rapid increase in output between 1920 and 1924 (see columns (2) and (3) of Table 4.3). By this standard, the German recovery was well below par, principally because of the continued disruption of activity due to the disputes over reparations, culminating in the occupation of the Ruhr, and the hyper-inflation of 1923–4.

For all four countries in the bottom block of the table, the initial post-war expansion was insufficient to offset the wartime destruction and disruption. They had not regained their pre-war level of output by 1924, and their recovery continued at a brisk pace in the late 1920s, though Poland had still not restored the 1913 level by 1929. Developments in the USSR deprived Poland of an important pre-war trade partner, and the expiration of agreements providing for large quantities of coal and other duty-free exports to Germany was followed from 1925 by a tariff war and a sharp fall in trade with Germany. The iron and steel industries and coal mining were particularly hard hit.

The very slow recovery in Austria was a direct consequence of the demise of the Austro-Hungarian Empire. Each new independent country wanted to locate varied production within its borders, and Austria's favoured position as the economic centre of south-eastern Europe disappeared.

1924–1929: the countries which restored pre-war parities

In the Netherlands, Switzerland, Denmark, Sweden, Norway, and the United Kingdom growth in the 1920s was restricted in varying degrees by the deflationary measures imposed in order to achieve an early return to the gold standard at the pre-war parity (see also Chapter 3.3). On the positive side it was expected that restoration of the pre-war values would provide a guarantee against inflation, contribute to domestic and international stability, and promote trade and prosperity. There was also a strong element of morality supporting the doctrine that a respectable country should not depreciate its currency.

However, significant costs were incurred in order to achieve this policy. High rates of interest depressed investment and impeded industrial expansion; and overvaluation of the currency made imports cheaper and exports less competitive. Price deflation also sustained the full burden of the interest charges on the large debts incurred by governments and private enterprises during and immediately after the war. The impact of these adverse effects during the post-war decade depended partly on differences in resource endowments, in the extent of dependence on foreign trade, and in the structure of production, and partly on the degree of flexibility with which economies adjusted to the parity restoration.

Neutral Sweden and the Netherlands both coped very well with the challenge posed by the high exchange rate, and both enjoyed a rapid expansion of industrial production in the late 1920s. In Sweden the problems created by the wartime malinvestment in some parts of heavy industry, and by the stabilization of the currency at the pre-war parity, were soon overcome and the economy surged forward. The transformation of industry was based on the exploitation of a very favourable resource endowment, including water for hydro-electric power, timber, and iron ore. Severe metal shortages during the war had encouraged the ore prospecting which laid the foundations for important developments in mining in the inter-war years. Wartime demands also hastened the development of lightweight metals, particularly aluminium, and these in turn gave rise to many new engineering products. Exports of iron ore, pulp and paper, machinery, and consumer durables expanded very rapidly in the 1920s, and provided an excellent platform for overall growth.

The Netherlands also did very well in the 1920s. By remaining neutral during the war it avoided both the financial problems and debt burdens which plagued the belligerents, and the destruction of its property and productive assets. The post-war increase in prices was considerably lower than in other countries and the extent of the deflation necessary to stabilize the guilder at the pre-war parity correspondingly limited. There was, nevertheless, a serious banking crisis in 1921–2, but the banking system emerged in good condition. From 1924 both industry and agriculture expanded strongly. The manufacturing sector was particularly successful in the development of new industries, including electrical engineering, artificial textiles, food products, and aeroplanes. On the basis of this performance the Netherlands achieved a high rate of growth of both industrial output and exports.

In sharp contrast, the growth of industrial production in the United Kingdom was painfully slow throughout the 1920s. Unemployment was very high and severe depression in the major industries pulled down the overall performance. The four large staple industries—coal mining, iron and steel, shipbuilding, and textiles—found themselves unable to compete in world markets during the 1920s, and all of them produced less in 1929 than in 1913. There is no reason to doubt that these industries suffered from the decision (effectively made as early as 1918) to return to gold at the pre-war parity of $4.86. It is generally accepted that this represented an overvaluation of about 10 per cent against the dollar. Against a number of European currencies, notably the French and Belgian franc, the German mark, and the Italian lira, the margin by which sterling was overvalued in the early 1920s was considerably larger.

However, there were other, more powerful, structural forces which were responsible for the depth and persistence of the problems facing British industry. 'Although the bulk of discussion about the problems of British industry in the inter-war period stressed British mistakes, faults, and short-comings, there can be no doubt that the basic causes were secular, impersonal and inevitable' (Kahn 1946: 72). The First World War dealt British overseas trade a savage blow from which it never recovered. In 1920, the volume of exports of all kinds that the United Kingdom was able to sell abroad was about 30 per cent less than it had been in 1913. Even in 1929—the best year for British exports in the entire inter-war period—export volumes still languished almost 20 per cent below their pre-war level. A detailed classification of United Kingdom exports of manufactures reveals a devastating loss of market share in all types of products and in all markets (Maizels 1965).

Before the war Britain had exported a very much larger proportion of its output of manufactures than any other country in Europe. Manufacturing as a whole depended on overseas sales for 45 per cent of its markets; cotton textiles for an extraordinary 75 per cent; woollen and worsted products, shipbuilding, and many types of machinery for about a half; iron and steel for roughly one-third. These high ratios made the United Kingdom especially vulnerable to external changes. Her markets shrank as a result of several features of this period, including the growth of import substitution in many traditional markets such as Canada, Australia, India, and western Europe; the imposition of higher tariffs; and the increase in competition from Japan, the United States, and other foreign manufacturers. This vulnerability was enhanced by the dominant position which the large export-dependent staples occupied in the British economy, accounting for roughly half of industrial output and employment.

Certain long-term trends had already started to weaken Britain's position in export markets before 1913. If they had continued at a normal peacetime pace it might have been possible for British exporters to respond by searching for new markets and developing new products and processes. Instead, the war severely curtailed British exports. Workers were recruited for the armed forces, production was diverted to meet military requirements, imports of raw materials for civilian products were severely restricted, shipping was unavailable to bring in supplies or to deliver goods to foreign customers.

This forced withdrawal from the market both accelerated the growth of import substitution and compelled importers to look elsewhere for the cotton cloth, machinery, shipping, and other goods and services they needed. While the United Kingdom was out of action, non-belligerents were able to expand their output in ideal conditions. The war thus presented rival manufacturers with a marvellous opportunity, and simultaneously prevented Britain from adjusting to these deeply detrimental developments. It compressed what might otherwise have been a long-drawn-out process of change into a few years, and made it difficult—in some cases impossible—for British industry to make a satisfactory response to the challenge.

The inevitable result of this check to adaptation to foreign competition was excess capacity, heavy losses, and high unemployment. In sectors such as iron and steel and shipbuilding, still further damage was caused by the huge increase in productive capacity undertaken in 1914–18 to supply armaments and other temporary military requirements. When peace came all these industries were left with excessive capacity built at inflated wartime prices, and they suffered from high unit costs and depressed markets. The resulting combination of financial weakness and unemployment in turn acted as a major constraint on the elimination of inefficiencies in industrial structure, organization, and practice which were essential if the economy was to prosper in the new conditions.

1914–18 was also a massive misfortune for the coal industry. Before 1914 Britain had enjoyed a substantial trade in exports of coal to Europe. The war, and the short-lived post-war boom, encouraged further expansion, often of old and inefficient mines. When the fighting ended it proved impossible to restore the previous level of exports. The Netherlands, Spain, and other former importers had developed their own mines during the war, and Britain also faced increasing competition from Germany and Poland. At the same time demand was reduced as a result of technical advances in fuel conservation and the growing use of substitutes, particularly in shipping, where oil replaced coal as the principal source of fuel. These trends were temporarily concealed by the disruption of German production and the closure of the Ruhr coalfields in 1923, but once Germany resumed production British coal exports dropped to four-fifths of what they had been in 1913. Domestic sales were also restricted by the depressed state of the major coal-using industries, and total output of coal thus remained well below the 1913 level throughout the 1920s.

It was widely recognized that Britain's early lead in industrialization had enabled her to build up a monopoly position in the supply of industrial goods which was not sustainable in the long run. As other countries developed their own resources, Britain's grossly disproportionate share of world trade and production would inevitably be eroded. However, the heavy commitment to the staple industries made adjustment more difficult, and no one expected the process to occur as abruptly as it did between 1913 and 1920.

Neither employers nor workers proved adept at adjusting to the scale and speed of the transformation made necessary by the war and the sudden deterioration in Britain's position. A difficult situation called for flexibility, intelligence, and vision, but the responses from the staple industries were typically stubborn, stupid, and short-sighted. Lord Birkenhead, a member of the cabinet, is reported to have said during the dispute which culminated in the General Strike of 1926: 'it would be possible to say without exaggeration that the miners' leaders were the stupidest men in England if we had not had frequent occasion to meet the owners' (Mowat 1955: 300). Together capital and labour aggravated the problems and impeded the necessary modernization and rationalization of industry.

Of course there were exceptions to the generally doleful British pattern. New science-based industries developed which were largely independent of export markets. Those which expanded rapidly in the 1920s included electric power supply, electrical machinery, and electrical goods and appliances; motor vehicles; rayon; and certain parts of the chemical industry, such as synthetic nitrogen, dyestuffs, drugs, and photographic chemicals. Some of these trades benefited from the first small steps taken in the direction of tariff protection at the beginning of the decade. The share of these industries in industrial output roughly doubled between 1913 and 1929, but they were still too small to compensate for the lack of progress in the old staples.

Another feature which differentiated the expanding industries from the old staples was the scale of their operation. The old industries typically consisted of very large numbers of small firms, whereas the new tended to have their output concentrated in a few large producers, and were thus able to enjoy important economies of scale. One significant example was the dominant role of Courtauld's in the production of rayon. A second was the formation of Imperial Chemical Industries (ICI) in 1926. According to Chandler (1990: 358) this merger 'provides one of the very few examples of systematically planned, large-scale, organization building in British industry before World War II'. It was the result of several factors: the earlier centralization of a major participant in ICI, Nobel Industries; the problems of British Dyestuffs, formed during the war to replace imported dyes; and the recent formation of IG Farben in Germany. The creation of ICI was followed during the later 1920s by administrative centralization. Although broadly following the American model, centralization at ICI was more complete due—Chandler suggests—to the British tradition of personal leadership.

For Denmark and Norway the costs of adopting a policy of financial deflation in order to restore the pre-war parity were also very high. Their exports consisted very largely of primary products (see Table 4.2): bacon, butter, and other foodstuffs from Denmark; fish and fish oil, wood pulp, and other raw materials from Norway. The markets for these products proved reasonably strong and exports from both countries increased rapidly in the 1920s despite the appreciation of the krone. However, the high taxes and tight credit policies imposed from the mid-1920s in order to avoid devaluation of the currency imposed a heavy burden on the domestic sector.

In Denmark the deflationary 'cure' was applied from 1925 to 1928, and was marked by severe depression, with widespread unemployment, declining production and prices, increased business failures, and the liquidation or bankruptcy of numerous banks. The results of a similar programme in Norway were even more drastic, with industrial production falling more steeply, and a bigger rise in unemployment. The banking system was also in crisis, with numerous bank failures in all regions reflecting the losses suffered by many farmers, manufacturers, and traders. By the end of the decade the attempt to restore the pre-war parity was seen by large sections of the business and farming communities to have been a serious blunder.

1924–1929: countries with depreciated currencies

France, Belgium, and Italy all delayed the stabilization of their currencies. This gave them several years in which their prices increased steeply and their currencies depreciated even more rapidly. During this period they benefited from low interest rates, an undervalued exchange rate, and a reduced burden of indebtedness. Industrial production in all three countries expanded rapidly, stimulated first by the post-war recovery from wartime destruction and dislocation, and then by the rapid growth of exports.

The contrast between the buoyancy of their trade, production, and profits, and the severe difficulties with which financially orthodox regimes such as the United Kingdom and the Scandinavian countries were struggling, was very pointed. Keynes (1972 edn.: 85) noted in 1928 that for Britain deflationary finance had brought a heavy burden of taxes and a million unemployed, and reflected that this was the price to be paid for remaining 'obstinately obedient to conventions':

Perhaps we deserve what we have got. France has abandoned principle and consistency alike, but she has always refused sacrifices which were avoidable . . . We in England have not submitted either to the warnings of theory or to the pressure of facts.

Currency undervaluation could be exploited either by gaining a competitive edge through lower prices expressed in dollars or other foreign currencies, or by accepting the international price and taking the benefit in higher domestic prices and increased profits. In 1929, prices for Italian exports of manufactures were no more than 11 per cent higher than in 1913; the increase was only 22 per cent for Belgium and 28 per cent for France. These levels represented a very substantial advantage over the United Kingdom, Sweden, and Switzerland, for all of whom the increase in export prices was approximately 50 per cent (Maizels 1965: 509). The favourable prices contributed to rapid export growth in all three countries.

This phase of inflation and currency depreciation eventually came to an end with stabilization in 1926. In France and Belgium the parities adopted are generally agreed to have reduced but not eliminated the competitive power derived from undervaluation. Although the surge in French and Belgian exports came to an abrupt halt with stabilization, the aggregate export series remained steady at about the level reached around 1927. There were signs of an incipient crisis in the sectors exposed to international competition, with falling profits and reduced sales, but industry acquired a new impetus from the expansion of domestic investment and growth was sustained.

This strong investment boom was stimulated by similar factors in both countries. The success of the currency stabilization and the end of the political uncertainty boosted business confidence. At the same time the achievement of a budget surplus, and the reflux of capital from abroad, led to lower interest rates and helped to end the 'crowding out' of private expenditure. In addition, the vigour of the previous phase of export-led growth strengthened the demand for additional capacity. These outlays enabled industry to install technically advanced plant and equipment, and so contributed to the process of modernization.

In Italy developments in the late 1920s followed a rather different and less satisfactory path. Exports peaked in 1925 as an acceleration of inflation threatened both domestic stability and the balance of payments. The value of the lira fell sharply: at the end of 1923 the rate was 112 to the pound sterling, by August of 1926 it had plunged to almost 150 to the pound. At that point Mussolini responded to his economic problems by electing to stabilize the lira at the *quota novanta* (90 lire to the pound). This large revaluation caused a decline in the volume of exports, and also increased the competitiveness of foreign manufactures in Italy's home market. These trends in international trade, together with the deflationary policies necessary to sustain the appreciated value of the currency, were responsible for a steep rise in unemployment and a slowdown in the growth of output.

German producers were cut off from many export markets during the war and hampered when it was over by the monetary chaos described in Chapter 3.1, which however had the advantage of clearing many firms of their debt and of lowering the costs of new

physical capital formation. After stabilization in 1924, German industry rapidly regained the international position it had held before
the First World War.

German industry made extensive use of cartels. Anti-trust
legislation was passed in 1923 but proved to be of little consequence. Many cartels evolved into trust companies or IGs
(*Interessengemeinschaften*). They were prevalent in chemicals, steel,
railroad equipment, and other heavy industries. The chemical IG
was merged into a giant firm, IG Farben, shortly after the German
stabilization. The resultant company dominated the chemical industry in Germany and rapidly became a major competitor on the
world scene.

The expansion of the Weimar economy after 1924 has been la-
belled unhealthy by many historians. One accusation is that wages
were too high to be sustained. Borchardt (1979) argued that
real wages outran productivity growth, taking 1913 as a standard.
This view, which makes the depression in Germany the result of
structural problems in the German economy, rather than of German economic policies, has become known as 'the Borchardt
thesis'. Holtfrerich responded that Borchardt's result was an
artefact of the way he did his calculations; when hourly wages are
compared with labour productivity per hour, no imbalance can be
detected.

Whatever the resolution of this calculation, everyone agrees that
wages were a larger share of national income in the 1920s than they
had been before the war. If this was not due to wages outrunning
productivity, then it was due to an increasing number of higher-paid
salaried jobs and a rise in the participation rate. In any case, the
profit and/or the rent share of income was reduced.

It is plausible to see such a change in income distribution as a
constraint on investment. Smaller capital income, in the absence of
changes in the workers' propensity to save, led to smaller investment funds. However, this inference is incomplete. Other critics of
the Weimar economy point to the capital inflows to be discussed in
the next chapter as a source of unhealthy capital expansion. The
problem, according to this contrary view, is that much Weimar
investment was 'unproductive'. Capital imports financed construction and particularly public construction which, so the story goes,
increased German foreign indebtedness without enhancing its productive capacity. The problem, in other words, was not that the
supply of capital in Weimar Germany was deficient; it was rather

that the demand for investment was skewed toward 'unproductive' purposes.

One final case which should be mentioned is the very successful performance of the Czechoslovakian economy in the 1920s. This new country inherited by far the most highly industrialized part of the former Habsburg Empire, and the capacity of the steel-making and engineering industries in the region had been considerably expanded during the war. However, the breakup of the empire shattered the pre-war trade links, leaving Czechoslovakia cut off from many of the traditional markets for its industrial products. Post-war inflation, the crisis of 1921, and the initial currency policy further delayed recovery. The attempt to revalue the depreciated currency to the pre-war standard of the Austro-Hungarian crown rapidly proved too painful, and was replaced towards the end of 1922 by a programme of currency stabilization at about 15 per cent of the pre-war parity.

This objective was successfully achieved and made possible a substantial expansion of exports and a healthy balance of payments surplus. From 1924 to 1929 industrial production increased at over 8 per cent per annum, probably the best performance of any country in Europe. A high level of domestic investment promoted the modernization and development of industry, with impressive advances in chemicals, textiles, footwear, glass, and ceramics and in some parts of heavy industry.

4.3 Agriculture in the 1920s

As can be inferred from Table 4.1, there were over 70 million men and women in Europe dependent on farming for their livelihood. In the immediate post-war years they enjoyed a fleeting period of prosperity, as prices soared while output was recovering from the ravages of the war. However, a crisis followed swiftly in 1920 when the post-war boom was brought to an end (see Chapter 3.1), and for the great majority of Europe's farmers the remainder of the decade was one of growing difficulty and deteriorating conditions.

The root cause of their problems was the excess supply of foodstuffs on world markets, created by continuous expansion of acreage outside Europe by countries able to produce competitive grains and other food crops at much lower cost. European producers were unwilling—or unable—to compensate for this by a corresponding reduction in their output. Given that there was also no prospect of a commensurate growth in consumption, the markets became progressively weaker. The downward trend in prices was briefly interrupted by crop failures in the mid-1920s, but then continued with renewed momentum. The final collapse came with frightening speed in 1930 and 1931. In Europe the two commodities which were most adversely affected were wheat and sugar. Both were especially important as a source of export earnings.

For wheat, the fatal interaction of increasing acreage and falling prices is illustrated in Figure 4.2.[2] As can be seen in graph (1), the long-run expansion of the area under cultivation by the four large overseas exporters—the United States, Canada, Australia, and Argentina—continued remorselessly. During the war and in the immediate post-war years a big reduction in European output and the collapse of Russian exports stimulated further expansion. Between 1909–13 and the mid-1920s the four overseas countries increased their output by almost 50 per cent. In contrast, acreage and output of wheat both in Europe and in the other producing countries was broadly the same in these two periods.

Unfortunately, however, this stability on the part of the European producers was not sufficient to prevent supply running ahead of demand on the world markets. Consumption of wheat was not increasing in step with rising incomes, and in the richer countries it was actually falling as consumers switched their spending to higher-quality foods such as meat and dairy products, fruit, vegetables, and eggs. In the United States, for example, wheat consumption per head of the population was approximately 15 per cent lower in 1924–8 than it had been in 1909–13. In France it dropped by 12 per cent, and in the UK by 8 per cent.

This imbalance between supply and demand was quickly reflected in mounting stocks of unsold wheat, with inevitable consequences for prices (see graph (2) of Figure 4.2). The steep fall in prices was temporarily reversed in 1924 and 1925, but only because of crop failures in each of these years in one or more of the main New World producers. As soon as overseas harvests recovered the

[2] The data on wheat production and consumption used in Figure 4.2 and the following paragraphs are from Malenbaum (1953). The price of wheat imported by Britain (Svennilson 1954: 246) is taken as a satisfactory measure of the trends in the world price in the light of London's free market and its role as the world's clearing house for wheat.

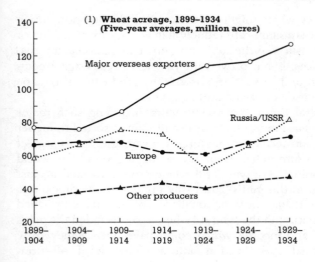

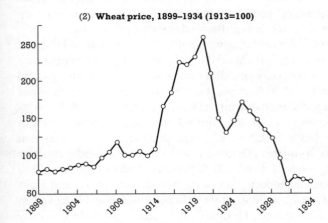

Fig. 4.2. Trends in the world wheat market, 1899–1934

decline continued. The prices of most products were falling in the late 1920s, but farmers suffered because the prices they received for their produce fell more sharply than those they paid. This adverse 'scissors' movement applied both to the relative prices of the equipment, fertilizers, and other goods purchased for use on the farm and to those of the goods and services they and their families consumed.

The one policy which might have prevented the deterioration in relative prices was a significant reduction in acreage by all the major producers. The issue was the subject of much discussion at international conferences, but it proved impossible to reach agreement. Every country found persuasive reasons why production should be preserved in their country and curbed elsewhere.

Instead, several European governments, including such major wheat importers as France, Germany, and Italy, resorted to higher tariffs and other protectionist measures in a vain attempt to protect their farming communities from the damaging trends in world markets. The initial post-war tariff barriers were erected against imported wheat in the mid-1920s, easily pre-dating the precipitate fall in prices in 1930. These nationalistic policies not only failed to restore prosperity; in the long run they also precluded the gains in productivity and income which could have been achieved by increased regional specialization and a higher level of intra-European trade. Furthermore, by artificially raising the domestic prices for agricultural products, the policies helped to restrict consumption and so exacerbated the fundamental problems.

The crisis would have been worse if output per unit of land had also been increasing, but this did not happen. For the world as a whole there were only modest fluctuations in yields around a broadly level trend. In Europe, the yield averaged 18.8 bushels per acre in 1909–14, declined during the war, and then recovered, but by 1924–9 had only reached 18.3 bushels per acre. These averages conceal very large differences in the productivity of European farms. In two countries (Denmark and the Netherlands) pre-war output already exceeded 40 bushels per acre, and in six others (Belgium, the United Kingdom, Germany, Sweden, Norway, and Switzerland) pre-war yields were above 30 bushels per acre. However, in Austria, France, Romania, Hungary, and Poland the yield was only about two-thirds of this, and in Italy, Spain, Bulgaria, and Yugoslavia it was no more than half this level.

Although a large part of these disparities can be explained by soil and climate, they indicate the potential improvements in yields that could have been reaped in the more backward countries by increased inputs of fertilizers, better seeds and crop rotations, and greater mechanization. Countries at a higher level of agricultural technology might also have been expected to make further advances. In fact, however, most countries made little or no progress in the 1920s, and in several yields actually declined. In the more developed regions of western Europe innovation was retarded by the slow recovery from the war, by the generally unfavourable economic conditions in agriculture, and by the adverse movements in the farmers' terms of trade. In eastern and southern Europe rural over-population, fragmentation of landholdings, and low levels of education and organization represented additional obstacles to the spread of better practices.

Land reforms were introduced in many parts of central and eastern Europe and in Greece by governments which saw this as a prudent response to rural unrest and the Bolshevik Revolution, but their effects on production were generally small. The most beneficial results were achieved in Czechoslovakia, where holdings of medium size increased in importance, raising the efficiency of production and marketings. In Poland, Bulgaria, and Hungary the reforms were extremely modest in scope and their effects correspondingly limited.

Even where the scale of redistribution was more radical it often had little impact on efficiency. In a number of countries the reforms essentially transferred ownership from landlord to tenant without changing the conditions of production, though it is argued that uncertainty regarding ownership rights discouraged investment and sales of land to more efficient farmers in Romania and Yugoslavia (Lampe and Jackson 1982: 352). The reforms also tended to reduce the marketable surplus, because the peasants preferred to increase the production of staple subsistence crops such as maize; in Romania the sharp fall in wheat production and yields has been attributed to the peasant's greater interest in cattle-rearing and fodder crops (Royal Institute of International Affairs 1932:149).

The problems faced by the European sugar producers were very similar to those just described in relation to wheat, except that in this case the destructive competition came from the tropical countries, especially Cuba and Java. During the First World War the output of European beet sugar fell sharply, partly because labour was not available, partly because of the closing of the British market. Production of cane sugar in the tropics expanded to take advantage of the new opportunities. When the fighting finished, there was a temporary shortage of sugar and a rise in prices, which encouraged further extension of the cane area in the tropics, but as soon as European production recovered to its pre-war level the boom came to an end. In 1913 beet sugar accounted for 45 per cent of a total supply of 20 million tons; in 1924 it accounted for only 33 per cent of an increased supply of 25 million tons.

By this point more sugar was being produced than could be

consumed, and prices tumbled. In 1924 the price in London was still 80 per cent higher than it had been before the war; one year later it collapsed with catastrophic speed to the pre-war level, and continued to fall. The producers nevertheless attempted to maintain their output, and looked to their governments for assistance. The constraints which had been agreed to at the 1902 Brussels Convention were quickly abandoned, and Europe returned to an era of protection and of bounties and subsidies for output and exports. These measures could work successfully for one or two countries, but when all producers attempted to rely on them they were self-defeating and simply served to aggravate the problems of over-production.

No country escaped the world crisis in agriculture at the end of the 1920s, but some suffered sooner and more deeply than others. The countries which were most badly affected by the decline in farm prices and conditions were the cereal and sugar beet exporters in eastern and central Europe. Other regions were able to escape the worst effects by increasing their output of products which were less vulnerable to competition from low-cost overseas producers, and those countries which were large importers of food, notably the United Kingdom, gained from the relative fall in food import prices.

In Italy, Spain, Portugal, and Greece farm incomes were partially sustained by sales of citrus fruits, wine, and tobacco. For Denmark, the Netherlands, and some of the other countries of western Europe, increasing consumption of meat and dairy products provided some shelter from the worst effects of the depression, and their farmers also gained from the steep fall in the costs of the fodder crops fed to their livestock. Nevertheless, for Europe as a whole the overall impact of the farm crisis was a severe set-back to economic progress, and retarded both industrial growth and international trade.

4.4 Aggregate productivity growth

Despite all the problems caused by the war and the post-war financial instability, there was a significant improvement in productivity in the 1920s. Table 4.4 portrays the rate of growth of both production per head of population and of productivity—measured by GDP

Table 4.4. Growth of GDP per head and per hour worked, 1890–1929 (average annual percentage rate of growth)

	GDP per head		GDP per hour worked	
	1890–1913	1913–29	1890–1913	1913–29
	(1)	(2)	(3)	(4)
Switzerland	1.4[a]	2.5	1.4[a]	3.2
Czechoslovakia	1.6	2.4	—	—
Netherlands	1.0	2.2	1.1	2.9
Norway	1.5	2.1	1.7	2.8
France	1.7	1.9	1.7	2.4
Spain	0.9	1.7	—	—
Denmark	1.9	1.6	2.1	2.6
Finland	1.9	1.6	2.2	2.2
Sweden	1.7	1.4	1.9	1.5
Italy	1.9	1.2	2.4	2.0
Belgium	0.9	1.1	0.9	1.8
Hungary	2.3	1.0	—	—
Germany	1.8	0.8	1.9	1.4
Portugal	0.4	0.8	—	—
Austria	1.5	0.4	1.7	0.8
United Kingdom	0.9	0.3	1.0	1.5
Ireland	0.9	0.3	—	—
Japan	1.4	2.4	1.7	3.5
USA	2.0	1.7	2.2	2.4

[a] 1899–1913.

Sources: (1) and (2) Czechoslovakia and Hungary: Good (1994); others, Maddison (1995: 104–8 and 180–4); (3) Maddison (1991: 274–5); (4) Maddison (1995: 249).

per hour worked—from 1890 to 1913 and from 1913 to 1929. In the period before the First World War there was normally very little difference between the two measures but this ceased to be true after 1913. In the later period GDP per hour worked increased much more rapidly than GDP per head (see columns (2) and (4) of Table 4.4).

While the performance of individual countries varies considerably, it is clear that in almost every case, both in Europe and in the United States and Japan, productivity growth accelerated between 1913 and 1929. The few countries which did not share in this process of productivity improvement included Germany, Austria, Hungary, and Italy. For Europe as a whole the average rate of growth of GDP per hour of labour input was a little over 2.0 per cent per annum over the years from 1913 to 1929, compared to about 1.5 per cent per annum between 1890 and 1913. The rate of increase in productivity was most rapid in Switzerland, Czechoslovakia, the Netherlands, Norway, France, Spain, and Denmark; but it was relatively low in two of the major economies, Germany and the United Kingdom.

It may at first seem odd that labour productivity grew more rapidly than production per head of population. This apparent paradox exposes one of the dominant trends of the twentieth century: the labour input from each person declined, while at the same time product per hour worked increased more than proportionally. The dominant explanation for this persistent tendency for total hours worked to rise more slowly than the increase in population, and thus for productivity to rise more rapidly than production per head of population, was the reduction in working hours which occurred in almost all industrialized countries in the years following the war. The working week was typically reduced from around 54 hours to about 48 hours in most industries and countries, and many more workers were able to take paid holidays.

This fall in hours worked reflected the universal and long-standing desire to take some part of the benefits of increased productivity in the form of more time for leisure rather than more consumption of goods and services. Further moves in this direction were made possible in the post-war period by the increase in the strength of the trade unions and the left-wing political parties, and also by the existence of favourable economic conditions for workers to exercise their greater bargaining power. The trend was thus in part a response to increases in productivity already achieved, but it also acted as a stimulus to firms to make further advances to compensate for the fall in labour input. Higher productivity also permitted increases in real wages, and in most countries the worker's lot thus improved due both to higher disposable incomes and to increased leisure.

However, as we shall see in Chapter 7, not all leisure was the result of free choice. Involuntary unemployment was generally quite high during the 1920s, and this rise above pre-war levels also helped to raise the rate of growth of GDP per hour worked above that of GDP per capita, most notably in the United Kingdom. Changes in the proportion of the population seeking work were a further contributory factor. For example, the larger-than-average gap in 1913–29 between the two measures for Denmark is accounted for by a fall in the participation rate, the small difference for Sweden and Germany by a sharp rise in this rate.

The growth of labour productivity is evidence not only that capital continued to be accumulated throughout this period—with interruptions—but also, what matters most, that there was no interruption in the incorporation of new knowledge into production techniques and in the formation of new human capital through better education. In fact, when economic historians of the inter-war years discuss supply factors and technical progress, they tend to portray a much more dynamic picture than when they focus on aggregate demand.

The distinguishing feature of modern economic growth identified by Kuznets, the 'extended application of science to problems of production', was not impaired during the 1920s. Just as life continues in the midst of great hardships, so modern industrial economies continued to introduce new products and production techniques, to improve managerial skills, to educate scientists and engineers and to diffuse literacy, even during the macro-economic chaos of the period. If anything the process gained advantage from spillovers of wartime technical progress. Seen in this light, the Great Depression at the end of the 1920s and the high unemployment rates of the inter-war decades seem to be an even greater tragedy in that there was nothing 'natural' in them. They were eminently man-made.

4.5 Technical progress and organization in the industrial sector

How can we account for the acceleration in technical progress achieved in the 1920s? One distinguished contemporary observer (Ohlin 1931: 66) referred to the decade in the following terms:

The rapid technical development during this period and the deep-going changes in organization, commonly called 'rationalisation', were factors which increased the need for adaptability. There would seem to be reason to believe that this rationalisation movement proceeded at a more rapid rate than before the war . . . New machinery was introduced on a larger scale than before, as shown by the enormous expansion of the machine-producing industries. The growth in output of manufactured goods took place in many countries with no, or only a small, rise of the number of workers.

It was a process of innovation, modernization, and mechanization which had begun in the late nineteenth century, and had proceeded most rapidly in the United States of America. Europe had made some headway before the war, but there were enormous opportunities for the Old World to exploit: in 1913 the average industrial worker in the USA produced roughly twice as much as his or her counterpart in the United Kingdom and Germany (Broadberry 1993). Many of the crucial advances made after 1919 had their origins in the earlier period, but were greatly improved and more widely diffused in the years between the wars. In addition, technical progress in sectors such as chemicals, motor vehicles, and aviation was strongly stimulated by the war, and this too created huge possibilities for increases in productivity in the inter-war period, in Europe and in the United States.

Of the numerous technological developments in this period, two were of quite exceptional importance: electricity for power, lighting, and communications, and the motor vehicle for transport. These two advances had the potential to bring about an immense rise in economic efficiency. They could dramatically reduce the cost and increase the flexibility of production, and their great benefits could be enjoyed across the whole economy: in the workplace and in the home. Cheap electric motors revolutionized the motive power for industry and agriculture and stimulated the mechanization of production; cheap motor cars, lorries, and tractors transformed transport costs for goods and people. Together they made possible the introduction of new products and new methods not only in large, centralized factories but also in small workshops and in remote villages.

Although small firms shared in the benefits of the new technology, the dominant tendencies favoured large plants, with substantial economies of scale. These were achieved by the application of techniques of mass production and standardization, introduced together with much closer control over the pace and continuity of the effort exerted by the labour force. Rationalization was, perhaps, just a fashionable catchword. It is indubitable, however, that in the 1920s considerable 'industrial restructuring' took place, often with the direct or indirect aid of the state. In Italy and Germany it was also promoted and sustained by the so-called 'universal banks'. In part such restructuring meant the creation of the cartels and combines to which we referred earlier, but it did not stop there. Measures to cut costs were adopted on a large scale.

These changes in turn allowed firms to lower prices dramatically, and so increase still further the market for their products. In Britain, for example, 55 employee weeks were required to produce a car at the Austin Motor Company in 1922, but only 10 were necessary in 1927 (Lewchuk 1987: 174). As a result of productivity improvements of this magnitude it was possible to bring down the price of an average passenger car from £550 in 1922 to less than £300 in 1929. At the Bat'a works in Czechoslovakia the introduction of American-style techniques of mass production in 1924–7 increased the production of shoes from 3.5 million to 15.2 million, with huge increases in labour productivity. These improvements permitted enormous reductions in price, and created vast new markets for the firm at home and abroad (Teichova 1985: 275).

It is not possible to discuss each breakthrough separately, but it may help to convey the scale and significance of the process to list some of the most important new products and processes which became available for widespread application in the years immediately before, during, and after the First World War. The selection made by Svennilson (1954) is reproduced in Table 4.5.

Striking gains in productivity were made in the production of capital goods, such as electrical and mechanical machinery, which thus helped to promote investment in a wide range of other industries; and also in goods purchased by consumers, including clothing, radios, refrigerators, and other household appliances. Some innovations transformed the distribution and packing of goods; others made their impact on the operation of financial and commercial offices.

Many of the advances were interdependent: progress in one field was stimulated by, and contributed to, developments in other fields. The expansion of production in the car industry needed not only the improvements to the internal combustion engine and the use of electric power, but also modern high-speed multiple machine tools that in turn depended on ball bearings, new alloy steels for the body, and new plastics for the interior fittings. Increased sales of cars and commercial vehicles then encouraged the construction of better roads.

Not everyone gained from this process. Productivity gains in one

Table 4.5. New products and processes (developed immediately before, during, or after the First World War)

Alloy steels (e.g. stainless steel); non-ferrous alloys; electric furnace technique; continuous rolling mills for steel production

The rotating cement kiln

New electrochemical processes

New methods for the fixation of atmospheric nitrogen

New methods for bleaching of wood pulp; the use of pulp in chemical production

Rayon

New methods of oil refining (cracking); hydrogenation of carbon; other synthetic methods for production of heavy organic chemicals

Synthetic solvents, plastics, and rubber

Ball bearings

Use of diesel motors for large ships

Electronic tubes; domestic radios

Aircraft

More efficient office machinery

New machinery in clothing industry

New methods of canning

Prefabricated material for packing; machinery for packing

Source: Svennilson (1954: 21).

industry could damage another; for example, large economies in the amount of fuel consumed in the generation of electricity severely harmed the coal industry. Old products such as gas lamps, woollen stockings, and horse-drawn carriages were displaced by new ones which were better and cheaper. There was also the danger that new methods of production and labour-saving equipment would reduce the demand for labour, and much was written about the threat of 'technological unemployment'. In the event, however, this did not normally become a reality, because lower demand in some sectors was more than offset by increased requirements in those which were expanding. The main causes of unemployment lay elsewhere (see Chapter 6).

It is interesting to note that the World Economic Conference held in Geneva in 1927 'unanimously recognized the benefits of rationalisation and scientific management and it asser[ted] the need of greater, more far reaching and better co-ordinated efforts in this field' (League of Nations 1927: 48). The statement reflects the intellectual climate of the time. On the one hand, the positivist faith in progress and technology, on the other the belief—widespread also outside the planned economies—that such progress requires an enlightened 'visible hand'.

5

INTERNATIONAL CAPITAL MOVEMENTS IN THE 1920s

O UR aim in this chapter is to ascertain the part played in the drama of the 1920s by the movements in international capital. We investigate the initial role of these capital flows in helping to promote the measure of stability achieved in the mid-1920s, and then their contribution to the detrimental developments which culminated in the crisis of 1931. We begin with an overview of the scale, origins, and destination of foreign lending during this decade, based on recently compiled estimates. These provide a more comprehensive picture than hitherto available. We then consider in more detail the special relevance of the inflow and withdrawal of these external funds to the position of Germany, including their relationship to the amounts paid in reparations, and to that of the producers of food and other primary products in central and eastern Europe and overseas.

5.1 An overview of foreign investment

Capital flows in the 1920s

The major sources of international finance and the destinations to which it went are shown in Figure 5.1 for the period 1924–30. In these seven years the flow of capital from the creditor nations, as measured by their records, amounted to at least $9 billion (equivalent in present-day prices to around $100 billion), and may have been appreciably more than that, perhaps between $10 and $11

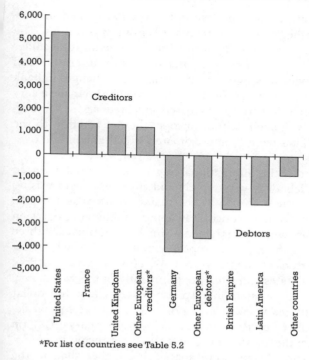

*For list of countries see Table 5.2

Fig. 5.1. Sources and destination of international capital flows, 1924–1930

billion.[1] Almost 60 per cent of this sum came from the United States of America, about 15 per cent each from the United Kingdom and France, and the balance, on a much smaller scale, from the other European creditors: Switzerland, the Netherlands, Czechoslovakia, and Sweden.

[1] For a more complete account of the estimates discussed in this chapter, and of the sources from which they are derived, see Feinstein and Watson (1995). They compiled independent estimates from the balance of payments records of both the creditors and the debtors. In principle these should agree; in practice it was found that the former were consistently lower. Feinstein and Watson argue that there are probably two major reasons for this discrepancy. First, errors in the data, including a systematic tendency for the major creditors to overstate their deficits and understate their surpluses. Secondly, the flight of private capital evading exchange controls and other restrictions on the free movement of capital in ways which distorted the current account statistics. They suggest a very arbitrary 15% as the likely order of magnitude of the addition required to the estimates based on the creditors' records.

About one-third of this massive outflow was invested in Germany, and a further quarter in the other European countries. The four British dominions and India together received a little under one-fifth, as did the countries of Central and South America. Much of this was intended as long-term investment, but changes in bank deposits and other forms of short-term investment also made a very significant contribution to the increased indebtedness of the borrowing countries. Indeed, within Europe, the net addition to the two types of capital were of approximately equal magnitude over the period 1924–30.

The high point of this international migration of capital occurred in 1928; it then fell away very rapidly and after 1930 there was no further net investment abroad by the major creditors as a whole. This aggregate movement conceals an apparent difference between the United States, which maintained a small net outflow for three further years, and the major European creditors, all of whom became net importers of capital from 1931. However, the outflow from the United States consisted predominantly of the withdrawal of foreign short-term assets in response to fears that the dollar would depreciate (as it did from April 1933 until the formal devaluation announced by Roosevelt at the end of January 1934); on long-term capital the United States was also a net recipient.

Interest rates in Europe were appreciably higher than in the United States, and those in Germany were among the highest in Europe. Capital flowed to selected European borrowers on a massive scale once stabilization had been achieved, and the adoption of the Dawes Plan provided—at least temporarily—a settlement of the dispute over reparations. In Europe, as elsewhere in the 1920s, it was the United States which was the dominant creditor, but the United Kingdom and France were also substantial net lenders.

The total inward flow (long- and short-term) to the 13 principal European borrowing countries amounted to approximately $10 billion in the seven years from 1924 to 1930, with over $7 billion going to Germany and the balance in much smaller sums to a number of other countries, notably Austria, Poland, Greece, and Hungary. At the same time many of these borrowers were themselves lending to others, and there was an outflow from them amounting to some $3 billion in the case of Germany, and about $750 million for all the other countries.

This movement of American capital to Europe in the 1920s initially contributed to international monetary stability by recycling the funds which flowed out to pay for the continent's current account deficits with the United States. In comparison with the pre-1913 period, Europe's trade balance had deteriorated because of the weakening in her relative industrial competitiveness. The net receipts on invisible account had also been greatly reduced. The loss of overseas assets as a result of the war and the Bolshevik Revolution had eliminated a large part of the pre-war inflow of interest and dividends from abroad, while the inter-Allied debts had increased the payments which had to be made to the United States. The inflow of foreign capital after stabilization thus helped to preserve the external value of the mark and other currencies. It also helped to sustain Europe's commitment to the gold standard.

But the gold standard that had worked so well before the First World War would not work nearly so well in the aftermath of that war. The capital flows of the 1920s masked many of the structural changes that had taken place during the war, changes in the fortunes of industries and of countries. As we have seen in Chapter 3.3, Europe attempted to regain stability in the 1920s by reviving the previous rigid system of international exchange. Capital flows were the lubricant that allowed people to ignore structural changes in the world economy for a few years.

Long-term foreign investment in 1914 and 1938

On the eve of the First World War long-term foreign investment in Europe amounted to about $12 billion, a little over a quarter of the total foreign assets accumulated by the world's creditor nations (see Table 5.1). Britain's interest in the Continent had declined in the late nineteenth century, as her investors switched their attention to the Empire and the developing regions of North and South America. By 1914 her holdings of European securities were little more than $1 billion, only 5 per cent of the UK total, and half what it had been forty years earlier.

In sharp contrast to this, the other European creditors had allocated some 40 to 50 per cent of their much smaller total foreign investment to Europe. France was by far the largest source of foreign capital on the continent, with European holdings amounting by 1914 to some $5.4 billion. Almost $2.5 billion of this was invested in Russia, with loans both to the tsarist government and to joint-stock banks and industrial companies. The total German investment outstanding on the continent in 1914 was about $2.5 billion, with the largest share allocated to Austria-Hungary, and less than

Table 5.1. Long-term foreign investment by creditor countries, 1914 and 1938 ($ million to nearest 50 million)

	1914		1938	
	Total investment	of which in Europe	Total investment	of which in Europe
United Kingdom	20,000	1,050	22,900	1,750
France	9,700	5,400	3,850	1,050
Germany	5,800	2,550	700	250
Netherlands	1,200	}	4,800	1,650
Belgium	} 4,300		1,250	300
Switzerland		} 3,000	1,600	800
Sweden	}		400	350
Italy	} 1,400		400	100
Other Europe[a]		}	650	150
Total Europe	42,400	11,300	36,550	6,400
United States	3,500	700	11,500	2,350
Other countries	200	—	4,750	600
Total	46,100	12,000	52,800	9,350

[a] For 1938 includes $400m for Portugal and $100m for Spain, and $150m for Czechoslovakia (all of it in Europe).

Source: Feinstein and Watson (1995).

$500 million in Russia. The remaining countries, including Belgium, the Netherlands, Switzerland, and Sweden, had total holdings in Europe of some $3 billion, but there is no information about the countries in which it was invested. The United States had as yet ventured into Europe on only a modest scale, with assets of some $700 million, almost all in the form of direct investment in manufacturing, oil distribution, and other commercial activities.

World War I and its immediate consequences played havoc with these investments. France and other holders of Russian securities lost their entire capital when the tsarist regime was overthrown. Investments in enemy countries either became worthless or were very severely depreciated. According to one estimate, only a quarter of the nominal value of France's pre-1914 foreign securities in Europe survived in 1919 (Meynial, quoted in Royal Institute of International Affairs 1937: 131). German losses were even more striking, and by the end of the war almost nothing remained of her previous holdings of foreign securities. Britain was left with little more than a third of its investments in Europe, and was also compelled to sell over $3 billion of her pre-war dollar securities in order to meet wartime obligations for equipment purchased in the United States. In total the foreign assets lost by the three main European creditors may have exceeded $12 billion, over a third of the investments they had accumulated abroad over the preceding century (Royal Institute of International Affairs 1937: 131; United Nations 1949: 4–5; Woytinsky and Woytinsky 1955: 199–200).

While European assets were thus being sharply diminished by these wartime losses and sales, the United States greatly strengthened its economic position. In 1914, long-term private foreign borrowing by the United States exceeded her investments abroad by over $3 billion. By 1919 the United States emerged from the war with foreign long-term assets of $6.5 billion, and liabilities of only $2 billion, and was from then on a substantial net creditor in respect of private long-term capital. The United Kingdom and the Netherlands also show a small nominal increase, but the transwar changes were dominated by the rise in the long-term external assets of the United States. Despite this, the United Kingdom remained the largest overall creditor, with long-term foreign assets double those of the United States.

Some two decades later, on the eve of the Second World War, the amount invested in Europe was a little over $9 billion, less than a fifth of the world total. Of the pre-First World War European creditors, only the United Kingdom shows any advance, even in nominal terms, on the 1914 level. However, Europe remained of limited interest to British investors. As in the pre-1914 period, the greater part of the long-term capital outflow from the United Kingdom was directed to the dominions and India. United States capital in Europe had increased to over $2.5 billion by 1938, outstripping investments of about $1.7 billion each for the United Kingdom and the Netherlands. The principal European borrowers from the United States were Germany, the United Kingdom, Poland, and Italy.

The 1938 figures in Table 5.1 provide a useful record of the level of foreign investment as it stood at the end of the period. However, the net change between the two benchmarks actually conceals some of the most crucial features of the capital flows in the inter-war period. First, it relates only to long-term investment. In 1914 short-term liabilities (and corresponding assets) were small, even for the United Kingdom, and were closely related to the financing of trading activities and to London's central position as banker for much of the world. During the inter-war period the extent and character of these short-term investments changed enormously: they grew very much larger and became far more volatile. The changes indicated by Table 5.1 omit all record of these developments, and thus give no indication of the violent fluctuations in short-term capital which occurred during the inter-war years.

Second, the character of the capital flows, both short-term and long-term, differed very markedly in the successive decades of the 1920s and 1930s, with radical changes in their origin, direction, motivation, and effect. Estimates of the stock of capital at the beginning and end of the period are thus a very inadequate basis for a full appreciation of the nature and causes of international capital movements in the intervening years.

5.2 European lending and borrowing

Relevant balance of payments statistics for the individual European borrowers and lenders, for the two periods 1924–30 and 1931–7, are summarized in columns (1) and (2) of Table 5.2. In the first period the records of the debtors show an immense net inflow of some $7.8 billion, an average rate of over $1.0 billion per annum, though, as noted above (see footnote 1), the true figures might be roughly 15 per cent lower than this. The movement of capital was dominated by foreign lending to Germany, which received more than $4 billion, over 50 per cent of the gross flow to Europe. Most of this capital came from the United States, and for a while it seemed that there was no limit to the appetite of American issuing houses and their investors for German bonds—regardless of the purposes for which the loans were raised—or for the interest to be earned from placing money on short-term deposit with German banks. The next largest destinations, a long way behind, were Austria and Italy, which together obtained about $1.5 billion. Roughly $1.3 billion was invested in eastern Europe, especially Romania, Poland, and Hungary. These were quite large sums relative to their national economies, giving foreign capital a significant role in their inter-war economic and political history.

On the other side, the payments accounts of the principal European creditors show a capital export of $3.8 billion, with France and the United Kingdom each contributing approximately $1.3 billion, and the Netherlands and Switzerland each a little under $400 million. As in the nineteenth century, Europe was a relatively unimpor-

Table 5.2. Balances on current account, gold and foreign currency, European creditors and debtors, 1924–1930 and 1931–1937 ($ million to nearest 10 million)

(+) = net capital export, (−) = net capital import

	1924–30 (1)	1931–7 (2)	1924–37 (3)
Europe: creditors			
United Kingdom	1,300	−4,000	−2,700
France[a]	1,340	−690	650
Netherlands	380	−290	90
Switzerland	370	−340	30
Czechoslovakia	250	90	340
Sweden	180	−20	160
Total	3,820	−5,250	−1,430
Europe: debtors			
Germany	−4,190	1,010	−3,180
France[a]	—	2,190	2,190
Austria	−860	−150	−1,010
Italy	−710	−50	−760
Romania	−440	−110	−550
Poland	−400	70	−330
Hungary	−320	20	−300
Greece	−310	−120	−430
Belgium	−240	230	−10
Norway	−140	0	−140
Yugoslavia	−80	−50	−130
Bulgaria	−50	20	−30
Finland	−40	150	110
Denmark	−40	60	20
Estonia, Latvia, and Lithuania	0	40	40
Ireland	30	−130	−100
Total	−7,790	3,180	−4,610
Total Europe	−3,970	−2,070	−6,040

[a] France is included with the creditors for 1924–32 and with the debtors for 1933–37; the estimates cover the French overseas territories, except Indo-China for 1924–30.

Source: Feinstein and Watson (1995).

tant outlet for British investors, most of whose funds were still directed to the Empire and South America, but their own continent accounted for a larger share of the foreign lending by France and the other European creditors. Taking the figures as they stand, there appears to have been a net inward flow for Europe as a whole during these seven years of about $4 billion but, as suggested earlier, it is likely that the estimates are subject to a bias tending to under-state the outflow from the creditors and overstate the inflow to the debtors, so the actual net import of capital by Europe from the United States was probably considerably lower than this.

For Germany the peak year for the inflow of capital was 1928, when it reached $1 billion; it then dropped very sharply. Wall Street stock prices, which had started to climb in 1927, were surging up-wards in 1928, luring more American investors away from foreign lending in the hope of a quick fortune at home. More seriously, there were growing doubts in the United States about the rapid expansion of Germany's external obligations, and the unproductive purposes for which some of the foreign capital had been raised; doubts partly stimulated from within Germany by those concerned about the increase in the country's indebtedness. From 1930, with the accession of Brüning, the adoption of deflationary policies inten-sified the economic depression and, after the success of the National Socialists in the general elections in September of that year, the sense of impending political crisis was a major deterrent to further foreign investment.

For the other European debtors the peak came a year earlier, when Austria, Italy, Poland, and Yugoslavia all raised large sums in the United States. Sizeable new bond issues were still possible for a few countries in 1928, including Denmark, Norway, and Italy in New York, and Greece and Hungary in London, but the boom was over and during the following years new lending fell away very rapidly. Economic conditions in many areas were already deterio-rating, particularly in the agricultural regions of central and eastern Europe. A sharp decline in prices for their wheat, sugar, and other farm products drove down export revenues and drastically weak-ened the ability of these countries to service their foreign debts. For the European debtors as a whole, annual capital inflow dropped from about $1.7 billion in 1927 and 1928 to $1 billion in 1929, and less than half that a year later.

A classification of European borrowing in the 1920s

Examination of alternative data sources provides a useful supple-ment to the story told by the balance of payments data. The alterna-tive data cover separate categories of foreign investment in either direction: new issues of long-term shares and bonds for foreign borrowers, purchases and sales of existing securities and of real property, amortization and repayment of debts, direct investment, and changes in short-term international indebtedness. There are serious gaps in these data which make it impossible to cover all items as fully or as accurately as would be desirable, but they provide more details about some items.

Estimates on this alternative basis were compiled for each of the 17 European debtors for the period of massive inward capital flow from 1924 to 1930. The results are given in column (1) of Table 5.3 for Germany, and in column (2) for the other European debtors as a group. Total capital movement as measured by the balance of payments data is given in row 3, and as measured by the capital transactions in row 12. The difference is shown in the final row as errors and omissions. The remarkably small size of this residual must be partly the fortuitous outcome of compensating errors in various components of the two estimates and, in column (2), in the estimates for the different countries. It is, nevertheless, an encouraging result, and suggests that the overall results are broadly reliable despite all the numerous uncertainties in the two sets of figures.

Row 4a shows that almost $3.5 billion of new long-term finance was obtained by the European debtors from external bond issues in the capital markets of the major creditors. The lion's share of this, 58 per cent, came from the United States; the United Kingdom provided 18 per cent, the Netherlands 9 per cent, Sweden 7 per cent, and Switzerland and Sweden each 4 per cent.

This classification of the origins of the long-term bond finance must, however, be qualified by the observation that it is possible to identify only the immediate, not the ultimate source of the funds. Thus if a loan was issued in Switzerland, but the shares were mainly purchased by French or German investors, the statistics would still show this as capital from Switzerland. For Germany, about 40 per cent of these loans were floated for governments and municipalities, and 60 per cent for private corporations; in the other countries corporate borrowing was responsible for only 30 per cent, and the bulk of the new issues was made by central and local government.

Investment in Germany from countries other than the six major creditors (for example loans from Belgium or Italy), and in other European countries from Germany and Czechoslovakia, are shown in row 8. The $450 million allowed for the estimated inflow under

Table 5.3. Comparison of the balances on current account, gold and foreign currency with direct estimates of capital transactions, European debtors, 1924–1930 ($ million to nearest 10 million)

Balance of payments: (−) = Deficit or increase in assets = Net capital import
Capital transactions: (+) = Decrease in assets/increase in liabilities;
                        (−) = Increase in assets/decrease in liabilities

	Germany (1)	Other European debtors[a] (2)	Total (3)
Balance of Payments			
1. Current account balance	−3,620	−2,810	−6,430
2. Gold and foreign currency	−570	−790	−1,360
3. Total Capital Movement	−4,190	−3,600	−7,790
Capital transactions			
Long-term capital			
4a. New bond issues abroad			
Central and provincial governments	470	1,030	1,500
Municipalities	160	210	370
Corporations	980	550	1,530
Total	1,610	1,790	3,400
b. New share issues abroad	90	240	330
5. *Less*: Repayments of debt	−260	−530	−790
6. Direct inward investment	120	200	320
7. Foreign purchases of domestic securities and real property	1,350	0	1,350
8. Other capital inflows	30	420	450
9. *Less*: Investment abroad by debtors	−1,050	−150	−1,200
Net long-term capital movement	1,890	1,970	3,860
Short-term capital			
10. Increase in assets	−1,050	n/a	n/a
11. Increase in liabilities	3,450	n/a	n/a
Net short-term capital movement	2,400	1,150	3,550
12. Total Capital Movement	4,290	3,120	7,410
Errors and omissions	−100	480	380

Note: Rows 4–6 cover the import of capital from the six main creditors; row 8 covers all forms of capital import from other countries, e.g. by Austria from Germany (offset by the increase in Germany's assets in row 9) and by Romania from Czechoslovakia.

 [a] See Table 5.2 for list of countries.

Source: Feinstein and Watson (1995).

this heading is very uncertain. The last entry relating to long-term capital, in row 9, covers the estimated outward movement of capital from these debtors; for example, investment elsewhere in Europe by Germany, and by Belgium or Italy in Africa. (The foreign lending by Germany is offset by row 8 to the extent that it was a movement of capital to the other European debtors.)

The enormous sums involved in short-term capital movements over this period are indicated in rows 10 and 11. There was a substantial outflow as banks and other concerns in the creditor countries built up their private external holdings of floating assets. In the case of Germany this amounted to over $1 billion. For Germany, this increase in net short-term finance was significantly more important than the supply of long-term capital, and accounted for about 55 per cent of the total inflow in 1924–30. For the other countries the proportion was rather smaller, but short-term capital still made up about 37 per cent of the total inflow.

5.3 Reparations and capital flows to Germany

The huge sums which poured into Germany were frequently portrayed by German politicians and financiers as the inward transfer necessary to permit the payment of reparations. In reality, however, reparations amounted to at most one-third of the gross receipts from abroad. In the period 1924–30 the total amount paid in reparations amounted to approximately $2,400 million (about 2.3 per cent of Germany's aggregate national income over these years), whereas the gross inflow of capital during the same period amounted to approximately $7,000 million, or 6.6 per cent of national income (Schuker 1988).

As long as United States bankers and investors remained eager to invest their capital in Germany, the much-debated transfer problem created by the demand for payment of reparations to the Allies was effectively solved. There were, of course, expressions of concern, both within Germany and outside, that at a later date these loans would have to be repaid and Germany would then face an impossible double burden. But the hunger for external capital was too powerful to be stemmed by such remote considerations.

A number of recent American studies have developed the theme originally stated by Mantoux (1946) in criticism of the campaign fought at the time by Keynes (1919). They have argued that the domestic burden involved in raising the necessary sums through taxation was also considerably exaggerated, and that after the downward adjustment made under the Dawes Plan—perhaps even before—the amounts were well within Germany's capacity to pay.

However, this analysis does not allow sufficiently for the fact that it was envisaged at the time that payments would be progressively raised as the German economy expanded, or for the extreme reluctance of Germans to accept even a modest increase in taxation to meet what was universally regarded as an unjustified and oppressive imposition by hostile antagonists. Thus, even if the economic aspects of the problem were not as crippling as had been assumed in the 1920s, the exaction of reparations was still of deep political and psychological significance for Germany. The issue thus remained a paramount cause of instability and a barrier to international economic co-operation.

The figures quoted above show that the average annual capital flow to Germany net of reparations was equivalent to over 4 per cent of her national income. Given the low level of domestic savings, the willingness of foreigners to fund German capital expenditure enabled the country to live markedly beyond its means. There were several reasons for the acute shortage of domestic capital. The years of war and hyper-inflation had wiped out virtually all liquid capital, including most of the reserves of the banking system; and fear of inflation remained a deeply inhibiting factor even when stability was restored. There was also considerable misallocation of available funds to unprofitable industries, including agriculture, and to desirable but not revenue-yielding social amenities.

Foreign capital thus permitted a higher level of investment and consumption in Germany than domestic resources would have supported; it enabled central and local government to spend more and tax less; the supply of imported goods was greater than it would otherwise have been; and the Reichsbank was able to add substantially to its reserves of gold and foreign exchange.

The liquidity of the banking system was also greatly improved by the funds received from abroad, although the banks were following a risky strategy to the extent that they relied on short-term deposits to make long-term loans. The massive foreign borrowing contributed to Germany's industrial rationalization and revival, notably in the coal, iron and steel, electrical, and chemical industries. However, only about 60 per cent of the long-term foreign capital issued in Germany in 1924–30 was taken by private enterprises, the remainder going to various public and semi-public bodies, such as the cities and municipalities. This enabled the local bodies to make substantial investments, partly in public utilities, urban transport, and housing, partly in social, cultural, and sporting facilities.

This position was stable only as long as the necessary imports of funds could be maintained, and the underlying problems and social conflicts meant that the economy was extremely vulnerable to any change in the preferences of American investors. The flow of long-term capital from abroad fell sharply in the first half of 1927, following a bitter attack on foreign borrowing by the Reichsbank president, Dr Schacht, and the withdrawal of the tax concessions previously enjoyed by foreign subscribers to German bonds. This subjected the economy to great pressures, and after a decline in gold reserves the tax exemption was reinstated and the bond flotations quickly revived. They reached a peak in the second quarter of 1928, then fell abruptly and had virtually ceased by the spring of 1929. The flow of capital from abroad recovered in 1930, but in 1931 the situation was transformed and there was actually a net outflow of over $600 million.

Several factors contributed to America's unwillingness to continue sending capital to Europe on the scale of earlier years. Internally, the tightening of monetary policy by the Federal Reserve referred to above raised interest rates sharply, thus weakening the incentive to lend abroad. With the stock exchange indices soaring upwards through 1927 and 1928 there was further strong encouragement to keep funds at home in the hope of more substantial gains from speculation on Wall Street. On the external side there was sharply growing alarm about the rising total of Germany's foreign liabilities, and her ability to continue to meet the obligations these imposed.

Did the end of the capital inflow cause the German slump?

In the late 1920s Germany went into a slump of unparalleled severity. Real domestic product fell by 16 per cent between 1929 and 1932, industrial production by over 40 per cent, the value of exports by almost 60 per cent. Unemployment raced from 1.3 million in 1927 (less than 4 per cent of the labour force) to 5.6 million in 1932 (over 17 per cent). The sudden contraction of capital imports from the United States has often been cited as the critical factor which precipitated this catastrophe (Lewis 1949; Falkus 1975; Sommariva and Tullio 1987). However, other scholars have argued strongly that the source of Germany's economic troubles was primarily domestic in origin (Temin 1971; Balderston 1983; McNeil 1986).

The latter theory is supported by the fact that nominal short-term interest rates were stable through the second half of 1928, fell in the first quarter of 1929, and only moved up in the second quarter. If the exogenous view of the depression was correct it might have been expected that they would have risen sharply as soon as the foreign inflow was cut off, but the observed pattern is easily explained if the German economy was already moving into recession before the import of capital from the United States dried up.

German industrial production recovered strongly in 1927 after the depression of 1925–6, but then showed virtually no further growth in 1928 or 1929. Similarly unemployment dropped to 1,600,000 in the six winter months of October 1927 to March 1928, and then increased sharply to 2,400,000 in the corresponding period of 1928–9. The same pattern is evident in the investment data. Gross fixed investment at current prices in the public sector (government and railways) expanded until 1927, and in other sectors the rise continued for a further year, though even at its peak in 1928 the investment ratio was low by comparison with the pre-war period. Moreover, information on investment intentions shows that both non-residential building permits and new domestic orders for machinery had already turned down in late 1927 or early 1928, well before the cessation of foreign lending.

Balderston (1983) attributes the low level and early decline in investment primarily to an acute and persistent shortage of domestic capital, and claims that this provides a 'thoroughly endogenous explanation' for the decline in fixed investment. Borchardt (1979) also finds a domestic explanation for the Great Depression, but as noted in Chapter 4.2 he argues that the root of the trouble was an excessive increase in wages relative to the growth of productivity. The socio-political distributional conflicts which emerged in the aftermath of the Great War are the focus of his analysis.

Although the virtual cessation of capital imports from the United States and the subsequent net outflow did not initiate the depression, it undoubtedly added greatly to the problems facing the German policy makers, and contributed to the adoption of measures which exacerbated the initial decline in activity. In principle, their options were either to abandon the gold standard, boosting activity by allowing the mark to depreciate, or to follow orthodox policies of retrenchment, reducing imports and expanding exports by deflating the economy.

From late 1929 long-term American capital was no longer available to sustain German budget deficits. German investors—with the experience of 1922–3 still deeply etched in their memories—displayed great reluctance to purchase long-term government bonds. The government and the Reichsbank were thus inexorably driven to resort to short-term borrowing. The more the short-term debt increased, the greater the perceived threat to stability, and the more energetic the efforts of domestic and foreign asset-holders to withdraw their capital from Germany. The deterioration in the political situation provoked by the steadily deepening depression and the opposition to tax increases gave added grounds for distrust of the currency.

The first of a succession of waves of capital flight occurred in the spring of 1929, and there were further massive losses of gold and foreign exchange in late 1930 and, on an even bigger scale, in 1931. The authorities were thus forced to adopt restrictive policies at precisely the point when the economy was in urgent need of counter-cyclical measures to stimulate revival. Short-term interest rates were raised in the second quarter of 1929, and the federal government, cities, and states initiated a succession of increasingly desperate efforts to raise revenues and restrict spending. From the end of 1930 and through 1931 Brüning introduced a succession of austerity decrees imposing progressively harsher increases in direct and indirect taxation, accompanied by reductions in civil service pay and in state welfare benefits. The descent was cumulative and catastrophic.

5.4 Capital flows to central and eastern Europe and to overseas primary producers

Elsewhere in central and eastern Europe the end of the foreign lending boom was an even more significant factor helping to initiate the depression and contributing to its severity. Unlike Germany, most of these countries—Czechoslovakia was the exception—relied primarily on exports of agricultural products for their foreign revenues, and were in trouble as soon as export prices began to tumble. They had borrowed heavily during the 1920s, frequently in the form of loans at fixed interest, and even when the funds had been productively invested—by no means always the case—they found themselves unable to service their debts from the rapidly diminishing proceeds of their exports. Thereafter they could only meet their external obligations as long as they could continue to attract fresh capital. After 1929, when the inflow of foreign capital ceased, the combined pressures proved intolerable, and painful adjustment was inescapable.

Hungary was more deeply affected than the other agrarian producers in this region and provides a good illustration of the difficulties they confronted. Together with Poland she had been the largest of the east European borrowers in the mid-1920s, and by the end of 1930 had an accumulated external debt of some $700 million, a great part of which had gone on unproductive expenditure. The export revenues on which she depended to service these debts came overwhelmingly from agricultural products, particularly wheat and maize. As their prices plunged the export proceeds went down with them; by 1931 their value was barely half the 1929 level and by 1932 less than a third.

The resulting balance of payments problem was insuperable. In a period of some ten weeks from the beginning of May 1931 the central bank was compelled to pay out more in gold and foreign exchange than it had possessed in April: a drain only made possible because rescue credits of $50 million were obtained from abroad. With bankruptcy threatening, urgent measures were required.

By mid-1931 Poland, Romania, Yugoslavia, and Bulgaria were in a similarly untenable position. Yet all five countries were inhibited by fear of inflation from following the example of other primary producers, such as Australia and Argentina, and depreciating their currencies. The deep prevailing fear of inflation in the minds of both politicians and the public is well indicated in the comment of a contemporary Polish economist, Edward Lipinski (quoted by Nötel 1986: 228): 'After this [repeated] collapse [of the Polish currency] its preservation became a sacrosanct principle of popular belief . . . It was duly realized that any devaluation could easily lead to panic, price manipulation, ruin of saving institutions, and a further sharpening of the crisis . . . Stability of the currency thus was turned into a popular myth.' Deprived of this solution they turned increasingly to moratoria, rigorous exchange controls, and commercial policy restrictions.

The role of the agricultural crisis in the Great Depression

The problems which beset the agrarian producers emerged early in the cycle of events culminating in the Great Depression, and were particularly severe in the case of the two crops grown in central and eastern Europe, wheat and sugar (see Chapter 4.3 for a detailed account). By 1925 it was impossible to find markets for the available supplies coming both from the restoration of output in Europe and from the recently expanded producers in North and South America. It thus seems clear that for agricultural foodstuffs a strong case can be made for the presence of overproduction, and for a downturn well before the break in activity in the industrial countries. For cotton, rubber, tin, and other industrial raw materials, however, as argued by Fleisig (1972), the causal sequence ran from the decline in industrial activity to the fall in prices.

If all economic adjustments took place automatically and without friction, this fall in agricultural prices would hardly matter from the standpoint of global economic stability. Any fall in the incomes of the producers of wheat would be offset by the rise in (real) incomes of the consumers of bread, and there would be no net effect on aggregate world demand. Unfortunately, this is not what happens in practice. The primary producing countries were forced to respond immediately to the deterioration in their international payments position, and to do so by contracting activity and cutting their imports. By contrast, the consuming nations were slow to appreciate the improvement in their purchasing power and were under no urgent pressure to expand their activity.

The loss of income to the food-growing countries and the cessation of foreign lending had substantial adverse consequences for others as well as for themselves. In the sphere of trade the decline in their export revenues undermined their ability to purchase manufactured goods from abroad, significantly reducing the exports of their customary suppliers, especially Britain. In the financial sphere, many of them were forced to devalue their currencies in 1929 and 1930, thus precipitating the period of instability on the foreign exchanges. Others turned to tariffs, exchange controls, and bilateral trading agreements, and contributed to the contraction in world trade. Countries with strong links to sterling, both those within the Empire, such as Australia and New Zealand, and those in Latin America, such as Argentina and Brazil, had traditionally kept their surplus balances in London. But now that they were in difficulty they were forced to run down these balances, thus adding to the pressures on the United Kingdom reserves.

6

THE ONSET OF THE GREAT DEPRESSION

From the late 1920s the descent into the Great Depression gathered pace in Europe—and in much of the rest of the world. Bankers, politicians, industrialists, farmers, all were seemingly helpless in the face of the successive banking crises, the growing stocks of unsold food, the collapse of export markets, the abandoned factories and ever-lengthening queues of men and women waiting desperately for work or for relief payments. In this chapter we first outline the general course of the depression, as reflected in the contraction of both output and international trade. We then trace the movement into the crisis as it developed in Austria and Germany and spread to other parts of central and eastern Europe, to Britain, and to the primary producing countries; and we examine the breakdown of the gold standard in the course of this process. We also look at the position of the banks in some other countries which avoided the severity of the crisis in Austria and Germany.

In the concluding part of the chapter we analyse the critical factor which eventually brought the slump to an end. We show that what was required to achieve this was a fundamental shift in policy—the abandonment of the gold standard—accompanied by a strong and public declaration of the change. We examine the working-out of this change in the policy regime in Britain and the United States, and consider whether a similar policy could have been adopted in Germany, thus forestalling the change in regime which Hitler introduced from 1933, with all its attendant costs for Germany and for the world.

6.1 The course of the crisis

A broad overview of some of the principal features of the world depression and of the magnitude of the crisis is given in Tables 6.1 and 6.2. As Table 6.1 shows, the collapse of international trade was extraordinarily swift and steep. The imposition of deflationary policies in pursuit of financial orthodoxy in the leading gold standard countries forced world trade into a vicious downward spiral. The problem was exacerbated by growing resort to tariffs and exchange controls, and by the impoverishment of the food producers resulting from the downward slide in agricultural prices (discussed in Chapters 4.3 and 5.4).

As restrictive monetary policies reduced output, and exports contracted, producers of manufactured goods naturally cut back their purchases of coal, cotton, metal ores, and other industrial raw materials. The producing countries were in turn forced to react to this deterioration in their exports by further restrictions on their imports of manufactured goods. The depression rapidly embraced both the advanced industrial countries and the producers of food and raw materials. Falling prices interacted with falling quantities, with catastrophic results.

As can be seen in the first row of Table 6.1, the value of world trade fell by almost 20 per cent in 1930, by a further 29 per cent in 1931, and yet again, by 33 per cent, in 1932. At the end of this staggering collapse the volume of goods traded (row 2) had fallen by a quarter, and their price (row 3) by half, leaving the value of international trade less than 40 per cent of what it had been three years earlier. The international economy was suffering the most severe contraction of demand it had ever known.

The movements in the output of industrial and primary products are shown in the first three blocks of Table 6.2. These series all

Table 6.1. World trade, 1929–1932 (index numbers; 1929 = 100)

	1929	1930	1931	1932
1. Value at current prices[a]	100	81	58	39
2. Volume	100	93	85	75
3. Price	100	87	68	52

[a] Index of the value of world imports and exports measured in pre-devaluation US gold dollars.

Source: League of Nations (1939a: 61).

Table 6.2. World production and prices, 1929–1932 (index numbers; 1929 = 100)

	1929	1930	1931	1932
1. Industrial production				
a. World[a]	100	87	75	64
b. Europe[a]	100	92	81	72
c. North America	100	81	68	54
2. Primary production—food				
a. World	100	102	100	100
b. Europe[a]	100	99	102	104
c. North America	100	102	103	100
3. Primary production—raw materials				
a. World	100	94	85	75
b. Europe[a]	100	90	82	73
c. North America	100	90	80	64
4. World prices				
a. Food	100	84	66	52
b. Raw materials	100	82	59	44
c. Manufactures	100	94	78	64

[a] Excluding USSR.

Sources: Blocks 1–3: League of Nations (1939*b*: 423–4); block 4: League of Nations (1939*a*: 61).

measure the quantities produced, and thus do not reflect the additional factor of falling prices; these are shown in the final block. For the industrial countries, the collapse of their real economies was swift and savage. In the world as a whole (row 1a), output plummeted in three years to less than two-thirds of the 1929 level. The descent was slightly less severe in Europe, even more catastrophic in North America. The volume of food produced (block 2) was not affected and remained broadly stable during this period; but, as noted above, the output of industrial raw materials (block 3) inevitably fell as industrial production declined, and again the reduction was worse in North America than in Europe.

The remarkable fall in world prices of all products is measured in block 4 of Table 6.2, with prices of primary products dropping most steeply. By 1932, prices of industrial raw materials had collapsed to only 44 per cent of their 1929 levels, foodstuffs to 52 per cent, and manufactures to 64 per cent.

As is immediately apparent from Table 6.3, no European country escaped the contraction in output and in world trade and prices between 1929 and 1932. The fall in industrial production in 1932

Table 6.3. The collapse of industrial production and exports from 1929 to 1932 (1929 = 100)

	Industrial production (1)	Value of exports[a] (2)
Poland	58	38
Germany	61	45
Austria	62	32
France	74	39
Czechoslovakia	75	36
Yugoslavia	76	35
Spain	84	35
Netherlands	84	42
Belgium	85	47
Hungary	86	32
Italy	86	44
Finland	88	44 (72)
Romania	88	58
Sweden	89	36 (52)
United Kingdom	89	36 (50)
Denmark	90	47 (67)
Norway	94	51 (75)
Greece	101	39
Switzerland	—	38
Total Europe	72	40

[a] Values measured in old US gold dollars; higher values in national currencies are shown in brackets for those countries which had devalued by 1932. Devaluation reduced the foreign exchange proceeds of a given quantity of exports but made the exports more competitive in foreign prices and so increased the volume of sales.

Sources: (1) As for Table 4.3, plus Yugoslavia from Kaser and Radice (1985: 573).
(2) League of Nations (1937: 53).

relative to 1929 is given in the first column, the corresponding fall in the value of exports in the second. In general 1932 was the trough year for output, but in many countries the value of exports continued to drop for two or three more years. For 11 of the 19 countries listed in the second column of Table 6.3, including the United Kingdom and France, the value of exports plunged by more than 60 per cent between 1929 and 1932. In six others, including Germany, Italy, Belgium, and the Netherlands, the decline was only slightly less severe, with exports falling by 1932 to well below half their 1929 values. For Europe as a whole, the value of its exports was reduced from $15.6 billion in 1929 to $6.3 billion in 1932. Every country was thus subject to a massive decline in demand.

The contraction of industrial production in the individual European countries between 1929 and 1932 can be seen in the first column of Table 6.3, where the countries are listed according to the severity of the depression. In the three countries which were most badly affected—Poland, Germany, and Austria—industrial output plunged almost 40 per cent in three years. In France the decline was delayed until 1931, but was then equally precipitous: 26 per cent in two years. Industrial production fell almost as steeply in Czechoslovakia and Yugoslavia, and in the former was unusual in that it continued to fall in 1933, finally coming to a halt at 59 per cent of the previous peak. Elsewhere in Europe the fall in industrial activity was more moderate, but in the majority of countries was still between 10 and 20 per cent. Of the 18 countries covered in Table 6.3, there is only one, Greece, in which output in 1932 was above the 1929 level, and then by only 1 per cent.

The decline in industrial output, in primary product prices, and in world trade drove unemployment to unprecedented heights, and we will devote the whole of Chapter 7 to a discussion of this aspect of the economic tragedy. We turn first to closer examination of the way in which the gathering crisis affected the banking system, and of the reaction of governments and central bankers as the world economy made its final descent into the abyss.

6.2 The failure of the banks in Austria and Germany

The United States ceased to supply capital for Europe on the previous lavish scale, and from 1931 was actually a net recipient of long-term capital. The only other country in a strong financial position was France, which attracted ever larger quantities of gold and foreign exchange. Both the American and the French authorities refused to take any steps to relieve the mounting crisis of confidence and liquidity in the rest of the world. The banking system was drawn inexorably into the gathering storm.

As noted in Chapter 3.2, a succession of bank failures had occurred throughout the 1920s, and there were problems of varying magnitude in Spain in 1925, in Poland in 1926 and 1927, and in

Norway and Italy in 1927. The problem then reached Germany in 1929, when the collapse of the Frankfurter Allgemeine Versicherungs was followed by the failure of smaller banks and withdrawals from savings banks in Frankfurt and Berlin.

These bank failures represented the inability of banking institutions to cope with the discipline of the gold standard. Banking systems differed greatly between countries, and there were many individual factors in any banking crisis. But the gold standard limited the freedom of banks—and governments—to deal with economic problems. This limitation is good when the world economy is in balance and problems are local. It turned from boon to burden in the 1920s when the world economy was out of balance, and problems spread from country to country as a result.

The crisis which ultimately undermined the banking system of central Europe emerged in Vienna in 1929 with the failure of the Bodencreditanstalt, the second largest Austrian bank. Under pressure from the government, the Rothschild's Credit-Anstalt agreed to a merger, but the rescuing bank was itself in a very weak position, and the enlarged institution could not provide a long-term solution. The Credit-Anstalt, Austria's largest bank, had unwisely operated during the 1920s as if the Habsburg Empire had not been broken up. In fact the Viennese banks had been cut off from their original industrial base, especially in Czechoslovakia. There was never a sound basis for their business in the 1920s, and their heavy commitment to unprofitable industries meant that failures and losses were inevitable.

In May 1931, after an auditor's report revealed the true position, the Credit-Anstalt went under; it was forced to reorganize with the help of international credit and a partial standstill agreement with its foreign creditors. This collapse set off a run on the bank that spread to the Austrian schilling. The government quickly ran through its foreign exchange reserves in a vain attempt to adhere to the gold standard and only belatedly imposed foreign exchange controls.

The problems of the German banks

The German banking system went into crisis two months later when one of the major German banks, the Darmstadter-und-Nationalbank (Danat), closed its doors. This threatened to precipitate the collapse of the entire German banking system, and a ruinous situation was only averted by government intervention and a banking moratorium. The German banking crisis of July 1931 is often seen as the consequence of the Austrian financial collapse in May. This presumption, however, has been hard to verify. The German crisis of July 1931 may well have been due to exclusively German causes, in which case the Austrian crisis foreshadowed— but did not cause—the more important German collapse (see Chapter 5.3).

German banks held the bulk of their reserves in cheques, bills of exchange, and Treasury bills that could be freely discounted at the Reichsbank. The bills earned more than deposits at the Reichsbank and were equally liquid as long as the Reichsbank stood ready to purchase them. The banks' reserve ratio fell sharply in June 1931, and again in July. Fully two-thirds of the fall in each month was accounted for by a reduction in the amount of bills held by banks. This reduction was concentrated almost entirely in the six great Berlin banks, and it was paralleled by a rise in the Reichsbank portfolio of virtually the exact same size. The large Berlin banks were selling their bills to the Reichsbank. They sold over half of their bill portfolio in those two months.

The problem created by the withdrawals was not primarily that the banks were losing reserves, except for the Danat Bank, which had heavily invested in a major failed firm. It was that the Reichsbank ran out of assets with which to monetize the banks' reserves as withdrawals continued. Despite some credits from other central banks, the Reichsbank had fallen below its statutory requirement of 40 per cent reserves by the beginning of July, and it was unable to borrow more. The Reichsbank could no longer purchase the Berlin banks' bills by mid-July.

The Reichsbank tried to replenish its reserves with an international loan, but tensions left over from the First World War disturbed the operation of the international credit market. The French, who had ample reserves to lend to the Reichsbank, were still fighting the First World War. They attached political strings to their offer of help that were unacceptable to the Germans. The Germans for their part tried to use the crisis to renegotiate the peace settlement and eliminate reparations, while the Americans pulled in the opposite direction to isolate the German banking crisis from any long-run considerations. The absence of international co-operation was all too evident; no international loan was forthcoming. There was no hegemonic lender of last resort.

Germany abandoned the gold standard in July and August 1931. A series of decrees and negotiations preserved the value of the mark, but eliminated the free flow of both gold and marks. In one of the great ironies of history, Chancellor Brüning did not take advantage of this independence of international constraints and expand. He continued to contract as if Germany was still on the gold standard. It is vivid testimony to the power of ideology that leaders like Brüning were induced to cling to orthodoxy even as the world economy collapsed. He continued to advocate gold standard policies after abandoning the gold standard itself. He ruined the German economy—and destroyed German democracy—in the effort to show once and for all that Germany could not pay reparations.

As a consequence of the German moratorium the withdrawal of foreign deposits was prohibited, and huge sums in foreign short-term credits were frozen. As other countries became aware that they would be unable to realize these assets, they in turn were compelled to restrict withdrawals of their credits. Many other European countries suffered bank runs and failures in July, with especially severe crises in Hungary, where the banks were closely tied to those in Austria, and in Romania. As a result of the extensive foreign withdrawals from the Budapest banks it was again necessary to impose a partial moratorium on external obligations and to declare a three-day 'bank holiday'.

In the same month a leading Swiss bank had to be rescued by a take-over. In contrast, French banks were generally in a strong position by the end of the 1920s, and largely avoided the crisis of 1929–31, with only mild failures in 1930–1. The British commercial banks were also largely unscathed, finding strength in their branch structure and security in their traditionally cautious policy towards involvement in industry.

6.3 Disintegration of the gold standard

Sterling under pressure

The stability of the British banks did not extend to the position of sterling. Almost immediately after Germany abandoned the gold standard the British pound was under pressure. The timing suggests that this was not the same process by which panic spread from Austria to Germany. German banks enjoyed a month of normal operation after the failure of the Credit-Anstalt. They felt pressure only after a delay and—we presume—from a new set of depositors. British banks had no such interlude. There was no internal drain. Pressure on the pound began as soon as the mark was restricted. Sales of sterling increased steadily after 14 July, and the Bank of England raised Bank rate on 22 July. The British troubles were accentuated when the standstill agreements froze some £70 million of British bankers' loans to Germany.

Although the banking crisis on the Continent had added to Britain's problems by simultaneously provoking a flight from sterling and freezing her foreign short-term assets, the extremely weak balance of payments position on both current and capital account was a more fundamental cause of her inability to sustain the gold standard. Britain's external financial position in the 1920s was undermined by several factors. On the current account, these included the abrupt transwar collapse of export markets for coal, cotton, and other staple products; the forced sale of a substantial fraction of her overseas investments to help meet the costs of World War I; the overvaluation of sterling as a result of the decision to return to gold at the pre-war parity of $4.86; and the adverse impact on her traditional Imperial and Latin American markets of the calamitous fall in primary product prices in the late 1920s.

The capital account was a further source of weakness because Britain had attempted to maintain her pre-1914 role as an exporter of long-term capital to the developing countries. In the 1920s, however, she could no longer achieve this by means of a surplus on current account, and was forced to offset the outflow by substantial borrowing from abroad. Much of the capital attracted to London was short-term, as described in Chapter 5, leaving Britain very vulnerable to any loss of confidence in sterling. The increasing deficits on the current accounts of Australia and other primary producers who normally held a large part of their reserves in London compelled them to draw on these balances; this further weakened Britain's position.

By mid-1930 the United Kingdom's gold and foreign exchange reserves amounted to some £175 million, and other liquid assets were approximately £150 million. Since the corresponding short-term liabilities amounted to some £750 million, this was only an adequate defence against withdrawals as long as confidence in the pound remained high. When confidence drained away in the course of 1931 it seemed to the British authorities that sterling's parity could no longer be sustained. After borrowing reserves from France and the United States in July and August, Britain abandoned the gold standard on 20 September.

As so often in the financial developments during the inter-war period, the influence of history was of critical importance. Foreign concern about the scale of Britain's budget deficit increased markedly with the publication of the Report of the May Committee in July 1931, and was the paramount reason for the final collapse of confidence in sterling. As Sayers observed (1976: 390–1), it is difficult today to understand this obsession with the deficit given the relatively trifling sums under discussion:

The explanation lies . . . in memories of the currency disorders of the early twenties, which were, after all, less than ten years behind. In those troublesome times it had become accepted doctrine that an uncorrected budget deficit is the root of forced increase in the supply of money and depreciation of the currency, and that such depreciations become almost if not quite unmanageable. This view was not a mere academic fetish: it permeated the atmosphere in all financial markets . . . The Bank [of England] itself, in all the advice it tendered to the struggling central bankers of recovering Europe, year after year preached the gospel. It was not to be wondered at, that in 1931 the physician should be expected to heal himself—and that when he seemed unwilling to set about it, his life should be despaired of.

Even so, it has been argued that the suspension of the gold standard was not inevitable and could have been averted if the authorities had been more resolute in their defence of the parity adopted in 1925 (Balderston 1995). This would have required a much more aggressive policy of raising interest rates and reducing the level of domestic activity. Such a policy might have involved severe damage to employment and enterprise, and perhaps to political stability, but if firmly implemented would have shown speculators that the United Kingdom was determined to maintain the gold standard. However, international economic organization is intended to be a means to an end, not an end in itself, and it is not surprising that the British government was ultimately unwilling to persist with their commitment to the gold standard regardless of the cost exacted in terms of lost output and increased unemployment.

In considering the factors underlying Britain's departure from gold, much contemporary and subsequent British comment attributed considerable significance to the undervaluation of rival currencies, especially the French franc. Recent research has shown that the importance of this factor was greatly overstated (Eichengreen and Wyplosz 1990). It was not the exchange rate policy which was the basis for France's prosperity at the end of the 1920s, or for her successful resistance until 1931 to the slump from which almost all other countries were suffering, and the share of exports in GDP was actually falling after 1927. Instead the strength of the French economy should be attributed to the crowding-in effect of Poincaré's fiscal policies, which induced an upsurge in domestic investment. Similarly in the case of Belgium, export growth on the back of a depreciated currency was not maintained after 1926, and the main sources of prosperity are to be found in the domestic economy associated with the expansion of the banking sector.

The Bank of England, after an initial delay to rebuild its gold reserves, sharply reduced interest rates in 1932. As in Germany, British monetary authorities continued for a time to advocate gold standard policies even after they had been driven off the gold standard. But while the influence of this ideology was strong in the immediate aftermath of devaluation, it wore off within six months. British economic policy was freed by devaluation, and monetary policy turned expansive early in 1932. The British devaluation was hardly the basis for international co-operation. The British did not seek international leadership; they did not champion their policies as hegemonic activity. Instead they backed into devaluation, arguing they had no alternative. And while many smaller countries followed the British lead, the other major financial centres sought instead to protect themselves from British policy. The British devaluation was a good policy—it broke the suffocating grip of the gold standard on economic policy—but it did not point the way toward international co-operation.

The British government had relinquished its pre-war role as steward of the international gold standard. More properly, it acknowledged in 1931, however backhandedly, that this leadership role could no longer be sustained. The domestic cost had become too great relative to Britain's diminished resources. If the international economic orchestra needed a conductor, it would have to be found outside London—presumably in America.

Collapse of the gold standard

By the time Britain was forced to abandon the gold standard seven other countries, including Australia, New Zealand, and Argentina, had already done so. After her departure another 24 countries followed rapidly, including Sweden, Denmark, Norway, Finland, the Irish Free State, Greece, and Portugal. As a British writer noted mournfully (Waight 1939: 1): 'If the foundations of the citadel of financial probity were unsound and the structure about to tumble, other centres could not remain for long unaffected.' In many other countries there was no formal suspension but the gold standard was made ineffective by the imposition of a range of exchange controls and restrictions. This applied ultimately to Germany, Austria, Hungary, Bulgaria, Czechoslovakia, Romania, Estonia, and Latvia.

By the middle of 1932 the institution which had been generally accepted as the best guarantee of international stability, trade, growth, and prosperity had been completely shattered. In Europe only France, Belgium, the Netherlands, Switzerland, Italy, Poland, and Lithuania remained on the gold standard. And only the first four of these were truly committed to its spirit, refraining from the imposition of exchange controls and allowing relatively free movement of gold. The inability to make the gold standard function successfully in the inter-war era was widely regarded as a symbol of failure even though the actual consequences for the real economy were highly favourable. Those countries which remained committed to gold did much less well subsequently than those which abandoned it.

At the same time as the gold standard was disintegrating there was also a renewed outbreak of tariff warfare, provoked by the deterioration in economic conditions and by the introduction of the Hawley–Smoot Tariff in the United States in 1930. Britain finally abandoned her long-standing commitment to free trade at the end of 1931, and numerous countries—including France, Italy, the Netherlands, Norway, Spain, Portugal, and Greece, and many others outside Europe—increased their tariffs in a desperate attempt to protect themselves from the deepening depression and the collapse of all attempts at international co-operation. In the judgement of the League of Nations (1933: 193–4): 'There was probably never any period when trade was subject to such widespread and frequent alterations of tariff barriers. . . . Currency instability has led into a maze of new protectionist regulations and private trading initiative generally has given way to administrative controls.'

The financial panic also spread from Britain to the United States, jumping instantaneously over the Atlantic Ocean in September 1931. Bank failures rose, and the Federal Reserve Banks lost gold. There were both internal and external drains. In one of the most vivid acts of poor monetary policy in history, the Federal Reserve raised interest rates sharply in October to protect the dollar—in the midst of the greatest depression the world has ever known. This was not a technical mistake or simple stupidity; this was the prescribed esponse of central banks under the gold standard. It shows how the ideology of the gold standard transmitted and intensified the Great Depression.

The pressure against the dollar eased, but the American economy accelerated its decline. The Federal Reserve Bank had chosen international stability over domestic prosperity. The result was intensified deflation and accelerated economic decline. Unlike Britain, which arrested the decline in 1932, the United States had to wait an additional painful year. This delay was not only costly for America; it added to the deflationary forces in Europe, delaying European recovery as well.

6.4 Banks in southern Europe, Italy, and Poland during the Great Depression

Spain stands as the prime example of a country that avoided the worst excesses of the Great Depression by staying off the gold standard (Choudhri and Kochin 1980). There was an attempt to fix the peseta in the late 1920s as France and Italy stabilized their currencies, but the deflationists lacked the political muscle. The government continued to run deficits which were monetized by healthy banks. There was a run on Spanish banks contemporaneous with the failure of the Credit-Anstalt in Austria. Martín-Aceña (1995) cites internal causes, but the peseta was under pressure as well. Very few banks failed, and the experience is not thought of as a panic. The Bank of Spain acted as a lender of last resort, enabled to do so by two factors. The banks held large portfolios of government debt that could be sold for cash. And, unlike the Reichsbank, the Bank of Spain was not bound by the inflexible norms of the gold standard. It did have to raise Spanish interest rates to protect the value of the peseta, but it continued to lend freely—as Bagehot (1873) had advised.

In Greece and Portugal the impact of the economic depression was relatively mild, and with minor exceptions the banks in each of these countries came through the period in reasonably good health. Where banking failures occurred in these countries it typically owed more to their involvement as universal banks with unsound or loss-making industries than to inherent financial difficulties. In Greece, as in Britain and other countries in which mixed banking was not the normal practice, the banks were much better able to sustain their liquidity and solvency, although problems were aggravated where the central bank was unable or unwilling to act as lender of last resort.

Italy and Poland

There were no general banking crises in Italy and Poland, even though they were on the gold standard. Differences in banking policy between them and other gold standard countries may well be the cause of the difference in financial outcomes. On the assumption that the causal relation runs in this direction, it is tempting to ask if Austria and Germany could have adopted the Italian and Polish policies.

The Credito Italiano, one of two large universal banks in Italy, found itself illiquid in 1930 as the economic downturn began. A holding company was formed to take the industrial assets of the bank, disguising its universal character without changing the fundamental financial status of the bank. This cosmetic change was not enough to deal with the problem. More action was needed at the start of 1931. The government reached an agreement with the Credito Italiano in February 1931, in which the bank gave up its holding company and its investment activities in return for a substantial grant of money from the government. The Credito Italiano was transformed from a universal to a commercial bank, but it was not allowed to fail.

Banca Commerciale, the other universal bank, needed help later in 1931 and a similar agreement was reached with them in October. In return for an even larger infusion of cash, this bank too allowed itself to be restricted to short-term activities. The banks were transformed. The government became actively involved in the finance of industry. But there was no banking crisis.

Secrecy was absolutely critical to the success of this policy. Depositors did not panic or move into cash; they did not spread difficulties from bank to bank in a contagion of fear. The lira was not subjected to unusual pressure. The policy decisions had been undertaken by a small group of men, and no word leaked out to the financial community. Such secrecy was possible in the Fascist government that ruled Italy; we can only speculate on why the secrecy did not result in the kind of self-serving policies usually associated with this kind of restricted decision making.

The story in Poland is similar, although less spectacular. There was no secrecy, and there were no secret agreements in the face of collapse. Instead there was a gradual state take-over of troubled private banks. The first test of Polish banking policy came in 1925 as the result of an agricultural crisis. The state responded by taking over troubled banks. Another crisis came in 1929, at the start of the economic downturn. The world agricultural crisis caused prices to fall in Poland, threatening banks who had loaned on the security of crops. Again, the government stepped in and took over troubled banks.

A third crisis in 1931 followed the failure of the Austrian Credit-Anstalt, in which the pattern of government expansion continued. Private banks held 40 per cent of Polish deposits and investments in 1926, but only 20 per cent by 1934. The Polish policy was not undertaken by a small group of secret financiers. It was not composed of a few large grants to banks. It was instead a policy stance extended to a large number of banks over a period of years. Its effectiveness came from the knowledge of its existence, that is, from the government's commitment to keeping credit markets stable.

Italy and Poland therefore were similar in the inter-war period in that their governments directly supported banks in trouble. The form in which this overall policy was implemented was vastly different—almost diametrically opposite—in the two countries. But government take-overs were common to both. Their common policies contrast sharply with those of Austria and Germany, in which failing banks were merged with other banks. This was a far less effective measure because the amalgamated banks then found themselves in trouble.

It would be comforting to report that Italy and Poland were spared the worst excesses of the depression as a result of their banking policies. But such was not the case. These countries were on the gold standard, and the gold standard was the primary transmission mechanism of the Great Depression. Unlike Spain, Italy and Poland experienced both deflation and falling production at about the rate of other gold standard countries. Only by breaking the 'golden fetters' of the gold standard, to use Eichengreen's term, was it possible to break the deflationary spiral.

6.5 The end of the contraction

Unhappily, it took a change of leadership to bring about a change in the policy regime. We can now see that restoration of the post-war gold standard was the problem, not the solution, in the 1920s because it imposed monetary constraints which prevented the authorities from taking the action necessary to contain the banking panics and failures. These crises amplified relatively modest initial disturbances and undermined the financial stability of the leading centres.

The ideology of the gold standard was very strong, and it was extremely difficult for leaders to abandon it in this time of crisis. Not recognizing that this ideology was a large part of the problem, they chained themselves to it as a drowning man holds on to a life-raft. Alas, these golden chains only dragged the European economy further under water. Only when national economies were freed of these constraints could the economic contraction be halted.

The change in policy regime can be seen most clearly in the United States. The Hoover Administration followed a policy regime that became more orthodox in 1931 and 1932. It was highly traditional in its support for the gold standard and its focus on efforts to bolster the credit markets rather than the economy directly. Although not initially deflationary, Hoover drew exactly the wrong lesson from the currency crisis of 1931 and became a strong deflationist.

The Federal Reserve maintained a passive stance in the early stages of the depression, replaced by active contraction in response to the run on the dollar in 1931. The Federal Reserve's steps toward expansion in March to July of 1932 were halted when the open market purchases alarmed other central banks and threatened the solvency of member banks by lowering the returns on bank portfolios. The Glass–Steagall Act of 1932 reiterated support for the gold standard at the same time.

No longer London, not yet New York. The Hoover Administration was not willing to lead the world economy out of trouble. Hoover remained committed to the policies that were depressing both the American and European economies. There was no chance for new leadership to emerge in America during the long contraction of the early 1930s. And when a change in leadership took place, in 1932–3, it happened slowly and with great confusion that magnified the problem. Without domestic leadership, the United States could not be a leader of the world economy.

The first sign that a new policy regime was on the way came after the election, in December 1932, when President-elect Roosevelt torpedoed Hoover's efforts to settle war debts and reparations multilaterally, signifying his opposition to continuation of the existing meagre international financial co-operation. A change in regime became more tangible in February 1933, when the President-elect began a serious discussion of devaluation as part of an effort to raise commodity prices.

This talk led to a run on the dollar and, once inaugurated, Roosevelt responded by declaring a 'bank holiday'. He also imposed controls over all foreign exchange trading and gold exports. He ended private gold ownership and took control over the sale of all domestic gold production. These controls allowed Roosevelt to avoid speculative disequilibrium when he began to devalue the dollar. At the same time he prohibited the private export of gold by executive order. The dollar, freed from its official value in April by the Thomas Amendment to the Agricultural Adjustment Act, began to fall. It dropped steadily until July, when it had declined between 30 and 45 per cent against the pound.

The clarity of the change in policy was unmistakable. The United States was under no market pressure to devalue. Despite the momentary pressure on the New York Fed, the United States held one-third of the world's gold reserves, ran a chronic foreign trade surplus, and dominated world trade in modern manufactures like automobiles, refrigerators, and other consumer durables. The devaluation was a purely strategic decision that seemed without precedent. Orthodox financial opinion recognized it as such and condemned it.

This was a change of regime of the type described by Sargent (1983) in his account of the end of several hyper-inflations. It was a dramatic change, clearly articulated and understood. It was co-ordinated with fiscal and monetary policies. The new regime clearly was designed to increase both prices and economic activity. It was supported by a wide degree of consensus—professional, public, and congressional—despite the vocal opposition of some financial leaders.

As with the British devaluation, the United States' action was the key to breaking free of the deflationary policies of the gold standard. It was also a national decision, taken without consultation or co-operation with other nations. Sequential devaluation was the best policy under the circumstances, but it was hardly a co-ordinated international response to the economic crisis. Devaluation was only one dimension of a multifaceted new policy regime. During Roosevelt's First Hundred Days, the passive, deflationary policy of Hoover was replaced by an aggressive, interventionist, expansionary approach. The New Deal has been widely criticized for internal inconsistency (Hawley 1966; Lee 1982). There was, however, a steadily expansionary bias in policy that added up to a marked change from the Hoover Administration (Temin and Wigmore 1990).

German deflation—was there an alternative?

The story is similar, although not as clear-cut, in Germany. As noted above, Chancellor Brüning continued to deflate the German economy through 1930, 1931, and the beginning of 1932, even though Germany had effectively gone off the gold standard in July 1931. The modern debate over Brüning's deflationary policy dates from 1979, when Knut Borchardt presented a case that Brüning had no alternative. (The original paper and two successors have been translated in Borchardt 1991; see also Borchardt 1984.)

Borchardt argued in three steps. First, there was no perception before the German banking crisis in July 1931 and Britain's departure from gold in September that the contraction was going to be more severe than those of 1921 and 1926. There consequently was no incentive to undertake any alternative economic policy before then. Second, there was no way to finance any expansionary measures. International capital flows could not have been increased, as discussed in Chapter 5.3, and the Reichsbank was barred by international agreement from extending domestic credit. Finally, expansionary measures would not have worked because the structural problems of the Weimar economy, discussed in Chapter 4.2, were too severe.

The question of whether Brüning could have acted differently actually has two parts. On the one hand, there is the historical question whether other plans were available for Brüning to choose. Holtfrerich has identified several proposals of expansionary measures. Prominent among these is the famous WTB (Woytinsky, Tarnow, and Baade) Plan of December 1931 to increase public works in what we would now call Keynesian 'pump priming' (see Chapter 7.4). Borchardt and his followers have responded that none of these alternative plans was in fact politically viable. The WTB Plan, for example, was not even accepted by the Social Democrats, for whom it was created. It was so watered down by the time it was formally adopted as party policy in April 1932 as to be not significantly different from Brüning's policies.

Another actual proposal was the cabinet discussion of devaluation following the British devaluation. It is clear that a German devaluation, like all devaluations in a gold standard, would have violated previous agreements. It is less clear whether anyone would have held Germany to its international obligations soon after Britain had defaulted on hers. And the credit controls initiated by Brüning after the banking crisis of July 1931 violated the spirit if not the letter of Germany's gold standard commitments. As noted above, these controls represented the abandonment of the gold standard just as clearly as a devaluation would have done. They gave Brüning the freedom to expand without risk of capital flight.

On the other hand, there is the general question whether any political leader can step out of historical context to do something different. No one, for example, expected Roosevelt to go off gold in 1933. Nothing that he had said in his previous career or his campaign for the presidency indicated this policy. There also was no extensive discussion of devaluation as an option—no 'WTB Plan' for an American devaluation. Nevertheless, as noted above, Roosevelt went off gold soon after taking office.

The second step in Borchardt's argument is that there was no way to finance a German public works programme in 1931–2. This also has been subject to extensive debate. One issue is whether the Reichsbank was able to extend credit to the government. Another is whether the bond market—if the government had tried to borrow directly from the public—would have responded well to a policy like the WTB Plan. If the public had applauded and bought the bonds eagerly, financing would not have been a problem. But if the public had decided that this expansion was the first step down the path toward a repetition of the 1923 inflation, then selling these bonds at any reasonable interest rate could have been a problem.

The third step in the Borchardt thesis is that the Weimar economy was 'sick' beyond recall. This was discussed above in Chapter 4.2. Here we need only note that all three steps in Borchardt's argument remain unresolved.

Papen succeeded Chancellor Brüning in late May 1932. The Lausanne Conference in June 1932 effectively ended reparations and cleared the major political hurdle from Germany's path. Brüning said later that he fell '50 metres from the goal.' The goal, that is, of ending reparations, not ending the disastrous economic contraction.

Brüning's deflation was replaced by Papen's first steps toward economic expansion. Brüning had initiated a small employment programme that had little effect in the context of his deflationary policy regime. This programme was expanded by Papen and complemented by some off-budget government expenditures. In addition Papen introduced tax credits and subsidies for new employment. These were steps in the right direction, but they did not alter the perception of the policy regime. They still appeared to be isolated actions, not regime shifts. The new policy measures (like the Federal Reserve's open market purchases earlier that year) nevertheless produced some effects. There was a short-lived rise in industrial production and shipments. The recovery was only partial, and the data are mixed, but there was a definite sign of improvement.

These tentative results seem to have had an immediate political impact as well. The Nazis had leapt to prominence in the 1930 election and increased their seats in the Reichstag from 12 to 107. They then doubled their large representation in the Reichstag in the election of July 1932. But that was their high point in free elections. They lost ground in the second election of 1932, in November, garnering 33 per cent instead of 37 per cent of the vote and reducing their representation in the Reichstag from 230 to 196 seats (Hamilton 1982; Childers 1983).

Further economic improvement could well have reduced the Nazi vote even more. If so, we need to ask whether the recovery begun under Papen could have continued. For if it had, then the political courage to hold out a little longer with the Papen or

Schleicher governments might have spared Germany and the world the horrors of Nazism. The question then is not simply about the recovery. It is also whether Germany—and hence the world—was balanced on a knife-edge in 1933 between the continuation of normal life and the enormous costs of the Nazis.

There is, however, only a slim case for believing that the recovery could have been sustained. The instability of politics mirrored the instability of the economy. The policy regime was in the process of changing, but there was no clear signal of change like the American devaluation. There was no assurance that Papen's tentative expansionary steps would be followed by others. The recovery of 1932 consequently was neither sharp nor universal. Even though a trough can be seen in some data, other series show renewed decline into 1933. The economy fell back to its low point in the brief Schleicher administration, and it appeared that the Papen recovery was abortive.

For Nazism to have been a transitory aberration, the recovery would have had to resume in early 1933. It would have had to be strong enough to repair the damage to the political fabric caused by the social and political effects of extensive unemployment. The expansive policies already undertaken would have had to have further effects—which they probably did—and the American recovery would have had to spill over into Germany. Both the Papen policies and the American recovery worked in the direction of German recovery, but neither had a strong effect, and the latter in addition could not have come for several months. One can argue that the future course of the German economy under elected governments would have limited the Nazis to continued minority status, but it is harder to argue that it would have led to a rapid decline in Nazi support.

Hitler was appointed chancellor at the end of January 1933, and sustained economic recovery began only thereafter. The advent of the Nazi government heralded the presence—as in the United States—of a new policy regime. Instead of focusing on the clear political discontinuity in 1933, we need to expose the clear change in economic policy. The Nazi government was truly a new (and horrible) regime, both politically and economically. The Nazis set out immediately to consolidate their power and destroy democracy. They obliterated democratic institutions. The evils of the Nazi regime must be accounted among the worst effects of the Great Depression.

They turned away from international commitments to the restoration of domestic prosperity. And they gave their highest priority to the reduction of Germany's massive unemployment (see also Chapter 7.4). Hitler conducted a successful balancing act. He reassured businessmen that he was not a free-spending radical at the same time as he expanded the job creation programmes and tax breaks of his predecessors. The First Four-Year Plan embodied many of the new measures and gave them visibility as a new policy direction.

Employment rose rapidly in 1933 as a result. The new expenditures must have taken time to have their full effects. The immediate recovery therefore was the result of changed expectations when the Nazis took power. It was the result of anticipated as well as actual government activities. Even though the specifics of the Nazi programme did not become clear—in fact were not formulated—until later, the direction of policy was clear. Hitler had been criticizing the deflationary policies of his predecessors for years, and the commitment of the Nazis to full employment was well known. As in the United States, a change in policy regime was sufficient to turn the corner, although not to promote full recovery.

7

UNEMPLOYMENT

THE inter-war years were very turbulent. Previous chapters have described the ups and downs of economic affairs and the vagaries of macro-economic policies. The narrative has focused on the national level, and co-operation has been discussed primarily with reference to central bankers.

The Great Depression, however, was not experienced at the national level. Individuals, families, and communities lived through a period of great hardship. Wealthy individuals lost money, and workers lost their jobs. Interpersonal comparisons are hard, and we cannot know the extent of any individual's suffering. But it is not unreasonable to assume that the unemployed workers and their families bore the brunt of the depression. Before we return to the national level and discuss the extent and variety of unemployment in the depression, it is appropriate to describe the nature of unemployment as experienced in the early 1930s.

We begin with some very specific accounts of the condition of the unemployed, and then look at the pattern as it affected different groups of workers. On a more abstract level we then analyse the behaviour of real wages and its relationship to unemployment, and consider the policies which were—or might have been—adopted by governments in an attempt to create work, particularly in Britain and Germany.

7.1 The experience of unemployment

The description of unemployment must be specific to be accurate; it cannot describe the experience of all Europe. Aggregate statistics have the virtue of generality and even universality, but they miss the detail of individual lives. Fortunately, a group of sociologists studied an industrial village in Austria during the winter of 1931–2 (Jahoda *et al.* 1971 edn.). First published in German in 1933, the results of their research described the intimate lives of an unemployed village, that is, an industrial village in which the factory had closed.

Marienthal was an Austrian village with about 500 families in 1931. It could be reached from Vienna by a half-hour train ride to a neighbouring village and then another half-hour walk over the flat countryside. A cotton mill had furnished the chief opportunity for employment in the village since its founding almost a century ago. The mill had progressed from cotton to rayon after the First World War. Despite industrial strife and a slowdown in demand in the mid-1920s, employment was at its peak in early 1929. By February 1930, however, production had ceased in the mill. The mill owners must have expected business not to pick up, for they started to demolish the mill almost immediately. Workers in Marienthal looked out in the early 1930s over the rubble of their former place of employment.

Unemployment relief was governed by a 1920 law. Workers were entitled to relief if they had worked at least 20 weeks in the previous year and had no other income. Aliens were not eligible. The amount of relief varied with the worker's work history, wage, and family situation. It lasted for 20 to 30 weeks. A worker's claim to relief was voided if any work at all was undertaken. Workers lost their benefits for activities as limited as cutting down trees in return for firewood, delivering milk in return for some of the milk, and playing the harmonica in return for a little money. The result was idleness supplemented by minimally illegal activity, such as stealing coal from the railway or potatoes from farmers.

Emergency assistance was available after unemployment relief ended. It was only slightly less generous and lasted for an additional 20 to 50 weeks. After that, assistance ceased. By the winter of 1931–2, therefore, most families were still on some kind of relief, but they were approaching the end. Fewer than 100 families in the village had income from work in Marienthal, neighbouring villages, or Vienna. The other 400 subsisted on relief of some sort, with the exception of nine families with no relief or assistance and eighteen with railway pensions.

Four-fifths of the families had allotments in the common land owned by the village authorities and the factory. Each allotment consisted of five plots, about two by six meters each, which were used to grow vegetables, varying with the season. Many families grew flowers as well, choosing cheerfulness over sustenance. About thirty families also bred rabbits. Despite the home-grown vegetables, diets were very monotonous. Meat was eaten only once a week by half the families, on Sunday. Very few families had meat more than twice a week, and what they had was usually horsemeat. This was an 'inferior good' in the language of economists; consumption had risen as income fell. Starches were the basis of most diets, and the flour used had changed from wheat to the cheaper rye. Sugar was replaced by cheaper saccharine. While almost all families had three meals a day, the evening meal typically was either coffee and bread or leftovers from the noon meal.

This poor diet consumed almost all the incomes of the families in the village. Families with children also bought milk; most families bought coal for heat. But there was little money left over for clothes and other expenses. Shoes in particular were a problem. Families typically could not afford to replace shoes that had worn out, and so they were patched and patched again. Some families even restricted the activities of their children to save the wear and tear on their shoes.

While comparisons across time and space are difficult, the income of the unemployed Marienthal workers appears similar to the Italian worker of 1890 mentioned at the beginning of Chapter 1. In both cases, the cost of food—even with limited meat and variety—consumed almost all the budget. Little was left over for recreation or for capital expenses.

While spending collapsed back into food, and food into bread and coffee, movement collapsed back into the village. Trips to Vienna had been frequent during the 1920s, to go to the theatre, to do Christmas shopping, or to attend school. With unemployment, the money to undertake these journeys vanished. Even the train fare became a burden, and people relied more heavily on their bicycles. The isolation of rural villages, which had been broken down by the railway and prosperity after the First World War, reappeared in the Great Depression.

The isolation was deepened by a decline in newspaper subscriptions. Subscriptions to the Social Democratic paper, which contained intellectual discussions as well as news, dropped by 60 per cent from 1927 to 1930. This was not entirely a matter of money, since the paper had a cheaper subscription rate for unemployed workers. Subscriptions to another paper with more entertainment value fell only 30 per cent. Detachment was hardly complete, however. Political organizations continued, albeit with reduced passion. Votes in the 1932 elections were almost identical to those in the 1930 election. And the National Socialists started organizing in the village.

Politics, like other leisure activities, should have benefited from the increased availability of time. But this advantage was heavily outweighed by an increase of apathy that reduced all forms of recreational activity. As noted, people stopped reading newspapers. It follows that they must have stopped discussing newspaper stories and columns with their friends and neighbours. Library usage also declined. Both the number of borrowers and the books checked out by each borrower fell. Card-playing became a popular way to pass the time.

One striking aspect of this lethargy was the fate of a park that had formerly belonged to the village manor and had become a focal point for village life. In more prosperous times, villagers sat on its benches and walked on its paths on Sundays. The grass and shrubs were neatly tended. Despite the increase in leisure, the park fell rapidly into disuse as unemployment rose. The paths became overgrown; the lawns deteriorated; the park became a wilderness.

Villagers became suspicious of each other as they reduced their activities. There always had been denunciations of people seen or suspected of doing illegal activities, such as working while receiving relief. The number of denunciations rose dramatically in 1930 and 1931, but the number which stood up under investigation did not.

The observing sociologists classified most families as resigned to their condition. The families were hanging on, preserving as much of their life and family as they could on their meagre budgets. All their activity was dedicated to getting by; no thought was given to the future. Some families still planned as before, but others collapsed entirely in mental and physical neglect and conflict. Almost three out of four families in the village were classified as resigned.

The unemployed men were exceedingly idle. They passed their time doing essentially nothing. They could not even recall much of any activity during the day when asked. They sat around the house, went for walks—walking slowly—or played cards and chess at the Workmen's Club. In a compilation of time cards, over half of the men's time was idle or unaccounted for. Another quarter was occupied in minor household tasks like shopping and getting water. Less than a quarter of the time was used in major household work, looking after children, or handicrafts.

Women were far more active. Although no longer working, they had the responsibility of keeping the household running and caring for the children. They spent time cooking, mending clothes to make them last longer, and managing their budgets. The men contributed less to the running of the household than before—sometimes not even turning up on time for meals—and the women had the full responsibility. Even though the women often had had a hard time completing their housework after working, they uniformly would have preferred being back at work.

One revealing key to the meaning of time for unemployed workers was their bedtime. While working, people generally went to bed around 11 o'clock. They came home from work, ate, put the children to bed, went to a political meeting or had some other activity, talked a bit, and then went to bed. In the early 1930s, the women still went to bed late in the evening, taking the time to complete their household tasks. But the men went to bed before 9 o'clock. There simply was no reason to stay awake; sleep expanded to take up the time.

The life of the unemployed worker in London and Wigan

Another classic survey examined the experience a few months earlier, in the summer and autumn of 1931, of unemployed workers in Greenwich, a borough of London (Bakke 1934). In this study a lone investigator lived among the workers, recording his observations and conversations. The results are less systematic than those from Marienthal, but similar in spirit.

The experience of a 28-year-old mechanic and lorry driver was reported in this Greenwich study. Three days after being out of work, the mechanic was very optimistic about finding another job. After all, he had never been out of work for much more than a week before. Three weeks later, he was not so sure. He had answered all the ads in the newspaper, but he was getting discouraged. 'You feel like you're no good, if you get what I mean,' he said.

After eight weeks he was reduced to walking to seek jobs to save the bus fare, even though he was living with his parents to avoid paying rent. And he had begun to lie about how long he had been without a job, to avoid being lumped in with the long-term unemployed. After eleven weeks, he was still actively searching, but now only randomly; answering ads did not seem promising any more. His comment at this point: 'There's one of two things, either I'm no good, or there is something wrong with business around here.'

By the seventeenth week, the mechanic was thoroughly discouraged and depressed. He was described as 'sullen and despondent'. Although not as depressed or idle as the workers in Marienthal, because there was evidence of work nearby that might be found, this English worker none the less saw his experience as similarly hopeless: 'It isn't the hard work of tramping about so much, although that is bad enough. It's the hopelessness of every step you take when you go in search of a job you know isn't there' (Bakke 1934: 64–7).

As in Austria, unemployed workers were eligible for unemployment assistance in Britain. It was set up with the same restrictions; any work disqualified the recipient from further aid. And the rules were policed by competing workers who reported real and suspected infractions.

Unlike Marienthal, productive activity had not closed down entirely in Greenwich. Workers consequently continued to search for work. The observer formed an early judgement on the effect of unemployment assistance on the willingness to search for work. He asserted that there was no effect at all; the benefit did not retard or reduce efforts to find jobs. Instead, 'It has removed the cutting edge of the desperation which otherwise might attend that search' (Bakke 1934: 143).

Our third report was made by the famous writer George Orwell. Orwell was commissioned by the Left Book Club to report on the condition of workers in northern England in the mid-1930s, and went to Wigan, a small town near Manchester (Orwell 1937). He reported that there was little evidence of extreme poverty in the industrial North. Everything, he said, was poorer and shabbier than in London, but there were fewer beggars and derelicts than in the metropolis. The communal nature of life in the smaller communities enabled unemployed workers to pool their resources and scrape by.

Orwell did, however, comment on the dreadful condition of unemployed single men. They lived in depressing furnished rooms in which they could not stay all day. Outside, their main concern in the winter was to keep warm. The cinema, the library, even a lecture offered refuge from the cold. Orwell said he was taken to hear the 'silliest and worst-delivered lecture I have ever heard or ever expect to hear'. But while he fled in the middle, the hall remained full of unemployed men.

The diet of unemployed families was based on white bread and margarine, corned beef, sugared tea, and potatoes. Orwell commented (1937: 95): 'the peculiar evil is this, that the less money you have, the less inclined you feel to spend it on wholesome food. . . . There is always some cheaply pleasant thing to tempt you. . . . Unemployment is an endless misery that has got to be constantly palliated, and especially with tea, the Englishman's opium.'

More recent authors have amplified these observations and provided details of unemployment in other countries. The general patterns are similar to those described here. Unskilled workers suffered more than skilled. Idleness and discouragement abounded. Unemployment relief often provided the margin between some semblance of the previous life and disruptive poverty.

It has been tempting to see unemployment in one country as special. The Nazis came to power in Germany; could this have happened because unemployment was worse in some respect there than in other countries? The historical record does not support this inference. As will be detailed shortly, unemployment was widespread throughout Europe in the 1930s. And studies of voting behaviour have revealed a complex pattern. As mentioned in Chapter 6.5, time-series evidence shows that the Nazi vote increased with unemployment, and decreased in November 1932 as unemployment dipped. But cross-section evidence, examining the voting patterns in the approximately 1,000 counties of the Weimar Republic, does not show that regions with high unemployment voted more heavily for the Nazis than those with low unemployment. The link between German unemployment and the rise of the Nazis is still obscure (Hamilton 1982; Childers 1983; Falter 1986).

7.2 The pattern of industrial unemployment

The available data on unemployment in this period are very imperfect, but a rough indication of the pattern of national industrial unemployment is shown in Table 7.1. Data for Italy are missing from this table because there are no reliable statistics. We know that industrial unemployment in Italy moved with the international trend, but its precise level cannot be determined.

The countries in Table 7.1 fall into three groups. The first group, consisting of the United Kingdom and the Scandinavian countries, had high unemployment throughout the inter-war years. The contrast between the 1920s and 1930s was not very pronounced; the later decade was only slightly worse than the 1920s had been. The second group consists of France, Germany, and the Netherlands. They had much higher unemployment in the 1930s than in the preceding decade. And the third group consists of Belgium alone—which had relatively low unemployment throughout, but the most marked contrast between the two decades.

These groups of countries correspond to the groups of nations to be identified in Chapter 8 as belonging to different trading areas. The sterling area, that is, the countries that followed Britain off gold in 1931, had the least severe increase in unemployment in the 1930s. Those countries that stayed on the gold standard (the gold bloc) and those in the Nazi area suffered much higher unemployment in the 1930s relative to the 1920s.

Before we conclude that devaluation was the sole cause of relatively low increases in unemployment in the 1930s, we should note that the countries abandoning gold in 1931 were those that had had the highest unemployment in the 1920s. Perhaps a discouraging record of unemployment in the 1920s made countries more willing to abandon the gold standard during the depression. In other words, the relatively good record of the devaluing countries in the 1930s

Table 7.1. Unemployment rates in industry, 1921–1938 (%)

	1921–9	1930–8	Ratio
United Kingdom	12.0	15.4	1.3
Sweden	14.2	16.8	1.2
Denmark	18.7	21.9	1.2
Norway	16.8	26.6	1.6
France	3.8	10.2	2.7
Germany	9.2	21.8	2.4
Netherlands	8.3	24.3	2.9
Belgium	2.4	14.0	5.8

Source: Galenson and Zellner (1957: 455).

was a reflection both of their policies in the depression and of their prior difficulties.

Unemployment was not evenly spread among all classes of workers when considered by age, sex, and occupation. Unfortunately, not much is known about this important problem for most countries. One exception is Britain, where more studies have been conducted than elsewhere.

In relation to age, Thomas (1988) found that the risk of becoming unemployed was very much the same for all adult age-groups, but that after about age 45 it was increasingly difficult to find a new job after losing the old one. In the words of a pioneering investigator (Beveridge 1937: 13): 'The older man has less power of recovery industrially, from loss of unemployment, as he has less power physically, from sickness or accident.' The result was higher unemployment, and higher long-term unemployment, among older workers.

On the other hand, there is evidence that it was young workers who were most liable to be without a job. According to a group of contemporary observers: 'the difficulty in retaining or securing employment appears to arise at the point when the change-over takes place between the juvenile and the adult wage' (Royal Institute of International Affairs 1935: 62). If they did find work, trade union customs and their lack of experience generally made them the most vulnerable when employers needed to dismiss workers.

Women accounted for only a small proportion of all those who were out of work: less than 14 per cent in 1933. In large part this was simply a reflection of the fact that they were a smaller proportion of the labour force, but it was also the case that women were less likely than men to lose their jobs. Surveys also found that women were more easily discouraged than men after losing their jobs and, therefore, more likely to leave the register than to continue to search for employment.

As far as occupation was concerned, unemployment was heavily concentrated in the semi-professionals on the one hand and in manual workers on the other, the unskilled ones being the worst hit. As Thomas put it (1988: 123): 'In general terms, the risk of unemployment fell as social class rose. Unskilled males were the most vulnerable, female higher professionals the least.'

Thomas's study also demonstrated that the increase in unemployment in the 1930s was not the result of increased job leaving.

Rather it was that workers were not being re-employed as rapidly as before. Some were not rehired at all—or at least not for a long time. The proportion of the unemployed in Britain who were out of work more than a year rose from about 5 per cent in 1929 to over 20 per cent during the 1930s. The result was a bifurcated labour market: one group went in and out of work with some frequency; the other remained unemployed.

The workers who were unemployed for long periods—or even permanently—and those who suffered the highest rates of unemployment were predominantly located in the areas dominated by Britain's traditional activities: coal mining, iron and steel, shipbuilding, textiles. The problems of these industries have been considered in Chapter 4.2. Here we note that declining production in particular industries, as well as in nations as a whole, meant declining employment. While it is true that greater aggregate demand would have reduced British unemployment (as it did after 1939), it also is true that even with higher demand many workers in traditional industries would have had to move to jobs in newer industries.

For various reasons they may well have been the last to be hired in these industries. Their skills may not have been transferable across industry lines. Employers may have wished to recruit younger workers, or ones without a previous history of employment in the declining industries with their specific trade union traditions and work practices. Or they may have been reluctant—or unable—to move to newer industrial locations. The result of these structural factors was that unemployment in Britain between the wars was particularly concentrated in certain areas. For instance, the male unemployment rate in 1932 was 36.5 per cent in Wales as against 13.5 in London, and the gap tended to widen as the recovery got under way (Thomas 1988: 124).

Unemployment in Germany and France

Germany suffered even more severely. In the worst year of the depression almost one in three of the workforce was unemployed, compared to one in five in Britain. In the winter of 1932, and again in 1933, the number registered as unemployed mounted to over six million. There were many more on the farms who were not officially classified as out of work, but who were equally victims of the contraction of output and the fall in prices. However, the higher total was more evenly distributed than in the United Kingdom, so that Germany escaped the heavy concentrations in particular areas and did not experience the sharp contrasts between prosperous and depressed regions.

The situation in France was less serious. For a number of reasons unemployment did not initially soar upwards in France as it had done in Britain and Germany. The onset of severe depression came much later, and it was not until 1932 that there was a sharp fall in the level of industrial production. As explained in Chapter 3.4, France enjoyed a strong balance of payments position in the late 1920s, and in these early years of the world depression she did not have to impose deflationary policies in order to protect her gold reserves. However, this advantageous position changed quite swiftly after Britain and other countries abandoned the gold standard and depreciated their currencies. From late 1933 unemployment did rise, and the position continued to deteriorate through 1934.

Even then, however, unemployment was neither as high, nor as concentrated in specific locations and industries, as in Britain. This was in large measure a reflection of the different pattern of activity in France. The proportion of the labour force occupied in agriculture was very much larger (see Chapter 4.1), and although peasant farmers suffered in other ways during the depression, they were not deprived of all sources of income, and were not forced into the ranks of the unemployed workers dependent on state assistance or charity for their survival. Within industry and trade, the structure of employment was also different, with a much larger proportion of small shopkeepers, outworkers, part-timers, and self-employed workers in small establishments. Many of these were also able to retain some sources of income during the downturn.

Two other factors also contributed to the more favourable position. Compulsory conscription eased the problem of youth unemployment. Much more important, a substantial part of the burden was shifted on to foreign workers by controlling the influx of immigrant labour. Admission from abroad fell from 221,000 in 1930 to 60,000 in 1933 (Royal Institute of International Affairs 1935: 74). To the question 'Who were the French unemployed?' it is thus possible to reply: 'They were the Italians, the Belgians, the Polish, and the Spanish.'

7.3 Unemployment, benefits, and real wages

Earlier in this chapter we reported the unemployed Greenwich worker's comments on the effects of unemployment assistance on his willingness to search for a new job. In a highly controversial article, Benjamin and Kochin (1979) argued that the increase in British unemployment in the 1930s was essentially due to the increase in the level of these benefits. Workers remained unemployed, in other words, because they had little incentive to find a new job. Benjamin and Kochin attempted to demonstrate this proposition econometrically, by estimating an equation that explained the unemployment rate by the ratio of the unemployment benefit to the wage, and the deviation of national income from its trend. This finding has been disputed by a variety of authors. But although the evidence adduced by Benjamin and Kochin has been shown to be deficient, their hypothesis has not been completely demolished, and it is now generally accepted that some weight should be given to the role of higher unemployment benefits in increasing the number out of work (Crafts 1987; Eichengreen 1987).

A further issue closely related to the question of unemployment is the behaviour of real wages. Keynesian explanations of the Great Depression start from the observation that workers bargain over nominal wages. When prices fall in a depression, real wages rise. The resultant profit squeeze intensifies the depression. This mechanism was evident during the Great Depression. As documented by Eichengreen and Sachs (1985), higher real wages in the mid-1930s were associated with higher unemployment.

This finding has created a problem for macro-economists because the Keynesian assumption of stable nominal wages has long since been abandoned. While Keynes saw wages as determined by tradition-bound workers and managers, modern macro-economics conceptualizes the wage bargain as the result of negotiations between highly sophisticated agents. These agents, particularly those acting for the workers, should have seen the demand for labour fading away and accepted lower nominal wages. The question for macro-economists is thus: 'Why did nominal wages not adjust to the rise in unemployment?' (Bernanke 1993).

One answer that has been proposed in the context of discussions of European unemployment in the 1980s is that the labour market does not work in the atomistic fashion of other markets. In the market for apples, for example, the trader who has apples left over at the end of the day lowers their price to clear his stand. But the unemployed worker in this story does not have the ability to force down wages. Instead, he has become an 'outsider' to the wage-setting process. Wages are determined by agreement between the employers and the employed workers—the 'insiders'. Insiders may care about the fate of the outsiders, but they also may not. Governments typically care about both insiders and outsiders; labour unions often consider only their current members, who are normally insiders. If the workers' agents care only about insiders, then the outsiders have no effect on wages. This could explain why increasing unemployment in the Great Depression failed to force down nominal wages faster than prices.

The only exception to this story is Germany. There, alone among European countries, wages fell faster than prices. Except for Germany, real wages in 1933 were higher than in 1929 in every European country for which data have been collected (as well as in the United States, Canada, and Japan). For the many countries with rising real wages, the range in 1933 (1929 = 100) was between 104 and 119. For Germany, by contrast, real hourly earnings in manufacturing, mining, and transport in 1933 were 5 per cent below their 1929 level (Eichengreen 1994).

This quantitative evidence has intriguing implications for the Borchardt debate, referred to in Chapter 4.2. If wages were too high in Weimar Germany, though this has not yet been firmly established, the problem was erased in the contraction. The conditions that allowed German wages to rise rapidly in the Weimar Republic evaporated with the onset of the depression.

An alternative explanation for the rise in real wages has also been suggested by some writers. In their view it was not the result of an independent fall in prices without a corresponding adjustment in money wages, but of an autonomous increase in nominal wages. In either case the rise in real wages would lead to higher unemployment, but there would be two quite different interpretations of why this had occurred. In the first case it would be necessary to explain why there was a fall in prices, in the second how workers were able to obtain the higher nominal wages. It is thus important for an analysis of the causes of the increased unemployment to establish which of these two versions was correct.

Dimsdale *et al.* (1989) attempted to do this by means of an elaborate econometric study of the British experience. They concluded that both the recession and the recovery in the 1930s were consistent with the consequences of a large exogenous demand shock (such as we have described in our account of the depression), accompanied by a large fall in the real price of imported goods. This led to higher unemployment because wages and prices were sticky, so that real wages rose when import prices fell, making it unprofitable to employ workers at that level of remuneration. Autonomous changes in wages were not an important factor.

Our search for the explanation for the mass unemployment of the depression thus leads back to the causes of the large demand shock, causes which we have attempted to analyse in the preceding chapters. It cannot be said that workers were themselves responsible for their own plight because they had initiated the process by exerting pressure for higher wages.

The fact that high real wages could be one of the causes of high unemployment did not escape policy makers. In order to solve the problem, countries that had devalued their currencies in 1931 implicitly counted on inflation, assuming some kind of upward rigidity of money wages. The governments of gold bloc countries, particularly Italy and France, tried to impose nominal wage cuts. Mussolini's Italy had adopted this policy as early as 1927, at the time of the stabilization of the lira at a revalued parity, and introduced it again in the first part of the 1930s. In the same vein, Laval attempted to make French workers take a cut in their nominal wages. Such attempts, however, met with strong opposition from the organized labour movements, and proved to be difficult to implement on a sufficiently large scale, even for dictatorial or authoritarian governments.

7.4 Policies to create work

Unemployment remained stubbornly high for many years. Much of the reason is that the Great Depression lasted so long. As long as demand remained depressed—for the host of reasons that we have seen in previous chapters—so did output and employment. The misguided macro-economic policy answers to the depression had perverse effects on unemployment. It is ironic, however, that some of them were advocated by governments and pressure groups precisely in order to alleviate the hardship of those without jobs. This is the case of the trend towards autarky that, particularly when applied by several countries simultaneously, resulted in work destruction rather than creation.

On the other hand, some policies went in the right direction, even if they probably did too little and too late. This is the case with public works programmes such as those undertaken by France and Italy. Moreover, the magnitude of the phenomenon postulated the establishment of unemployment insurance and of some kind of relief for those not covered by such insurance.

At the micro-level, steps were taken to reorganize the labour market. In some cases these included attempts at improving employment exchange offices, in order to ease the possible mismatch between demand and supply of labour, and to organize seasonal and casual labour more effectively. In the same policy category fall efforts to provide better vocational guidance to new entrants in the labour markets, and retraining for those who had lost their jobs.

Government intervention in these areas was more or less active in the individual European countries but nowhere was it really able to make a quantum difference. Rather, in this, as in many other areas, it signalled a new interventionist stance shared by all European governments albeit with different intensity, a stance that was to take root and develop on a much wider scale during and after the end of the Second World War. If anything, the 1930s created a widespread belief in the electorates of most countries that unmitigated *laissez-faire* was the cause of inter-war unemployment and that appropriate state policies could deliver full employment.

Keynes and the campaign in Britain

The attempt to persuade the government to adopt a large-scale public works programme funded by borrowing was conducted most vigorously in the United Kingdom. The issue first emerged in the 1920s, when unemployment soared after the collapse of the post-war boom, and it gathered strength in the trade union and labour movements, with support from the Liberal party. By the time of the general election of 1929 it had become the dominant issue dividing the parties, and the campaign was notable for the active participation of Keynes. He penned a brilliant pamphlet in support of the Liberal leader's proposals for a public works programme, *Lloyd George Can Do It*, but despite his sparkling critique of the Conservative party's opposition to such expenditure, neither the electorate nor the government were persuaded.

The issue remained at the centre of political and intellectual debate as the depression deepened. In 1931 Keynes gave a detailed elaboration of his ideas in evidence to a Royal Commission, but was unable to overcome the resistance of those whose views were still rooted in orthodox economic thinking. The theoretical break-through was not to come until he had completed his great work, *The General Theory of Employment Interest and Money*, first published in 1936, and even then the process of conversion was generally very slow and partial, particularly in Whitehall and in the City.

The government ministers and their advisers in the Treasury had a number of different reasons for their steadfast rejection of all proposals for state spending aimed specifically at reducing unemployment. Some of their objections were practical and administrative: it took time to draw up plans for road-building, land had to be acquired, it was the responsibility of local authorities, not of central government, and so on. These were convenient debating points to make in political campaigns, but could not be sustained when unemployment persisted for so long.

A second line of attack was that the causes were structural and long-term—the problems of the declining industries discussed in Chapter 4.2—and would not be alleviated by short-term measures. There is more merit in this argument, but inability to solve a problem completely is not sufficient justification for not doing what can be done. With unemployment rising to about three million by 1932, even the removal of a few hundred thousand workers from the dole queues would surely have been worth while.

This was not done because there were deeper levels to the opposition within the Treasury and in the financial and business community. One powerful and permanent component was the belief that it was essential to limit government spending, and that the only effective way to do this was to constrain it within the level that could be covered by taxation. Once this fundamental principle was breached, as it would be if the government acceded to the demands for deficit spending on public works, it would be impossible to resist other demands for higher expenditure—and there was no end to the list of potential worthy causes, from higher pensions and unemployment benefits to improvements in education and health care.

Still more fundamental, though probably too technical to be appreciated by more than a minority, was the argument that a programme of government expenditure would not actually be an effective cure for unemployment. This proposition rested on what has since come to be known as 'crowding-out': any spending by the government would simply displace a corresponding amount of spending by the private sector. This would hold even if the increased government spending was not matched by an equivalent increase in taxation, but by borrowing. There would thus be no net gain in output or employment. At a time of mass unemployment and idle factories this negative prospect could scarcely be attributed to shortages of labour or other physical resources. Rather, the argument was psychological and financial.

The source of the psychological crowding-out was the private sector's belief that budget deficits were a sign of financial profligacy and irresponsibility. If the government committed such sins, financiers and industrialists would lose confidence in the future stability and prosperity of the economy. Businessmen would refuse to invest in their enterprises. Bankers at home and abroad would refuse to buy the securities the government would have to sell if it was to cover its deficit. Such views might be irrational in the prevailing conditions, but they were deep-rooted and powerful.

Financial crowding-out was a more abstract proposition, and was the most fundamental determinant of the view held by the Treasury and their supporters among academic economists. According to these theorists, this displacement would occur because there was a limited supply of savings. If more of this finite fund were drawn on for public investment, less would be available for private investment. A possible escape from the logic of this doctrine might be available if there was a compensating reduction in investment overseas. That apart, public spending could only be effective in raising total spending if it was associated with a relaxation of bank credit and lower interest rates. However, if the authorities wanted to do that, it was not necessary for them to accompany it by public works. In the words of the original and most influential proponent of this doctrine (Hawtrey 1925: 48): 'The original contention that the public works themselves give additional employment is radically fallacious.'

But, of course, the Treasury and the Bank of England did not want to relax credit in the 1920s. On the contrary, it was an imperative requirement of the restoration and preservation of the gold standard that interest rates should be kept high. It was not until the country had finally abandoned the gold standard in 1931 that they could begin to think in terms of a different strategy. From mid-1932, the fact that it was no longer necessary to defend sterling made cheap money a possibility for the first time since the war.

The bank rate was lowered in stages from 6 per cent in September 1931 to 2 per cent in June 1932, and then remained at that low level until the outbreak of war in August 1939. A reduction in long-term interest rates followed after the collapse of the Labour government, and the formation of a coalition dominated by the Conservatives, with the ultra-orthodox Philip Snowden as Chancellor of the Exchequer. The new government's cautious financial stance generated a significant increase in confidence in financial circles, enhanced the willingness of the public to hold government securities, and enabled the authorities to bring about a fall in long-term interest rates. For the remainder of the decade cheap money (about 3 per cent) for industry and for housing was the principal element in their policy, and the means by which they hoped to encourage economic recovery and industrial restructuring.

Before we leave this topic we should note that modern research has demonstrated that even if the programme of public works advocated in 1929 had been adopted, the impact on employment and output would have been somewhat less than Keynes and his colleagues had anticipated. We now know that the value of the multiplier—the expansion of expenditure as a result of the initial increase in spending—was not as great as they had thought. The benefits in increased activity at home would have been rapidly curtailed by higher imports, and an outlay of the magnitude proposed by Lloyd George would probably have created jobs for only about 300,000 of the more than one million who were out of work in 1929 (Thomas 1981; Hatton 1987). Those who would have found work if the programme had been adopted would no doubt have welcomed even this modest increase.

Policy in Sweden and Germany

The depression made its main impact on Sweden from 1931, primarily because exports could no longer be sustained once production activity and trade collapsed elsewhere. The fall in exports then caused a reduction in activity and a rise in unemployment. The attitude of the government at that time was similar to that in the

United Kingdom, and they were not willing to adopt measures which required deliberate budget deficits. In 1933, however, a new government was elected, based on a coalition of the Social Democrats with the Farmers' party. They were more responsive to proposals from a group of distinguished Swedish economists, notably Myrdal, Lindahl, and Ohlin, for a deliberate counter-cyclical fiscal policy, with deficits to be financed through government borrowing. A policy of this nature was implemented from 1933 to 1935, but only on a modest scale and its effects were relatively limited.

Monetary policy thus remained the more important weapon in the attempt to mitigate the effects of the depression in Sweden. The initial policy consisted essentially of an attempt to prevent any further fall in prices and thus to stabilize the domestic purchasing power of the Swedish krona. When Sweden left the gold standard in September 1931 the authorities expected prices to rise, but by the end of the year they again saw falling prices as the major source of instability. To counter this a more expansionary monetary policy was introduced, and this succeeded in offsetting the contractionary forces and creating public confidence in the Swedish financial system. Unemployment reached a peak in 1933 and then declined steadily as production recovered.

In Weimar Germany, as described in Chapter 6.2, government policy accelerated the drop in employment as the depression deepened. Determined to balance the federal budget, successive governments reduced unemployment benefits as tax revenues declined. The Brüning government regarded reparations as its primary problem; unemployment would be taken care of once reparations were cancelled.

The conflicts of German policy can be seen in the discussions during early 1932. The depression was at its worst by then, and unemployment was very severe. The General German Trade Union Federation (ADGB) sponsored a plan of job creation that was known as the WTB Plan after the initials of its three authors, as described in Chapter 6.5. The first author, Wladimir Woytinsky, was the chief source of the ideas in the plan, which—in retrospect—are quite Keynesian in their emphasis on direct job creation.

The ADGB requested a meeting with Chancellor Brüning to present this plan. The government however was only willing to undertake a work creation programme if the budget was balanced. So expenditures for unemployment relief, welfare, and job creation had to be cut rather than increased as the economy and tax revenues declined. Brüning refused to meet with the trade union federation.

The labour minister nevertheless proposed a modest plan for work creation in several areas, chiefly government enterprises and agriculture. Even this was vetoed by the Reichsbank on the grounds that it required credit expansion. The government plan was leaked to the press, which did not help its progress in the cabinet, but it provided a fig-leaf for the labour minister when he met with the ADGB in April.

The government failed to respond to the trade unions because Brüning was determined to deal with Germany's external problems—that is, reparations—first, and its internal problems second, as discussed in Chapter 6.5. Inaction in the latter sphere appeared tolerable, both because deflation seemed to correspond to the short-term interests of business and because the government failed to appreciate the corrosive effect of unemployment on the social institutions of the Weimar Republic.

When Brüning was replaced by Papen in May 1932, the existing work creation plan could be implemented. It was introduced in June, while the Lausanne Conference deliberated the fate of reparations (see Chapter 8.1). Only in September, after the conference had ended reparations, was an expanded programme introduced. It emphasized incentives for private employers to hire workers over direct government employment. Among these incentives were lower wages for new employees, which the trade unions saw as being against rather than for the workers' interests. Although this programme was modest and had no discernible immediate effects, it was the model for succeeding plans.

Schleicher followed Papen in December and built on the existing plan. He also changed the focus from the private economy back to the ADGB focus on government employment, decreasing public support for the programme. The Reichsbank of course opposed the extension of credit and sought to limit the programme. The government therefore created an intermediate institution to extend credit, leaving the Reichsbank to guarantee the bonds. The Reichsbank budget was unaffected! This was the blueprint for the larger work creation programme introduced under Hitler.

Hitler of course was not bound by either reparations (which had ended) or by the need to satisfy the populace (which was controlled by terror). The Nazi work creation programme was a precursor of rearmament, and it had a military component from the start. The army's demands were so modest, however, that the Nazi government extended the programme in a variety of ways. The result was a rapid fall in measured unemployment. Part of the reduction was due to the programmes, but part also was due to a decline in the quality of the statistics as faithful Nazis replaced civil servants in the unemployment agencies.

8

THE FRAGMENTED WORLD
OF THE 1930s

OUR central theme in this chapter is the disintegration of the international economy which followed the onset of the Great Depression. We look first at the extent of the disharmony and rivalry displayed by the European nations and the United States at the World Economic Conference of 1933. Co-operation was desperately needed to mitigate the effects of the slump, but it was not forthcoming. Each country had its own agenda, its own economic and political priorities, its own preferred solutions.

The next three sections examine the operation of the three rival trading areas which emerged in this decade: the sterling area around Britain; the gold bloc, with France, Belgium, Switzerland, and the Netherlands as its principal members; and the Nazi trading area, with Germany at its centre.

8.1 Attempts at international co-operation

President Herbert Hoover of the United States had imposed a one-year moratorium on payments of reparations and war debts in July 1931 in an effort to avert the German crisis. But the Hoover Moratorium was not sufficient to end the German financial panic. A Special Advisory Committee of the Bank for International Settlements reviewed economic conditions in Germany in late 1931, and found that the schedule for reparations payments established by the 1929 Young Plan was no longer feasible. The plan had expected trade expansion and recovery, not worldwide depression and the collapse of trade.

The British government led an effort to convene a conference to discuss reparations. Chancellor Brüning stated in January 1932 that Germany would seek their complete cancellation. The French vehemently responded that they would not easily cede their right to reparations. The British and the Italians supported the Germans, leaving the French nearly isolated. The United States remained uninterested in reparations, but adamantly opposed war debt repudiation. Even in their last moments, reparations were a source of discord. There was no international leadership and no cooperation.

Brüning's January statement and its repercussions in other capitals delayed the conference. Impending elections in France and Germany also contributed to the delay, as neither government would be in a position to make concessions prior to elections. The delay in convening the meeting contributed to the collapse of Chancellor Brüning's government. Brüning had launched Germany on a programme of deflation to end reparations by demonstrating to German creditors that the nation could not pay. He succeeded in destroying the German economy along with reparations, a truly Pyrrhic victory.

The Lausanne Conference on reparations

The Lausanne Conference finally opened in June 1932 with statements of national views, with the French opposing substantial concessions, and the Italians, British, and Germans favouring a clean slate. The proceedings at Lausanne were complicated by a disarmament conference concurrently meeting in Geneva, where the United States informed England and France that it would not allow European default on war debts while funds sufficient to cover the payments were being used for armament spending. The Germans expressed willingness to offer compensation, but they wished to avoid mention of the word reparations. The British and the French favoured a clause linking reparations with an American war debt settlement. Germany objected to the American argument that there was no link between the two obligations, and that an agreement had to be definite and independent of America.

A breakthrough in negotiations led to the Lausanne Convention.

An annex to the agreement addressed the German reparations conflict, directing Germany to deposit bonds worth RM3 billion (£125 million) with the Bank for International Settlements (BIS). The bonds were to be issued by the BIS after a three-year moratorium if Germany was judged to be capable of paying; their allocation was to be settled in a future meeting of the creditors. (The bonds, printed but never issued, were burned in 1948.) Beyond the issue of the bonds, Germany was permanently relieved of reparations obligations.

Another annex of the Convention called for a world economic conference to address the major remaining international economic issues. The British Treasury had favoured such a conference since late 1930. France had blocked Britain's attempts to co-ordinate an international conference in 1931, fearing both pressure to join in an artificial international redistribution of gold and German manipulation of the conference to obtain a reparations reprieve. After the sterling devaluation of September 1931 removed British pressure for gold redistribution, and the Lausanne Conference of June 1932 ended German reparations, both these obstacles to co-operation had been eliminated.

The 1933 World Economic Conference

The French and British asked President Hoover to postpone the December 1932 war debt payment, but he refused. France and several other European nations defaulted on the instalment, and the English paid by earmarking gold in the Bank of England, angering American public opinion and increasing President-elect Roosevelt's determination to keep war debts off the agenda for the World Economic Conference. Despite agreement to end reparations with the face-saving bonds held by the BIS, war debts remained as an internationally divisive issue. Neither co-operation nor effective leadership was possible on the eve of the 1933 economic conference.

The Lausanne Convention had called for a committee of experts to meet in advance of the large conference to establish an agenda. The British staked out a position requiring higher prices and the revival of trade as conditions for a stabilization agreement. The French cautiously guarded their continued adherence to the gold standard, which remained free of attack, and their trade barriers, which provided protection from depreciated currencies. The Hoover Administration, represented at the meetings of the experts, sympathized with the French arguments, while Roosevelt, initially unsure, eventually drifted towards the English policies.

As the London conference approached, prospects for success grew ever dimmer. As the value of the dollar fell during May, Roosevelt became less interested in stabilization, reversing the cooperative policies that he had advocated. Meanwhile, the French government conveyed to the United States and British governments its belief that exchange stabilization was a prerequisite for success in London. The French sought not recovery, but security, in a world over which they exercised little control.

Central bank representatives from Britain, France, and the United States decided in June 1933 that exchange stabilization was possible. Each agreed to buy and sell gold to keep their currencies within prescribed limits of 3 per cent either way. The provisions of the stabilization were to be kept secret, and the agreement would be nullified if the details were made public. Declarations were prepared stating that the three governments intended to limit fluctuations of the dollar and sterling for the length of the conference, that stabilization on gold was the ultimate objective, and that they would avoid measures that might interfere with monetary stability.

Unfortunately, the news of dollar stabilization leaked to the press, and American markets responded quickly. The dollar strengthened, and commodity and share prices fell as investors anticipated a return to deflation. Roosevelt telegraphed his negotiators in London to reject the agreement, claiming that he did not wish to restrict his domestic policy options and that he was not certain at what level the dollar belonged. After attempts to sway the President failed, Roosevelt's rejection was announced at the World Economic Conference, causing turmoil and intensifying speculation against the Dutch florin and the Swiss franc, but restoring the recovery of American markets.

After the collapse of this agreement, the French concentrated pressure on the British to stabilize and join the gold countries, warning of impending monetary anarchy in Europe. In response, the British asked for a currency declaration, which was quickly drafted and approved by the gold countries. To the consternation of the French, however, the British invited American participation in the agreement. The United States representative revised the document until the only remaining points were a call for monetary stability, recognition that an eventual return to the gold standard was desirable, and a statement that individual nations would take action to avoid speculation. He advised Roosevelt to accept the document, fearing that the United States would be held responsible for the collapse of the conference.

Roosevelt none the less sent a message to London on 1 July rejecting the declaration. His infamous bombshell exploded in the face of the conference and the public two days later. The message, loaded with inflammatory rhetoric, accused the stabilization discussion of interfering with the real issues that the conference should address. In Roosevelt's words (Nixon 1969: 269): 'The world will not long be lulled by the specious fallacy of achieving a temporary and probably an artificial stability in foreign exchange on the part of a few large countries only . . . The sound internal economic situation of a nation is a greater factor in its well-being than the price of its currency.'

Roosevelt later admitted that the message was too heavy in rhetoric, but several economists agreed with his general argument; Keynes even said that Roosevelt was 'magnificently right' (Feis 1966: 238). None the less, much of the logic of Roosevelt's message was contorted. His concerns about a United States gold drain were offset by the fact that the country possessed one-third of the world's gold reserves. His qualms about only two or three nations stabilizing were contradicted by the fact that the rest of the world would stabilize in terms of the dollar, franc, and pound. And the distinction he stressed between governments and central banks was essentially irrelevant in considering a stabilization agreement. However, his central message that domestic conditions needed to be given priority was correct.

The failure and collapse of the World Economic Conference is traditionally attributed to Roosevelt's message. But the conditions for international economic co-operation were not present in mid-1933. Each of the major countries had its own view of the economic crisis and was trying to formulate its own remedies. Instead of initiating international co-operation or leadership, each of the major European industrial and financial powers was becoming the centre of a currency and trading bloc of its own. The major industrial countries were moving away from, not toward, agreement and co-operation.

Britain's devaluation, however badly executed, allowed Britain to lower interest rates and expand the economy. Devaluation both improved the trade balance and, more importantly, freed macro-economic policy from the 'golden fetters' of the gold standard. Many of Britain's trading partners followed Albion's example. They too benefited from the relaxation of constraints on expansionary policy. While none of these countries reached full capacity in the 1930s, they grew more and suffered less than the countries that clung to the gold standard.

8.2 The sterling area

Once Britain had devalued, the pressure to follow suit was especially great among countries with export-based economies for whom the United Kingdom was the primary market. Denmark, Sweden, Norway, and Finland followed Britain off gold, but did not immediately peg to sterling. By January 1932 Japan, Venezuela, and Bolivia were adopting policies that increasingly seemed to tie their economies to sterling. The countries that pegged to sterling between 1931 and 1933 formed the sterling area, composed of the colonial empire and India, semi-independent nations including Iraq and Egypt, the dominions excluding Canada, and other foreign nations, particularly in Scandinavia.

The reasons for choosing to link with sterling varied among these groups. India and the colonial empire were compelled to do so by Britain; this was not unusual, as a sterling peg had previously been used to stabilize these currencies. Australia and New Zealand had already suffered exchange depreciation, and needed to be tied to sterling to retain competitiveness in the British market. South Africa, after initially trying to maintain its gold parity, was forced to devalue and peg to sterling for similar reasons.

Many smaller European and Latin American countries chose to link to sterling both because Britain was a primary export market and because they held large reserves of sterling for exchange transactions. The Brussels Conference of 1920 and the Genoa Conference of 1922 had encouraged holding foreign currency instead of gold, and unless these countries devalued and repegged to gold, they would suffer large capital losses on their sterling reserves.

Just as there were multiple reasons for pegging to sterling, there were multiple mechanisms for maintaining this new parity. The currency board system implemented for the colonial empire, Egypt, and Iraq provided an automatic relationship with sterling. A system of semi-independence, in which the exchange rate was rigidly fixed and maintained through large sterling reserves, was adopted in India, Australia, New Zealand, South Africa, and Portugal. The third policy, an autonomous system of preserving a target sterling parity without holding large sterling reserves, was attempted in Scandinavia.

The British government studiously avoided encouraging countries outside the colonial empire and India to devalue or to peg to sterling because it wished to avoid responsibility for other nations' difficulties. Even though Britain avoided formal arrangements, it supported nations that voluntarily committed themselves to the sterling area. In December 1931 the Bank of England provided a credit of £500,000 to the Bank of Finland, which was trying to maintain sterling parity through exchange controls. In the same month a credit of £250,000 was granted to Denmark. Throughout the 1930s Australia received sizeable credits which, while never used, demonstrated British willingness to stabilize exchange rates within the sterling area.

Soon after the devaluation of sterling in September 1931, British Treasury officials began to consider a monetary policy for the Empire. The British authorities shared the opinion of the leaders of the Empire that prices were too low, but they feared that the Empire countries might promote inflationary programmes of deficit monetization, public works, and deliberate credit expansion which could potentially destabilize sterling. In early 1932 the discussion of Empire monetary policy developed into preparations for the forthcoming British Commonwealth conference to be held in Ottawa.

Trade and the 1932 Commonwealth Conference at Ottawa

In the 1932 Ottawa meeting, the monetary policy issues were confined to a committee through which the British advanced their policies, reassuring the dominions and India that monetary policy would be directed towards higher prices and recovery, but avoiding discussion of stabilization. The principal discussions at Ottawa were devoted to trade agreements. In February 1932 the United Kingdom had finally deserted its long-standing commitment to free trade. The national government introduced the Import Duties Act, providing for an immediate 10 per cent duty on all goods except basic foodstuffs, raw materials, and goods already subject to duty. It also established an Import Duties Advisory Committee with power to recommend higher duties for specific goods, and the nominal tariff on most manufactures was quickly raised to 20 per cent.

The United Kingdom delegates had hoped to obtain improved entry for British manufactures in the Commonwealth markets, but Australia, Canada, India, and other members were unwilling to take any measures which would harm their emerging manufacturing industries. Despite their initial expectations the agreement did little to help increase Britain's sales of manufactured goods. The best that could be agreed was that the dominions would give preferential access to British producers by raising even higher tariffs against imports of manufactures from non-Commonwealth countries, and Britain would in turn grant Commonwealth producers preferential access to the British market for food and raw materials.

The policies adopted at the Ottawa Conference helped to bring about a considerable shift in the pattern of United Kingdom trade, with a marked increase in the importance of both purchases from, and sales to, the dominions. This reinforced other trends operating in the 1930s to increase her trade with the British Empire and the sterling area at the expense of other countries. The broad picture can be seen in Table 8.1. The share of United Kingdom imports purchased from the four dominions increased dramatically from 13 per cent in 1929 to 23 per cent in 1938, and there was also a rise in the proportion acquired from India and from Britain's colonies in Africa and Asia. In Europe only the sterling area countries, the Scandinavians, and Portugal were able to maintain their share of the United Kingdom market.

The rest of the world, including the United States, the gold bloc countries, the exchange control group associated with Germany, and the Argentine and other Latin American countries, all lost ground. In total the share of the countries which were in neither the Empire nor the European sterling area group fell from 63 per cent in 1929 to 49 per cent in 1938. Since the actual value of United Kingdom imports in the later year was still well below the 1929 level, this meant a large absolute fall in the amounts sold to Britain by these countries.

On the export side there was a very similar story. The share of the much-reduced United Kingdom exports sold to the four dominions rose from 20 to 25 per cent, and the proportion taken by the colonies and by the Scandinavian countries also increased. The striking

Table 8.1. Changes in the direction of United Kingdom trade, 1929 and 1938 (%)

	UK Imports		UK Exports	
	1929	1938	1929	1938
British Commonwealth				
Dominions[a]	13.0	22.5	19.7	25.4
Ireland	3.9	2.5	5.0	4.3
India, Burma, and Ceylon	5.5	7.4	11.5	8.5
Other British Commonwealth	4.5	7.0	8.3	11.7
Total Commonwealth	26.9	39.4	44.5	49.9
Rest of the world				
Scandinavian countries and Portugal	10.2	11.1	5.2	9.3
Gold bloc[b]	14.2	10.1	11.5	9.6
Exchange control group[c]	8.2	5.4	8.4	6.4
Other Europe	5.2	4.6	4.2	5.1
Total Europe	37.8	31.2	29.3	30.4
United States	16.5	13.0	6.3	4.3
Argentina	7.2	4.3	4.0	4.1
Other Latin America	4.5	3.9	5.9	3.5
Other countries	7.1	8.2	10.0	7.8
Total foreign	73.1	60.6	55.5	50.1

[a] Australia, Canada and Newfoundland, New Zealand, and South Africa.
[b] Belgium, France, the Netherlands, Poland, and Switzerland.
[c] Austria, Czechoslovakia, Germany, Hungary, and Italy.

Source: Board of Trade (1940: 374–81).

exception to this general trend within the Empire and sterling area was the fall in British sales to India, where competition from both Japan and from domestic producers continued to hit British textile exports. Despite this, the share of United Kingdom exports to the Empire and sterling area countries increased from 50 per cent in 1929 to 59 per cent in 1938.

Cheap money and the sterling area

When the World Economic Conference ground to a halt following Roosevelt's attack on attempts to stabilize currencies, the formation of the gold bloc led by France, with its intent to deflate world prices, caused alarm among the primary producing nations of the sterling area; they feared that the British might join the gold bloc. The Chancellor of the Exchequer's response was to reaffirm his commitment to cheap money and higher prices, but also to express concern that Europe, which eventually must abandon gold, should not fall apart in chaos during the conference. The British Commonwealth Declaration was signed on 27 July 1933, resolving to raise prices, to ease credit and money without monetizing government deficits, to eventually restore the gold standard, and to keep exchange rates stable within the sterling area. The declaration succeeded in quieting talk of public works and further depreciation in the Empire, in distracting attention from the general failure of the World Economic Conference, and in reaffirming the Ottawa agreements.

As the dollar became more unstable and the United States did little to encourage pegging to the dollar, this declaration formalizing the sterling area made it a more attractive option for countries seeking to stabilize their exchange rates. Denmark, Sweden, and Argentina formalized their sterling pegs soon after the British Commonwealth Declaration. Norway had officially pegged to sterling in May 1933, having devalued 9.5 per cent from the sterling gold parity rate.

From late in 1933 to 1938, the sterling-to-dollar exchange rate was reasonably stable, meaning that a large part of the world enjoyed five years of exchange stability. Following devaluation of the franc in September 1936, France associated with the sterling area by trying to maintain a fixed sterling rate, much as the Scandinavian countries had from 1931 through 1933. In late September both Greece and Turkey devalued slightly and linked to sterling, and Latvia moved from a franc to a sterling peg, with a substantial devaluation.

The cheap credit policies of Britain allowed the sterling system to accommodate the cheap money policies of Scandinavia, Australia, South Africa, and other devaluing nations. London facilitated the operation of the system by supplying sterling area nations with the sterling reserves they needed. The stability of the pound throughout the decade encouraged a willingness to hold sterling balances, and the combination of increased production in South Africa and dishoarding in India supplied gold to the sterling area, ensuring convertibility.

While British policy could not create the international co-operation necessary to initiate worldwide recovery, recovery was possible for any nations that wished to join the sterling area. Adherence to the gold standard had spread the depression; relaxing the harsh discipline of this rigid system was the first step to recovery.

8.3 The gold bloc

The gold bloc of the 1930s had its origins in the Latin Monetary Union of 1870, in which the French, Belgian, and Swiss francs were established at equal parities. In response to Roosevelt's message to the World Economic Conference and the turmoil that emerged in its aftermath, the representatives of France, Belgium, Holland, Switzerland, Italy, and Poland released a joint declaration. This stated that their governments would strive to maintain the gold standard and the stability of their currencies at their current parities, both to create a stable gold platform for the recovery of international exchange market stability and to promote social progress at home. Representatives of their central banks met in Paris, and on 8 July they pledged to support each other's currencies, reimbursing each other in currency or gold.

While the gold bloc was to develop a reputation for possessing little cohesion and no organization, its initial declaration successfully ended the speculation against the Dutch florin and the Swiss franc that had persisted during the proceedings of the World Economic Conference. Despite this strong beginning, however, the gold bloc remained a symbolic organization. No progress was made in developing the connections between the central banks or the government policies of the gold bloc nations after the 8 July meeting.

Of all the trading blocs that emerged in the aftermath of the London Economic Conference, the gold bloc was the only one still constrained to follow the stringent deflationary policies demanded by the gold standard. The continuing efforts in these countries to hold their economies to this harsh course produced ever more economic declines. Unemployment stayed high and troublesome in these countries, as described in Chapter 7.2. The commitment to the gold standard revealed by these actions in the presence of the recovery beginning in other countries was deep indeed. It is no wonder that this misguided ideological purity prevented international co-operation and inhibited the emergence of leadership.

Exchange controls or stringent deflation

Within the constraints of the existing gold parities, countries had only two options to protect their trade balances: exchange controls and deflation. Among the central European nations, including the emerging trading bloc around Germany, tariffs were supplemented by exchange controls, nominally leaving the countries on the gold standard but effectively rendering the system meaningless. In contrast, the gold bloc regarded exchange controls as incompatible with the workings of the gold standard and completely against the spirit of the system. Continued deflation was the only available policy, therefore, and the core gold bloc countries sustained this for as long as they could.

Czechoslovakia, a minor member of the gold bloc, devalued its currency in February 1934. Unemployment in Italy had risen to levels at which deflationary measures were no longer feasible. Mussolini placed pride in the stability and strength of the lira and was unwilling to devalue. Italy therefore gradually imposed exchange controls, maintaining only the illusion of retaining gold standard parity. In July 1935 the Italian government prohibited gold exports. Not all the original members of the gold bloc could stand the strain of deflation for very long.

The other gold bloc nations pursued policies of stringent deflation. The French had been successful in the early years of the decade in keeping their current account deficit small through trade barriers, but by 1933 the situation was steadily growing worse. The decline in economic activity was accompanied by lower government revenues, resulting in budgetary deficits that caused great alarm among the French populace, who still bore the memory of the inflationary cycles of the mid-1920s. The political effects of expenditure cuts and new taxes created a situation of turmoil in which there were four governments in 1932, three in 1933, and four in 1934. Even though the decline in prices left the real wages of pensioners, veterans, and government employees higher than their original levels, attempts to reduce fiscal expenditures by cutting payments to these groups were highly unpopular.

Within the gold bloc, the high prices resulting from the overvalued gold standard parities of the currencies discouraged trading among the bloc's members. French trade with Belgium decreased 13 per cent between 1933 and 1934, and French trade with Switzerland decreased by 40 per cent. To encourage trade among themselves, the gold bloc nations met in Geneva in September 1934, and signified their agreement to increase trade and tourism within the bloc and to arrange another conference to meet in Brussels in October to discuss trade policy. Poland was not allowed to participate in either the Geneva or the Brussels conferences, ostensibly because its economy was structured differently from those of the other members of the gold bloc, but more likely because the other members were reluctant to include a nation whose economy was in as desperate need of assistance as Poland's in 1934.

The Brussels conference convened in an atmosphere of pessimism and reluctance to co-operate. The Italians were not interested in the conference and tried to use the absence of Poland as a pretext for postponing or cancelling it. Eventually Italy sent only one delegate to Belgium. The Dutch were reluctant to limit their preferential trade agreements to the members of the gold bloc. They favoured extending any trade barrier reductions to Germany and Britain, especially as they were concerned about German retaliation which might cost them the German steel market, one of their most important export markets. The Belgians, hosting the conference, were openly discussing devaluation, and there was speculation in the French government that the Belgian government wanted the conference to fail in order to provide a justification for devaluation.

France was constrained by limitations similar to those placed on the Dutch. While the French were interested in promoting the gold bloc, their most important export markets were in countries in other exchange blocs. The French were limited by most-favoured-nation trade agreements in the concessions that they could offer to their gold bloc trading partners.

The conference opened with the Italian and Dutch delegations expressing reluctance to reaffirm their countries' commitment to maintain the gold standard and their currency parities. Under French guidance the conference was brought to a close with an agreement for gold bloc countries to continue bilateral negotiations to allow for a 10 per cent increase in gold bloc trade by 30 June 1935. The conference therefore was successful to the extent that the gold bloc survived intact. But the results of the proposed negotiations were not the least bit encouraging for gold bloc unity. The French agreed in principle to increase Belgian trade, but the proposed 10 per cent rise was unattainable.

Belgium devalues, France struggles on

Belgium had been severely hurt by its loss of competitiveness in British markets with the sterling devaluation in 1931. In September 1934 the Belgian government asked for French assistance, but neither loan arrangements nor proposals to lower French quotas on Belgian goods were enacted. In March 1935 the British government limited steel imports, worsening Belgium's plight. In desperation, the Belgian government reopened talks with France to seek economic assistance. Again, the French could not offer more than token assistance. Returning from Paris essentially empty-handed, the Belgian government was forced to impose exchange controls. A new government devalued the Belgian franc on March 30, repegging it 28 per cent lower at a level calculated to restore the prices of Belgian goods to the level of British and American prices.

When the gold bloc was officially declared in the aftermath of the World Economic Conference, French opinion was firmly opposed to devaluation of the franc as an alternative to deflation. Memories of the inflation and currency crises of the early 1920s were still an extremely powerful force. However, as the disparity between the recovery of countries with depreciated currencies and the stagnation of gold bloc countries became apparent, individuals within French political and journalism circles began to support devaluation, although public opinion remained strongly opposed. The primary danger to the franc was perceived to be the budget deficits that threatened to resurrect the debt monetization and the resulting inflationary cycles that had caused the economic chaos of the 1920s. Fearing these consequences, successive French governments struggled with programmes to reduce expenditure and augment decreasing revenues, but economic contraction and budget deficits persisted.

The Popular Front, a coalition of the Radical, Communist, and Socialist parties led by Léon Blum, took office in June 1936 with a plan to restore economic growth with a French New Deal. Blum renounced deflationary policies, but did not devalue. France consequently suffered serious depletion of its gold reserves. The Popular Front introduced a shortened work week of forty hours without a reduction in wages, and raised wages to stimulate consumption and ignite the economy. The Matignon Accords, which forced employers to sign a package of wage increases, were the Popular Front's solution to widespread labour unrest.

By mid-1936, there was widespread support for devaluation among politicians, publicists, and banking and financial experts, but still not among the general populace. The opposition to devaluation during 1934 and 1935 had so effectively convinced the French public that devaluation would cause a return of inflation that this opinion persisted among the populace through 1936, initially precluding a unilateral devaluation. Ultimately, however, it proved impossible to withstand the pressure against the franc; this final episode in the disintegration of the inter-war gold standard is taken up in Chapter 9.4.

Clinging to the gold standard, France and the other remaining members of the gold bloc were helpless to alleviate the depression in their countries. The professed cure for disequilibrium was the persistent source of the disease.

8.4 The Nazi trading area

After the banking and currency crises of July 1931, the German government allowed banks to reopen only after freezing foreign deposits and limiting foreign exchange transactions to the Reichsbank. Germany abandoned the gold standard by imposing controls on foreign exchange transactions, but did not devalue the mark. These initial exchange controls were ineffective, and were replaced in September, following the sterling devaluation, with more stringent measures. These required owners of gold and foreign assets to sell them to the Reichsbank, restricted the amount of foreign exchange available to importers, and compelled exporters to surrender their foreign exchange proceeds to the Reichsbank.

In January 1933 Adolph Hitler and the Nazi party came to power. As described in Chapter 6.5, many of the Nazis' policies, including exchange controls, work creation projects, government intervention in banking, and the programme for agriculture, were inherited from the Weimar Republic. Germany had always had a high degree of government involvement in the economy and in foreign trade policy. But the Nazis used terror, the threat of concentration camps and possible death, to enforce compliance with economic controls, including exchange and trade controls.

The deterioration of world trade in the 1930s was magnified in Germany by the devaluations of sterling and the dollar relative to gold and the mark; by the rise of protectionism; and by capital flight resulting from Jews fleeing persecution, and from domestic and foreign response to Nazi policies (see Chapter 9.1). For the short term, the response in 1934 was increased foreign exchange restrictions and a moratorium on interest payments on debt to foreigners. A long-term strategy was devised with the 'New Plan' of Hjalmar Schacht, the president of the Reichsbank and the Minister of Finance, which encouraged autarky by restricting imports and provided commodity boards to create greater administrative control of trade. In 1935 a scheme was initiated to extend subsidies to German exports that were not competitive on world markets because of the overvalued mark.

The trade policies of the Nazis, moving towards autarky, were unique among the western economies because they were directed towards preparing for a war economy. German goals included military preparedness and administrative control over the domestic population, with politics taking precedence over economics. The price paid for this was fewer available import goods and increased labour intensiveness.

Bilateral trade and exchange clearing agreements

The Nazis initiated bilateral trade agreements that were to take several forms during the decade. One of the first systems was the private compensation procedure, which created agencies that attempted to balance imports and exports by matching private exporters and importers to ensure offsetting trade. One characteristic of this system was the use of blocked marks, frozen funds held by foreigners and used at a discount to buy German exports. Through the use of blocked marks, German exporters could obtain higher prices in terms of marks for their products, and foreign importers purchasing these marks at a discount could purchase German exports at a lower price in terms of the foreign currency. Because this system was highly profitable for German exporters, its use was limited to additional exports, those goods that were not competitive in foreign markets due to the overvalued mark.

A second, more flexible method was the bilateral exchange clearing system, which attempted to balance credits and debits on a national level. The mechanism of this system was conducted through clearing accounts in the Reichsbank. German importers paid marks to the Reichsbank account of the trading partner, where the funds were held until they could be used to pay German exporters for goods sold to the other country. If the accounts held insufficient funds, the exporters had to wait for imports to increase, and if there were excess funds, importers had to wait for increased exports. The central bank of the trading partner held similar clearing accounts for its exporters and importers. After the initial agreement with Hungary, arrangements of this type were made between Germany and Estonia, Latvia, Bulgaria, Greece, Yugoslavia, Romania, Czechoslovakia, and Turkey. While the details of each arrangement were different, all of these clearing agreements shared the common goal of opening trade controls to help export industries.

The central banks of Germany's trading partners with clearing balances were forced to intervene to prevent the blocked marks from depreciating, which would decrease the competitiveness of the trading partner's exports in the German market. One alternative, pursued by Hungary and Bulgaria, two nations politically favourable to Germany, was to pay exporters in domestic currency for their holdings of blocked marks. A second alternative, pursued by Romania and Yugoslavia, two nations wary of German influence, was to allow the blocked marks to depreciate slightly until domestic importers purchased German goods and depleted the balance of blocked marks. Hungary, following the financing principle, experienced consistent trade surpluses with Germany, while Romania, following the waiting principle, experienced alternating surpluses and deficits. Germany's trading partners found political opposition to Germany economically costly and acquiescence rewarding.

Germany's trade with western Europe, traditionally an area of export surpluses, was limited by the decline in international trade and the rise of exchange controls. Germany negotiated so-called Sondermark Agreements with France, Belgium, the Netherlands, Switzerland, Italy, the Scandinavian countries, Spain, and Portugal to preserve these valuable export markets. These agreements involved partial rather than full clearing systems, with the establishment of clearing accounts for additional trade. Normal levels of trade were conducted according to foreign exchange quotas, and the special accounts for additional trade, the trade that developed beyond normal levels, operated in the same manner as the bilateral exchange clearing agreements between Germany and south-east Europe.

In 1934 the ASKI (Ausländer Sonderkonten für Inlandszahlung) procedure was introduced, replacing the private compensation procedure, which had been less restrictive and had been used to avoid strict exchange controls. The ASKI procedure established accounts at German banks where foreign exporters' proceeds were held. Foreign exporters needed to secure permission from German exchange control authorities to trade with Germany, with German imports limited to only those deemed necessary by the commodity control boards. ASKI balances could be used to purchase certain non-essential German goods, but the goods had to be shipped to the country of the account holder. Two types of ASKI accounts developed: accounts for individual foreign exporters, and accounts for foreign commercial banks which represented a group of foreign traders.

The New Plan also created a system of payment agreements with Great Britain, Belgium–Luxembourg, Canada, France, and New Zealand. These agreements provided for the release of free foreign exchange to pay for imports and to transfer payment on old German debts. In addition, Germany agreed to import goods equal to a specified fraction of its exports to each country. The effect of the New Plan was to extend and develop the exchange controls of the early 1930s, replacing the ineffective ones with more stringent controls.

The exchange control system in place after the New Plan consisted of three different arrangements: the stringent ASKI agreements, the more moderate clearing agreements, and the laxer payments agreements. Germany's free trade was limited to only a small group of countries, including the United States, because the overvalued mark doomed Germany to a trade deficit where trading agreements were not in effect.

The reorientation of Germany's trade

Germany's bilateral trading agreements accounted for 50 per cent of Germany's trade by 1938. German trade with south-east Europe often is overemphasized, as the Balkans bought only 7 per cent of Germany's exports in 1935 and 11 per cent by 1938. While these parts of Europe were regarded as prime areas for German economic and trade expansion, there was significant resistance to any kind of limiting relationship with Germany. Germany incurred trade deficits with most of her Balkan neighbours during the 1930s, and the largest German trade was conducted with western Europe, Latin America, and the Middle East.

Kitson (1992) concludes that Germany sacrificed terms-of-trade advantages that could have been won from its position as monopolist in export markets and monopsonist (dominant or sole purchaser) in import markets. Other objectives replaced improvements in the terms of trade, as isolation from the world market, reduced dependence on imports, and the reorientation of trade to safe, adjacent countries took precedence. According to Neal (1979: 392) it was relatively costless, and often politically rewarding, for Germany to forgo the advantages of monopoly exploitation.

While England, France, the Netherlands, Italy, and other economic powers increased trade within their empires, Germany, which had no empire, was forced to develop a currency bloc, altering its pattern of trade. The pattern of changes between 1929 and 1938 is shown in Table 8.2. German trade was reoriented in favour of southern and eastern Europe, the countries with which it

Table 8.2. Changes in the Direction of Germany's Trade, 1929 and 1938 (%)

	German Imports		German Exports	
	1929	1938	1929	1938
Europe				
Southern and eastern Europe[a]	9.8	18.7	11.2	20.8
Scandinavian countries	7.4	11.3	10.2	12.9
Austria[b]	1.5	—	3.3	—
Gold bloc and Czechoslovakia	23.6	16.1	35.2	26.0
United Kingdom	6.4	5.2	9.7	6.7
Total Europe	48.7	51.3	69.6	66.4
Rest of the world				
British dominions and colonies	12.5	10.3	4.3	6.1
United States	13.3	7.4	7.4	2.8
Latin America	12.1	16.8	7.8	12.1
Other countries	13.4	14.2	10.9	12.6
Total rest of the world	51.3	48.7	30.4	33.6

[a] Bulgaria, Greece, Hungary, Italy, Romania, Spain, Turkey, and Yugoslavia.
[b] Not shown separately after unification with Germany in 1938.
Source: League of Nations (1939: 278 and 300).

conducted the stricter policies of ASKI and clearing agreements. As trade between Germany and south-east Europe increased, these nations became more dependent on exports to Germany's market for basic foodstuffs and raw materials. These countries were isolated in the post-depression trade world, and Germany, paying prices 20 to 40 per cent above the world level for agricultural commodities, was the most attractive market. A trading bloc was effectively established, providing Germany with a dependable source of necessary commodities.

Between 1929 and 1938 Germany's exports to south-eastern Europe, Spain, and Italy rose sharply from 11 to 21 per cent of the total, and the proportion of her imports from this region increased from 10 to 19 per cent. There was also an increase in the share of German trade with the Scandinavian countries, especially Sweden, and with Latin America. By contrast, the trade with the gold bloc countries, Czechoslovakia, and the United Kingdom became relatively less important as these countries turned to other sources and markets, especially within their own empires.

Although successful in reorienting German trade, the Nazi policies never made south-east Europe one of Germany's major trading partners, and some of the increase which did occur was simply the re-establishment of older trading patterns broken by the inflations and upheavals of the 1920s.

9

INDUSTRIAL PROGRESS
AND RECOVERY

THE failure of aggregate demand in the 1930s meant that employment and output in the European economy declined. But the capabilities of the economy did not disappear with jobs. Idle capital reduced the need for net investment, but replacements still offered the opportunity for improvement. And new products and new methods continued to be introduced even in the worst of times. This chapter shows first that the abundant capital inflows of the 1920s vanished completely in the Great Depression. It goes on to record the progress of individual economies and industries in this more hostile economic environment, and to review the policies adopted to promote recovery in some of the major economies. It closes with the final attempt at international co-operation before the Second World War, the Tripartite Agreement of 1936.

9.1 Capital outflows from Europe

From 1931 the nature and direction of the movements in international capital changed dramatically. The overall dimensions of the process were about the same as they had been in the previous phase, but the content and dynamics of the flows were completely different. In the 1920s the net movement of capital was predominantly from the rich creditor countries to the less-developed debtors in Europe and elsewhere. This pattern of international capital movement thus conformed very broadly to that of pre-1914 foreign lending, even though it was supplemented to an unprecedented degree by short-term investments. In the 1930s, this traditional pattern was sharply reversed. Vast sums now flowed from the less-developed nations to their former creditors, from countries with deficits on their balance of payments to countries in surplus, from capital markets where interest rates were high to those where they were lower.

The flood of bonds and shares which had poured out of the capital markets in New York, London, Paris, and other financial centres now dwindled to a thin and irregular trickle. Potential lenders retreated in the face of the rapid deterioration in economic conditions and prospects, damaging financial crises, and numerous defaults by debtors unable to cope with the collapse of primary product prices and of their foreign earnings. The occasional new issues of long-term capital which were made in the 1930s were outweighed by the amortization of former loans by those debtors who maintained their repayments. The migration of capital characteristic of the new phase consisted predominantly of short-term funds, moving swiftly and on a vast scale, and determined almost entirely by speculative forces and the threat of war.

The banking crises of 1930 and 1931, the loss of confidence in the stability of various economies, and the loss of value of their currencies played the major role in stimulating the seemingly perverse flows of 'hot money' from the debtors to the creditor countries. Enormous sums were withdrawn by asset holders, who simply wished to preserve their investments in the face of currency depreciation and the domestic inflation associated with it. These movements were swelled by a very high level of activity by speculators, some trying to avoid losses when they anticipated depreciation of their own currencies, others looking for capital gains from the short-term purchase of a foreign currency which was expected to appreciate.

To protect their limited reserves of gold and foreign exchange against these mounting pressures more and more countries were compelled to impose exchange controls. This in itself provoked further withdrawals before the available loopholes were closed. Repatriation of German and other securities was made increasingly profitable by the widening disparity between the prices quoted for these securities on domestic exchanges and the lower levels at which they were valued abroad. The strong recovery of security prices on Wall Street from the spring of 1935 provided a further inducement to move capital to the United States.

From the middle of the decade these economic factors were powerfully supplemented by political concerns. A succession of developments, including the Italian invasion of Ethiopia, the German reoccupation of the Rhineland, and the Spanish Civil War, raised the alarming prospect of world war, with its attendant dangers to wealth from seizure or destruction by the enemy, and from the imposition of increased taxes, capital levies, and exchange restrictions. As the panic spread, Great Britain and the United States came to be seen increasingly as the only safe and reliable havens for capital.

The result of these tendencies was a transfer of capital to the United States of almost $5.5 billion from 1934 to 1937, and further large movements across the Atlantic in 1938 and 1939. The flow towards the United Kingdom began a little earlier, and over the seven years 1931–7 the net import of funds amounted to roughly $4 billion. In the same period there was also a small net movement of about $600 million to Switzerland, Sweden, and the Netherlands (Feinstein and Watson 1995). The countries responsible for sending these vast sums cannot be identified reliably from the available data, but it seems likely that the great bulk of this capital, perhaps $6–7 billion, was an outflow from continental Europe, with France, Germany, and Belgium leading the exodus. Switzerland and the Netherlands also remitted large sums to the United States, though much of this may have come initially from other sources.

As the economic climate darkened, both foreigners and nationals became increasingly anxious to transfer their funds to stronger and safer currencies; and the resulting withdrawal of short-term capital put the central monetary authorities under enormous pressure. In Germany, Austria, Hungary, Poland, Italy, and many other countries the inevitable step was the imposition of progressively more stringent and comprehensive exchange controls. In itself, this further intensified the eagerness of asset holders to escape from such currencies, and the extent to which they succeeded in doing this will not be reflected in the records of the debtor nations, but can be seen in the massive accumulation of gold by the recipients, notably the United Kingdom and, after the stabilization of the dollar, the United States.

The change in France's international financial position was particularly striking. In the late 1920s, the undervaluation of the franc and the weakness of sterling enabled France to make massive additions to its reserves of gold and foreign exchange, and also to lend abroad, albeit on a modest scale—French investors having lost much of their enthusiasm for foreign investment after their experiences in 1917. From 1931, when Britain left the gold standard and devalued the pound, the franc lost its strength, and capital ebbed away as investors became progressively more pessimistic about future economic and political conditions in France. The outflow in 1931–7 was over $2 billion, and may have been considerably larger.

The German accounts show a net outward movement in this period of over $1 billion. For the most part this was not the result of speculative flows, but a deliberate programme for the reduction of foreign indebtedness. The transformation of exchange controls from 'an emergency measure to a totalitarian institution' (Ellis 1941: 158) gave the regime tight control over all current and capital account payments, and provided the context in which securities could be repurchased and debts repaid.

Financial conditions were also problematic and painful for many of the other European debtors even though the net capital movements were relatively small. Belgium experienced similar problems to France and was forced to devalue in 1935; and there were net outflows from Finland, Poland, and a number of other countries. However, a few of the debtors continued to receive a net import of capital against the general trend. In the case of Austria this reflected the success of her economic policies, the reduction in external debt, and the abolition of exchange controls from 1935. In the following two years Austria was unique in again being able to secure short-term credits on the London market. Romania continued to attract direct investment for the expansion of oil production, and Greece was also a net importer of capital, reflecting the more favourable economic circumstances she enjoyed during and after the Great Depression.

9.2 An overview of a limp recovery

The climate in which Europe attempted to make its recovery from the depths of the depression could hardly have been less favourable. The adverse factors included the flight of capital from continental Europe described above, which made balanced trade more urgent; the imposition of exchange controls, multiple exchange rates, bilateral trade agreements, quantitative restrictions, and other barriers to normal international commerce (see Chapter 8.4); the persistent stagnation in the income of millions of farmers and raw material producers; and the stubborn continuation of deflationary policies in the gold bloc countries which was stressed in Chapter 8.3.

All these tendencies were clearly highly detrimental to the revival of international trade from the catastrophically low levels to which it had collapsed in the early 1930s (see Chapter 6.1). Relief from the contraction would thus have to come primarily from the expansion of domestic demand. Lower prices, and thus higher real incomes, would contribute to this for those in work, but this alone would not be a sufficient stimulus. Before turning to consider the policies adopted to promote recovery in some of the leading countries, it will be helpful to set the scene with a brief review of the overall picture.

The sustained weakness of world trade can be seen in Table 9.1. There was some recovery in the volume of world exports and imports (row 2), but it was not sufficient to regain the 1929 level. Prices (row 3) continued on their downward course until 1935 and then managed only a very weak recovery. By 1937, the best year in the 1930s, the value of international trade was thus still only a miserable 46 per cent of what it had been in 1929.

The trends in output of industrial and primary products are traced in the first three blocks of Table 9.2. The recovery in industrial production (block 1) was slightly better in Europe than in the United States of America and Canada. Even there, however, the revival had only enough strength to carry the volume of output in 1937 some 10 per cent above the 1929 level, a growth rate for this important sector of the real economy of only 1.2 per cent per annum over a period of eight years. Production in North America was unable to achieve even this much, and the level in 1937 was still 7 per cent below the previous peak.

Table 9.1. Indices of world trade, 1932–1937 (1929 = 100)

	1932	1933	1934	1935	1936	1937
1. Value at current prices[a]	39	35	34	35	38	46
2. Volume	75	75	78	82	86	96
3. Price	52	47	44	42	44	48

[a] Index of the value of world imports and exports measured in pre-devaluation US gold dollars.

Source: League of Nations (1939a: 61).

Table 9.2. World production and prices, 1932–1937 (1929 = 100)

	1932	1933	1934	1935	1936	1937
1. Industrial production						
a. World[a]	64	72	78	86	96	103
b. Europe[a]	72	77	86	93	101	110
c. North America	54	64	67	76	89	93
2. Primary production— food						
a. World	100	102	101	101	103	106
b. Europe[a]	104	106	107	107	107	109
c. North America	100	100	98	91	96	97
3. Primary production— raw materials						
a. World	75	81	87	95	106	119
b. Europe[a]	73	77	85	91	98	109
c. North America	64	69	71	78	91	108
4. World prices						
a. Food	52	46	42	40	42	46
b. Raw materials	44	40	40	39	42	47
c. Manufactures	64	56	50	48	48	51

[a] Excluding USSR.

Sources: Blocks 1–3: League of Nations (1939b: 423–4); block 4: League of Nations (1939a: 61).

Production of food continued to be broadly stable (block 2) but with food prices stagnant at around 40 per cent of their 1929 level, farm incomes remained very depressed. Producers of industrial raw materials fared rather better in terms of the recovery in output between 1932 and 1937 (block 3), responding to the revival in production in the industrial economies, but this was not sufficient to lift prices (row 4b), so that their incomes—and capacity to import manufactures—languished well below the level of the more prosperous 1920s.

Industrial production recovers in some countries, not in others

The strength of the revival in industrial production varied markedly between countries within Europe, as can be seen very clearly in Table 9.3. By 1935 most countries had managed to achieve some degree of recovery from the depth of the slump; the expansion was rapid in some countries, slow or negligible in others. By far the best progress was made by the group around the United Kingdom which broke away from the gold standard in 1931 and devalued their currencies. All five of these countries made a good recovery by 1935, and by 1937 industrial production was at least 30 per cent above the 1929 level; for the most successful, Sweden and Finland, the increase was over 50 per cent.

The currency depreciation made some contribution to the advance achieved by this group, but its impact was limited by the generally depressed state of world markets. A more important consequence of their departure from the constraints of the gold standard was that they were no longer compelled to impose deflationary policies. The introduction of cheap money facilitated recovery and

Table 9.3. Industrial recovery, 1932–1937 (1929 = 100)

	1932 (1)	1935 (2)	1937 (3)
Countries which devalued in 1931			
Sweden	89	123	152
Finland	88	121	152
Denmark	90	124	135
United Kingdom	89	113	130
Norway	94	108	130
The exchange control countries			
Romania	88	122	132
Germany	61	100	127
Italy	86	96	111
Hungary	86	102	108
Yugoslavia	76	90	107
Austria	62	80	106
Czechoslovakia	75	74	93
The gold bloc			
Netherlands	84	91	103
Belgium	85	99	101
Poland	58	75	97
France	74	72	81
Other countries			
Greece	101	141	152
Spain	84	86	52
Total Europe	72	86	103

Sources: As for Table 4.3, plus Yugoslavia from Kaser and Radice (1985: 573).

created favourable conditions for the expansion of housebuilding, and of new industries which needed to borrow capital to initiate their activity.

By contrast, industrial output stagnated in all five gold bloc countries as long as they persisted with their deflationary programmes. More competitive exports from the United Kingdom and the Scandinavian countries added to their problems. By 1935 output in France and Poland was still at least 25 per cent below the 1929 level. Two years later production in the Netherlands and Belgium had just crept above the 1929 level; the other two countries were unable to achieve even this.

Experience in Germany and the other countries which resorted to exchange controls rather than devalue generally fell between these extremes. Romania showed the best performance, rising rapidly by 1935 and continuing the expansion to 1937. This reflects the stimulus of a successful import-substitution policy and also the continued growth of the oil industry. The major economy in this group, Germany, only just matched the 1929 level in 1935, after the very severe depression of 1932, and subsequent expansion carried production in 1937 to 27 per cent above the previous peak. In Italy the improvement was only 11 per cent by 1937, and the other countries did less well. Czechoslovakia was especially vulnerable to the contraction of her export markets, and was still unable to achieve the pre-depression level by 1937.

Policies to promote recovery in Germany and Italy

While the main pattern of German recovery was set by its exchange rate regime—neither devaluation nor the gold standard—there are some special characteristics that deserve mention. It is important to recall that the unique aspects of the Fascist economy do not seem to have made much impact on the aggregate statistics in Table 9.3, although they did affect the composition of production.

The Nazis quickly moved to take control of the economy. They had achieved electoral support in 1932 partly because the other political parties seemed powerless to arrest the economic decline. It should not be supposed that the Nazis had an economic plan when they took power in January 1933; in fact they continued the exchange rate policies of the Brüning government and the small government stimuli of the Papen government. But they also did a variety of other things that cast these existing policies in a new light.

Indeed, the whirlwind of activity under Hitler looked to some contemporary observers like the New Deal of Roosevelt in the United States. They hailed these two 'new men' as identical saviours of the world economy. Nothing could be further from the truth. Roosevelt moved to preserve a democratic and pluralistic society, Hitler to destroy it. In economics, Roosevelt acted to improve (as he saw it) the competitive economy; Hitler acted to replace it with administrative controls.

The Nazis dealt with unemployment in characteristic fashion (see also Chapter 7.4). They declared it illegal to be unemployed. They replaced the bureaucrats who collected unemployment (and other) statistics by the party faithful, who had neither the training nor inclination to discover that Nazi policies were not working. While Germany did start recovery in 1933, the rapid fall in recorded unemployment in that year should be viewed with scepticism.

The Nazis did not like to use prices as economic incentives. They upheld farm prices in 1933–4 when international surpluses threatened to force them down. And they kept them from rising in the next few years in the face of rising demand. In 1936 they issued the famous Price Stop Decree, freezing all prices. Competition and variable prices were not allowed to allocate resources in the Nazi economy.

Administrative controls were used to direct investment into favoured areas instead. Interest and dividend rates were frozen with the rest of German prices; heavy profit taxes reduced the availability of retained earnings. The government sold government bonds and directed the funds into the areas they chose. When they did not want the government budget to look in deficit, they issued off-budget ('Mefo') bonds that only slightly disguised the heavy central direction.

The Nazis used Four-Year Plans to organize their investment programme. These plans were imitations of the Soviet Five-Year Plans, but they were even more chaotic than the beginning of Soviet central planning. The Four-Year Plans did not replace other bureaucracies; they were added on top of, and competed with, them. They stretched into every corner of the economy, but the Nazis did not have enough administrators to implement the ambitious plans effectively. There were monetary incentives for managers to comply with the economic plans, although they were limited by the constant prices and control of the capital markets. The Nazis extended their rule of terror to business enterprises, compelling compliance by threatening arrests and even concentration camps for managers who put their interests or the interests of their company ahead of the interests of the Reich.[1]

The aim of the Four-Year Plans clearly was to prepare Nazi Germany for war. Nazi economic policy initially was directed at putting people back to work; after a few years their concern shifted from reviving the whole economy to shifting resources into military and supporting activities. Historians have debated whether specific investment projects—like the famous autobahns—were part of the war effort. But there can be no doubt that the Nazis increasingly favoured heavy industry, airplane manufacture, and armaments in their plans. If they did not expand munitions production immediately on taking power, they did so within a very few years.

There were several results of the Nazi economic programme. Steel production grew rapidly. Consumer goods production did not. The share of consumption in GNP fell from 69 per cent in 1928 at the peak of the previous business cycle to 56 per cent in 1937. And the quality of consumer goods fell as well. Scarce resources were allocated to the war effort, and consumers made do with ersatz materials. Viewed as a private economy, the Nazi programme did not lay the foundation for continued expansion.

Italy's Fascist regime was eleven years older than Germany's. In the 1920s, after a brief spell of free-trade and market-oriented policies (1922–5), Mussolini slowly moved to a more controlled economy. As we have seen, in 1927 the lira had been brought back to gold at an overvalued parity that foreign observers considered untenable. Contrary to expectations, however, the Fascist regime was by then well established in power, and it produced enough

---

[1] A word needs to be said about the experience of IG Farben under the Nazis. As a major German firm, it was intimately connected with the Nazi government. As a producer of chemicals, it was part of the Nazi military buildup. The question has been raised of IG Farben's culpability in Nazi savageries. The picture is mixed. On the one hand, executives of IG Farben were not immune from the terror of the Nazis. No company, however large, could withstand the totalitarian state. On the other hand, IG Farben employed slave labour from Auschwitz during the war. There was no compulsion to do so; it was a decision to get cheap labour. Even though IG Farben was not a totally free agent, it participated far more than it needed in the Nazis' persecution of Jews and other disfavoured groups (Hayes 1987).

deflation to allow the exchange rate to be roughly consistent with the purchasing power parity of the currency. An orthodox policy of tight money was accompanied by tariff measures to protect those domestic industries, such as iron and steel, that stood to lose most from an overvalued currency. Coercive measures typical of a consolidated dictatorship were taken both to reduce wages and control prices.

While the Fascist propaganda tried to deny that a depression even existed, it actually turned out to be quite severe, due also to Mussolini's stubborn determination to keep the lira on the gold standard after Britain's departure in 1931. Between 1929 and 1932, industrial production fell by 10 per cent, while agricultural incomes were severely curtailed by a colossal fall in the export price of the main Italian staples. Urban unemployment and underemployment in the countryside rose to unprecedented levels, in spite of a timid public works policy.

Italy's recovery policies were constrained before 1935 by the political decision to keep the lira on gold even after the United States left in 1933, adhering to the gold bloc led by France. Two sets of policies were attempted in order to try to offset the costs of an overvalued currency. Exchange rate controls were extended, and an *ad hoc* administration was created that was eventually raised to ministerial rank. In addition, across-the-board wage cuts were introduced by decree. These measures were unable to produce a rapid upturn in economic activity. The recovery was therefore slow until Mussolini's 'orthodox' policies were reversed by his decision to conquer Abyssinia.

Government spending was stepped up in 1935. Large orders for military equipment generated enough demand for industrial goods to absorb excess capacity. Industrial production rose considerably, and unemployment fell back to pre-depression levels. In fact, inflationary pressures were felt in 1936. In the new circumstances, the gold standard remained in place for official and propaganda purposes only. In practice, it was deprived of much of its meaning by lifting the reserve requirement whereby the central bank had to keep reserves in gold and foreign exchange equal to 40 per cent of its outstanding circulation. Nevertheless, the lira was not officially devalued until October 1936. Pegging to the French franc was made possible by new and more binding exchange rate controls, and by extensive use of bilateral (or clearing) agreements in foreign transactions. Import quotas were established.

When Italy invaded Ethiopia in the autumn of 1935, the League of Nations imposed economic sanctions on the aggressor. They proved to be rather ineffective. Germany did not participate in the sanctions, and the United States, not a member of the League, did not strongly enforce the trade ban even though it approved of the sanctions. Coal and oil continued to flow into the country. Thus the sanctions, rather than weakening Mussolini, enhanced his popularity. Even Italians who opposed the regime rallied around the government, putting patriotism before party.

The sanctions provided unexpected popular support to a policy of 'national autarky'. The latter was aimed not only at sparing the slim gold reserves, but at introducing a 'planned' war economy as well. Exchange controls, quotas, and clearing agreements became policy tools for the allocation of resources to the desired war-related industries. At the same time, the government undertook the reorganization of a number of large enterprises in such sectors as metal-making, shipbuilding, and engineering that had fallen under its wing as the result of the 1931–3 support granted to the major German-type banks in order to avoid a major banking crisis, as discussed above.

To sum up: Italy's recovery policies, dictated as they were by the political considerations of a strongly established dictatorship, followed a course halfway between French monetary orthodoxy and German planning for war purposes. When measured in terms of activity levels the results were not as bad as those of France; when measured in terms of war preparations they were not nearly as 'good' as those of Germany.

9.3 Technical progress in agriculture and industry in the 1930s

Productivity continued to improve through the 1930s, despite the unfavourable conditions in many countries. For Europe as a whole, the rate of growth of GDP per hour worked was approximately 1.5 per cent per annum from 1929 to 1938, compared to 2.2 per cent per annum from 1913 to 1929 (see Table 1.5). In addition to the underlying process of technical progress and the possibility of benefiting from earlier advances in the leading countries, the actual performance in individual countries was affected by movements in employment and in hours worked. Developments in some of the individual sectors are noted in the following paragraphs.

Agriculture was the classic victim of increasing supply and decreasing demand. The long-run trend was for the demand for agricultural products to decline relative to the demand for other products as incomes rose. The demand for grains fell absolutely as diets improved with income and people ate more meat. In addition, the demand for European products fell in the inter-war years, due to both the influx of agricultural imports from the Americas and the fall in demand during the depression.

Despite the sustained agricultural depression of the inter-war period, technical change continued. The use of fertilizers increased output per hectare; the use of tractors increased output per worker. Svennilson (1954) commented that the tractor was to agriculture what the steam engine was to industry. The diffusion of the tractor however was slow, particularly compared to North America. Europe started off the 1930s with only one-sixth as many tractors per hectare as North America. The number of European tractors doubled in the 1930s, but the North American tractor density was still over four times as high at the end of the decade.

The clash of increasing productivity and reduced demand meant lower prices and fewer agricultural jobs. The share of the labour force engaged in agriculture continued its long-run decline in industrial countries, but the rural population were reluctant to leave the countryside. Many farmers, instead of looking for alternative work when farming was no longer profitable, sought government aid to preserve their incomes as farmers. Each country has its own myth of its agrarian past, and each country has a slightly different way of embedding this legacy in the distribution of political power. But the uniform outcome has been government support of agriculture.

Coal mining followed a similar path after the First World War. Coal was, of course, the industrial fuel *par excellence* in the nineteenth century. It was coal-using activities that were replacing agriculture. But the consumption of coal reached its peak during the boom years of the late 1920s. As with agriculture, there was a short-run fall in demand during the depression that accentuated a long-run shift of demand away from coal. The combination reduced miners' income and pushed them into other activities.

Britain had gained from being the workshop of the world in the nineteenth century. And most of the new activities of that period relied on coal. Textiles were manufactured in Lancashire because coal was mined there, not because cotton grew there. Railways used coal; steamships did too. And just as Britain was the first to produce these products, it was the first to engage in large-scale coal mining. The consequence of this early start was that British coal-mines were the oldest in the world when the demand for coal stopped growing after the First World War. They had the deepest shafts and the highest costs. British miners therefore felt the decline in demand most keenly. The social unrest that was such a prominent part of inter-war British history was the result.

After the General Strike of 1926 and a series of investigations by government commissions, Parliament passed an Act in 1926 to encourage the collieries to amalgamate voluntarily, but with little success. The industry continued to suffer from the existence of an excessive number of small and inefficient collieries, using outdated methods and equipment. In 1930 the government made another attempt to improve the position. An Act set up a compulsory cartel scheme, and although this did not succeed in eliminating all price competition, it did eventually help to sustain prices and profits—a necessary condition for modernization of the industry. The Act also attempted to promote the reorganization of coal mining by amalgamations and concentration of production, but this was resisted by the fiercely individualistic owners. Exports and output of coal continued to decline.

Germany had newer coal-mines, but was still subject to the general fall in the rate of growth of demand. The Ruhr coalfield was successfully cartelized and 'rationalized', that is, smaller inefficient mines were closed, and machines were introduced. The results were that productivity and profits rose—in sharp contrast to British mines. But the mining labour force fell in Germany as in Britain. The increased mechanization substituted for the age of British mines in reducing the demand for labour.

Other traditional industries—especially textiles, steel, and shipbuilding—had similar problems. Their growth slowed markedly in the inter-war period, due to a mixture of short- and long-run influences. British industries suffered more during the 1920s than those in other countries. They all suffered in the 1930s. There were, however, some useful improvements in the United Kingdom. In particular, a protective tariff was granted to the iron and steel industry in 1932 on condition that there would be a thorough reorganization, and for the remainder of the decade the industry was sheltered from foreign competition and able to invest with greater confidence. The ore-fields of Lincolnshire and the East Midlands were exploited more fully, and large, integrated modern plants were constructed close to these fields and in Scotland. There were improvements in the scale of production and in the degree of concentration, and although exports remained stagnant, output expanded strongly to meet the increasing home demand from the vehicle and other industries, and productivity improved. Far greater changes were still needed before Britain would be able to compete with the leading foreign producers, but the industry had taken a few steps in the right direction.

The growth of the new industries

Not all industries had such cheerless experiences. The problems of the traditional industries were partly offset by the promise of new industries, though their special contribution to the growth in productivity and real income during the 1930s should not be overstated. For example, Aldcroft and Richardson stated (1969: 270): 'It is obvious that without the new industries—motor-cars, rayon, household appliances, radio and electrical engineering, for example—the increase in productivity and real income [in Great Britain] would have been very small compared with what was actually achieved in the inter-war period.' Von Tunzelmann (1982) subjected this assertion to a test utilizing admittedly imprecise input–output data. He found that if these new industries had grown only at the average rate for all industries, gross output in 1935 would have been reduced by less than 4 per cent.

The chemical industry was not a new industry in the inter-war years, but it did re-create itself. The industry began early in the nineteenth century with the production of inorganic chemicals (soda ash, sulphuric acid, superphosphate, etc.). It transformed itself toward the end of the century with the production of organic chemicals (dyestuffs, pharmaceuticals, photographic chemicals, etc.). It began a third generation during the First World War with the attempt to replace imported products by domestic production.

New methods of producing nitrogen led the way toward new methods of synthesizing organic chemicals. The yield from oil refineries was raised by new methods in the 1930s, leading to the beginning of plastics industries. The giant firms formed in the 1920s—ICI and IG Farben—dominated in various international agreements. Economies of scale in the production of chemicals by these new methods guaranteed that independent companies from other countries could not offer effective challenges to these cartels.

The automobile industry came of age in the inter-war years. Mass production had been introduced by Henry Ford just before the First World War with the famous Five-Dollar Day, but only began to spread after the war. Unified production and marketing with periodic model changes was introduced by General Motors in the 1930s. These changes transformed the automobile industry—leading to countless smaller changes in the design and production of cars—from a speciality craft to a modern central industry.

These changes came later to Europe than the United States. Incomes were lower in Europe, reducing the demand for cars. And public transportation was better—in part because distances were smaller—further reducing the demand. Automobile production in the four largest European producers—Great Britain, Germany, France, and Italy—together never reached half the American production in the inter-war years.

Electric power generation in Britain originated in the activities of numerous separate power companies. Recognizing that the fragmented British electric supply was falling behind the Continent—only about 6 per cent of British households had electricity at the end of the First World War—Parliament created a Central Electricity Board in 1926. The Board designed and constructed a national power grid for which selected private generating companies provided the supply. The bulk of the grid was constructed in 1929–33, when it provided an inadvertent fiscal stimulus. Its main aim was to increase the efficiency of intra-regional power flows, not yet to make a truly national power supply.

The use of electricity in Britain increased steadily during the inter-war years. The construction of the national grid is not visible in a break in the series. Instead the cumulative effect of better technology, national distribution, and lower charges brought an increasing electrification of society. Residential use grew the fastest, reaching two-thirds of households by 1938, but industrial and commercial establishments also converted to the new power source, as did urban transport systems and the railways.

Electrification of homes in turn increased the demand for consumer durables—the new products of the inter-war years. Initially, electricity was used solely for illumination. Heat was the next use, in cookers, irons, and space and water heaters. Vacuum cleaners and radios followed rapidly during the 1930s. As with electricity itself, the wider distribution of these new appliances reduced the costs of producing them, further stimulating their use.

Developments on the Continent were similar, albeit at different rates. The French and Germans were more centralized from the start, avoiding the characteristic British fragmentation. The Italians started out well, but failed to construct a national power grid during the 1930s. The hilly Italian terrain had made hydro-power important, and each plant generated its own electricity from local water-wheels or turbines. The diversity of standards and organization made national unification even harder to achieve in Italy than in Britain.

With radios came a market for radio programmes. Messages had been transported over cables since the middle of the nineteenth century. Wireless communication made its entry early in the twentieth century through Marconi's efforts to promote ship-to-shore communication. Broadcasting was a creation of the inter-war years, supplementing the previous systems of point-to-point communication by telegraph and telephone.

The birth of broadcasting created immediate issues of public policy. Recognizing at least dimly the importance of this nascent communication channel, European governments wanted to keep control of it. They were opposed by technologically aggressive entrepreneurs who wanted to reap private gains from their new innovations. The struggle was a continuing one, resulting in uneasy compromises that differed between countries and shifted over time in several countries.

The private industry structure quickly reduced to a stable oligopoly. The Marconi, CSF, and Telefunken companies in Europe vied with the American RCA for a worldwide market. The contest was only partly like a traditional oligopoly. The uneasy balance between public and private control was a characteristic of many countries, and the companies had to compete for political favours as often as for technical edge.

Point-to-point wireline communication also increased during the inter-war years with the extension of telephone service. Germany held an ambivalent position in the development of European telephone service in the 1920s. Politically isolated and in conflict with her neighbours, Germany nevertheless was a vital part of emerging European telecommunications. The Germans were invited to meetings on technical standards because they and the Americans were in the technological vanguard. And Germany sat in the centre of Europe making connections for many other countries that wished to communicate through Germany by means of German telephone cables. Like broadcasting, telephonic communication was dominated by political concerns. And like power generation, construction of a co-ordinated system was impeded by local technical conditions.

9.4 The Tripartite Agreement

French gold losses mounted in the spring of 1936 as noted in Chapter 8.3. Blum's Popular Front government, whose appeal was largely based on its repudiation of deflation, was forced to make emphatic declarations that it opposed devaluation. Even while Blum was defending the franc by publicly announcing his opposition to devaluation, his opinions were drifting towards devaluation and he privately began to explore the possibilities of an international accord to prevent competitive devaluation of the dollar or the pound in the event of a French devaluation. To defend the French gold reserves, the government was faced with a choice between deflation, devaluation, and exchange control. Deflation was eliminated as an option by its failure to achieve recovery, or even stability, during its many reincarnations during the first half of the decade.

Faced with the choice between exchange control and devaluation, the financial and banking communities favoured devaluation as the lesser of two evils. Imposition of exchange controls would lead to French autarky, isolating France from its allies, the western democracies. Exchange control was regarded as a Fascist option, requiring extensive controls and administration, and severe penalties, to be effective. While many members of the right-wing press and of financial circles favoured devaluation, the French public remained resolutely opposed, as were the Communist party and many members of the Radicals and the Socialists.

The French government's problem was unprecedented in the need to negotiate internationally before devaluing. Unlike the devaluations of the dollar and sterling, which were relatively simple, largely domestic decisions, the franc devaluation was jeopardized by the prospect of competitive devaluations or increased trade barriers in the devalued nations. The floating pound and the dollar were likely to respond to a French devaluation.

The United States asked France in the summer of 1936 whether a joint American and British statement that the dollar and the pound would not depreciate in the event of a reasonable franc devaluation would ease the process of French devaluation. The French opposed this tripartite declaration as merely amounting to a unilateral devaluation, which the Blum government could not accept so readily after campaigning with the promise not to devalue. The British also did not want any commitment that would force them to support the franc and would link the pound to gold. They did not want France pegging to sterling; they wanted France to peg the franc on gold to allow continued British operations in francs. The British did express their willingness to unofficially keep the pound as stable as possible, while retaining control of the sterling rate. In the spirit of co-operation they agreed to devise some formula for the rates, preferably a meaningless one.

France did not pursue negotiations immediately, expecting an improvement in the domestic situation, but the anticipated calm never developed. The government announced a 21 billion franc rearmament programme in September 1936 and proceeded to experience a massive gold outflow. France then responded by presenting a draft pre-stabilization agreement to Britain and the United States. This called for nations to direct monetary policies toward maintenance of stability and consideration of the international effects of domestic policies.

Washington and London objected to the excessive references to co-operation and stability. They also disliked any reference to the gold standard. The United States objected to a reference to social classes, which would not be palatable to the American public, and to a formula for the French devaluation that would adjust the franc to world prices. The British were uneasy that the new French proposal did not clearly define the extent of the franc devaluation, which the Treasury feared might exceed 100 francs to the pound.

A revised French draft offered a compromise suggesting that the French and British co-operate daily, allowing each to convert holdings of the other's currency into gold. This compromise was the basis of what became known as the 24-hour gold standard. The two exchange authorities subsequently agreed that each morning they would inform each other if they intended to engage in currency operations during the day. If they agreed on the operation and the rates that would be used, a gold price would be established at which currency could be redeemed for gold at the end of the day.

The United States rewrote the second French proposal and submitted it to Britain and France on 19 September. The American version, which was to form the basis of the final agreement, retained flowery French allusions to peace and liberty, while offering reasonable dollar stability, accepting the French devaluation, and promising co-operation with the French and British governments. But with an agreement appearing imminent, an American confusion emerged to jeopardize the negotiations. The American officials had misinterpreted the British position on stabilization of currencies.

Washington informed London that the United States was interested in a $5 pound, plus or minus ten cents. United States officials assumed that the British would consider it a reasonable level, as $5 had been the average rate for the past year while the British Exchange Equalization Account managed the exchanges. In fact, the British disliked the $5 parity, but had maintained that rate to avoid forcing devaluation of the franc and other gold bloc currencies. The American message was immediately rejected by the British, who replied that no such agreement had ever been implied or arranged, and that there would be no stabilization of the dollar–pound exchange. In order to salvage the Tripartite Agreement, the Americans responded to the British objections by agreeing to disagree. The United States retained the view that a $5 pound was appropriate, but was willing to concede the point to allow the announcement of the declarations.

The British, French, and American governments released the Tripartite Agreement on 26 September 1936. A large fraction of the declarations was devoted to the avowals of belief in peace, prosperity, increased living standards, truth, beauty, and goodness that the French favoured. While the British were sceptical of this phraseology, the Americans took it seriously. Secretary of the Treasury Morgenthau believed that the declaration would be significant in restoring peaceful conditions to the world.

More significantly, the declaration included the references to relaxing quotas and exchange controls that the British wanted, although France was not specifically mentioned, and the French did very little to lower trade barriers after the release of the agreement. The British agreed not to retaliate against the French devaluation, but there were no promises about rates because the British refused to constrain their domestic policy. The agreement also included announcements calling for increased co-operation among the central banks and the equalization funds of the Tripartite Powers.

The Tripartite Agreement marked the total failure of the gold standard to stabilize the international economy. The tangled negotiations needed to produce even this minimal agreement showed the tattered remains of international organization. Minimal and partial co-operation was possible with great strain, but more was unattainable. Germany and Italy were not interested and not welcome in international forums. The French and British were too weak to provide effective leadership. And the United States under Roosevelt had turned inward, providing more of an obstacle than an opportunity for co-operation.

The agreement did avoid a round of competitive devaluation. Currency movements were generally mild in the few remaining years of peace. But it would have been far better for all of Europe if an agreement for a co-ordinated devaluation could have been concluded five years earlier, when Britain abandoned the gold standard.

The Netherlands and Switzerland followed France off the gold standard in September 1936, officially ending the gold bloc, three years after its inception. Recovery was quick in these two nations, as it had been in Belgium. Export markets recovered and expansionary policies were implemented. The Italian government used the occasion of the French devaluation as an excuse to devalue the lira and reduce exchange controls, and Czechoslovakia devalued the crown a second time. The Tripartite Agreement was received negatively in France, where it was commonly believed that the Blum government had reneged on its promises not to devalue, and where the international accord was seen as a sham hiding the French devaluation.

The benefits of devaluation were largely offset in France by the increase in French prices. In June 1937, under the pressure of gold losses and budget deficits, the Blum government resigned and was replaced by a government that allowed the franc to float. The French economy remained stagnant from 1936 to 1938 until a new government ended the forty-hour work week, imposed new taxes and budgetary economies, and attacked fiscal fraud. The French economy then rebounded rapidly, but it was too late; the Nazi menace was at the door.

10

EPILOGUE: THE PAST
AND THE PRESENT

....

THIS book has argued that the shock of the First World War,
coupled with the policies adopted after the war, led to the
economic disasters of the inter-war years: more specifically, that it
was the gold standard—reintroduced in the 1920s to cure the instability of the immediate post-war years—which prevented the world
economy from dealing with the problems which emerged at the
end of the decade and deepened in the early 1930s. The failure of
institutions was exacerbated by failures of leadership and co-
operation. Policy failures were more important than they would
have been in other circumstances because the underlying situation
was so difficult, the need for enlightened and constructive policies
so great.

We began our history of the period by placing the developments
between the wars in historical perspective, showing how far inter-
war economic growth fell short of the standard achieved in earlier
and later periods (Chapter 1.2). We close by looking back at that
period in comparison with the aftermath of the Second World War,
and with the current situation created by the collapse of the centrally planned economies of central and eastern Europe, and the end
of the cold war. The comparison suggests two fundamental ques-
tions which might fruitfully be addressed in the context of our
analysis of the primary determinants of the failures of policy and of
performance in the inter-war period. First, if the result of the First
World War was economic crisis and severe depression, why were
the consequences of the second, larger conflict not equally disastrous? Secondly, are there any parallels between the position after

the two world wars and that created today by the breakup of the Communist regimes, the end of the cold war, and the new economic and political attitudes and policies emerging among the governments and people of the European Union and the United States?

10.1 The aftermath of two world wars—similarities and differences

As is well known, economic and political developments after the Second World War effectively avoided the crises which followed the First World War; instead they ushered in a period of remarkable success. Reconstruction was very rapid. Three to six years after the end of hostilities, even those countries whose economies were most damaged by the conflict had recovered to their highest pre-war GDP levels. Moreover, and more importantly, reconstruction was followed by a quarter of a century of exceptionally high rates of growth, more rapid than anything ever experienced before or since. This was particularly true of continental Europe and of Japan.

Not only was economic growth extremely rapid, but fluctuations were very mild and unemployment extremely low. So exceptional and unexpected was this stream of events that the years 1950–73 came to be known as the 'golden age', and in countries like Germany and Italy people talked of an economic miracle. Why was the outcome of the so-called 'second post-war settlement' so distinctly different from that of thirty years earlier? We discuss three possible contributory factors: the scale of the shocks created by the wars; the nature of the international economic organization created after the wars, and the degree of international co-operation and aid both within Europe and between Europe and the United States.

The scale of the shocks

The magnitude of the two world wars in terms of the relative scale of military spending can be seen from Table 10.1. In the First World War the share of net national product allocated to the war effort reached a peak in 1917 at 53 per cent in Germany and at 38 per cent in the United Kingdom. In the United States, a late and reluctant

Table 10.1. Military expenditure as a percentage of net national product at factor cost, selected countries, 1913–1920 and 1937–1951

	UK	USA	USSR	Germany	Japan
First World War					
1913	4	1	—	—	—
1914	9	1	—	14	—
1915	34	1	—	41	—
1916	38	1	—	35	—
1917	38	6	—	53	—
1918	32	13	—	32	—
1919	13	9	—	—	—
1920	4	3	—	—	—
Second World War					
1937	—	—	9	—	13
1938	7	—	—	17	—
1939	16	2	—	25	—
1940	49	2	21	44	17
1941	55	12	—	56	25
1942	54	34	75	69	36
1943	57	44	76	76	47
1944	56	45	69	—	64
1945	47	38	—	—	—
1946	19	10	—	—	—
1947	11	5	—	—	—
1948	8	5	18	—	—
1949	8	6	17	—	—
1950	8	5	16	—	—
1951	10	11	17	—	—

Sources:
1938–45: UK, USA, USSR, Germany: Harrison (1988: 184).
Other: UK: Feinstein (1972: tables 1, 3, 12, and 33 and supporting worksheets);
USA: US Department of Commerce (1975: series F1, F6 Y458–9);
USSR: Bergson (1961: 128 and 303);
Germany: Stolper *et al.* (1967: 57), Sommariva and Tullio (1987: 226–7);
Japan: Milward (1977: 85), Ohkawa and Shinohara (1979: 269 and 375).

entrant into the war, war expenditures peaked at 13 per cent of NNP in 1918. When the war was over the proportion of resources devoted to military expenditure fell swiftly to a quite low level.

The pattern of expenditures in the Second World War was more uniform and more dramatic. All five of the countries shown in the lower block of Table 10.1 devoted more than half their national product to the war. Germany and the Soviet Union devoted as much as three-quarters to this end. At the end of the war military spending again declined rapidly, but continued to absorb about 10 per cent of NNP in the United Kingdom and the United States, less in Germany. In both global conflicts the wartime rise and the post-war decline in military spending were large shocks to the world economy. It is clear, however, that the end of the Second World War was a considerably larger shock, forcing a reallocation of close to half the national product in many of the major industrial countries in a very few years.

A second element in the assessment of the impact of the wars is the extent of the destruction, damage, and economic dislocation which they caused. Here too, the set-back to the economies of the belligerent countries during the Second World War was much more severe than in 1914–18. By 1945 the level of GDP per head of France, the Netherlands, Germany, Italy, and Japan had fallen back to late nineteenth- or early twentieth-century levels; the position in Austria was even worse. One or two generations of work were lost. Of the major powers, only the United States and the United Kingdom managed to end the war with per capita GDP higher than it had been in 1938.

It is thus evident that the Second World War was responsible for a far more severe shock to the world economic system than the First. Other institutional and policy developments must therefore have been sufficiently favourable and conducive to good economic performance to more than offset this adverse initial position.

Institutional changes and a new international monetary system

The real shocks resulting from the wars were massive. Even in the absence of other problems, they would have posed formidable challenges to economic policy makers. But they were not the only problem. After each war, the international monetary regime lay in shreds and needed to be reconstructed.

The gold standard was suspended at the start of the First World War. Even before the conflict ended, policy makers were anticipating its resumption. Alternatives existed but were firmly rejected. The argument in favour of its restoration seemed to be reinforced as prices accelerated and Germany and other countries suffered the ravages of hyper-inflation (see Chapter 3.1). The gold exchange standard was formally revived in 1925 with the British return to gold, but it did not achieve what its advocates had predicted. On the contrary, we have argued that its rigidity was a prime cause, and even *the* prime cause, of the Great Depression; its abandonment was the way out of the depression (Chapter 6.5). A further consequence of the depression which it created was the disintegration of the world monetary system. The international economy split into competing currency and trading blocs. Trade barriers between the blocs rose dramatically (Chapter 8). Bilateral barter often substituted for multilateral arrangements; international trade and capital flows essentially vanished (Chapter 9.1).

Why was the situation so different after 1945? In a broad historical perspective, it is possible to see that both the United States and Europe had changed since 1919. The former emerged from the Second World War as undisputed world leader, and this time was ready to accept the responsibility. The lesson of Versailles had been absorbed: if stability and prosperity were to be achieved a sufficient degree of international co-ordination and co-operation had to be established. The United States could provide the relevant preconditions for a new international order based upon mutual trust and collaboration, but it could not impose this; Europe also had to be ready to play its part.

European societies had long been divided. The blame for the unsatisfactory first post-war settlement cannot be laid solely at the door of incompetent politicians and central bankers: its outcome was deeply rooted in Europe's history and its social and political structures. The changes required in order for the post-1945 settlement to yield a better outcome were finally possible as a result of a long historical process inaugurated with the crisis of European liberal capitalism at the end of the nineteenth century. It has been persuasively argued by Maier (1987: 162) that reversing that crisis took half a century: 'the cumulative achievement required the institutional flux that was left in the wake of not one but two wartime upheavals.'

The military, political, and social situation of 1945 was so much more favourable to the creation of pre-conditions for stability and consensus than that of 1919 precisely because it came at the end of this long and tragic historical process. There were two components of the mid-century settlement, international and domestic, and they were mutually reinforcing. This created a virtuous circle, in sharp contrast to the previous occasion when the mistakes made at

Versailles amplified the domestic fragility which afflicted European countries in the aftermath of the war.

The international part of the second post-war settlement rested on the determination of the United States and the United Kingdom to reverse the conditions which had prevailed in the inter-war period. The bitter lessons of the 1930s were well learnt. The aim this time was to create a radically different framework of international economic relations, one which would enable countries to co-operate in trade and investment to their mutual advantage, and so help to sustain high levels of domestic activity. The economic advantages of such co-operation were powerfully reinforced by the belief that this would also promote world peace.

As early as 1941 Roosevelt and Churchill recognized the need to avoid the problems which the enormous burden of war debts had created after 1918. The outcome was the generous scheme for Lend-Lease, under which supplies required by the United Kingdom for the war effort were in effect provided free of charge by the United States and Canada. In 1942 the two powers also reached a preliminary agreement to set international economic relations on a new footing. The Bretton Woods Conference which followed in 1944, and gave rise to the system of that name, was a deliberate attempt to avoid the deficiencies of the inter-war gold standard. It is noteworthy that consensus on the broad lines of the whole project 'derived from a shared interpretation of the inter-war years, which owed much to the analysis of the League of Nations' (Foreman-Peck 1995: 240).

Bretton Woods set the framework for a new international monetary system based on fixed exchange rates, with the dollar as anchor currency. It was accepted, however, that there might be special circumstances in which it was necessary for a country to adjust the relative value of its currency, and procedures were created under which this could be done. Britain took advantage of this in 1949, France in 1955 and 1957. Two international bodies were established. The International Monetary Fund (IMF) was designed to allow the smooth adjustment of temporary balance-of-payments disequilibria; the International Bank for Reconstruction and Development (normally known as the World Bank) was to take care of longer-term development needs. Commercial policy was dealt with under the auspices of the General Agreement on Trade and Tariffs (GATT), signed in Geneva in 1947. This initiated the lengthy process of reducing tariff barriers on manufactured goods.

When even the moderated discipline of the Bretton Woods system proved too harsh for the still-prostrate western European economies in the immediate post-war period, they were exempted from the requirements of convertible currencies. The European Payments Union allowed its members to discriminate against outside suppliers for over a decade after the conclusion of the war. It was a vital first step towards reconstructing multilateral trade and eventually bringing about full currency convertibility.

Aid and co-operation

As soon as the war was over, it became clear that implementation of these plans for a new international economic system would need robust transitory measures if the colossal task of reconstruction and conversion to peacetime economies was to be successfully achieved. In another far-sighted departure from the attitudes which prevailed after Versailles, the United States recognized its responsibility for providing the essential bridge to prosperity. There was inevitably some friction in the discussion of the terms on which aid and loans would be granted, but the contrast with the post-1918 wrangling over war debts and reparations was enormous.

Immediate relief aid (UNRRA) was provided to avoid major hardship in devastated Europe. A large loan was made to the United Kingdom. More than this was needed, however, if trade was to revive to the extent necessary. Europe's foreign exchange reserves were virtually exhausted and exports to the dollar area were still very low, making it impossible for Europe to import vital supplies and equipment from the United States and Canada. What was needed was a major injection of purchasing power into the international economy *in dollars*. A similar problem had arisen after 1919, and in that era it was left to private capital markets to take care of, with the destabilizing results that we have seen (Chapter 5.3 and 5.4). This time, the United States government made available a total of over 13 billion dollars in grants and loans to Europe between 1948 and 1951 through the so-called Marshall Plan (officially the European Recovery Programme).

While scholarship has failed to uncover specific links between American aid and European investment, it seems clear that the Marshall Plan kept the nascent investment plans of the western European countries from being strangled, either by foreign exchange scarcity or by planning bureaucrats. The Marshall Plan also eased the harshest post-war living conditions, fostering a relatively peaceful social context in which reconstruction could be more easily effected; and it contributed to the creation of a new climate of confidence and co-operation within and between the nations of Europe, which was a critical element in the domestic aspects of the new post-war settlement.

One other contrast between the two post-war settlements is also of great importance. The 1920s were dominated by disagreements between the former enemies, most conspicuously the bitter disputes between France and Germany over reparations and territory. The political leaders who came to power after the Second World War were determined to avoid such divisive and destructive policies and instead initiated the successive measures which led by 1956 to the formation of the European Common Market. At that point it included only six countries—with the United Kingdom, the Scandinavian countries, and others outside—but it provided economic and political unity at the heart of Europe.

However, all these constructive measures also sharpened the distinction between the Atlantic economy and the centrally planned economies led by the USSR. Although invited to join in the Marshall Plan, the Communist nations were not willing to allow the Americans to have the say in their affairs this would have involved. After initial hesitation, the Soviet Union and its allies also declined to participate in the arrangements established at Bretton Woods. The post-war international system of which we speak therefore refers to only a part of the world economy. Trade and finance among the Communist nations was organized quite separately and was not part of the system of free multilateral trade and payments.

It would be claiming too much to say that the monetary flexibility which the Bretton Woods system provided in place of the rigidities of the inter-war gold standard was the principal key to European prosperity after the Second World War. Numerous problems had to be overcome in order for this to be achieved. We have emphasized certain changes in policy and institutions, but numerous other factors also changed between 1919 and 1945. Because we are observing history, not conducting a controlled experiment, we cannot be certain which subset of these changes was responsible for enabling the world economy to escape a repetition of the disasters of the inter-war period. We can say, however, that macro-economic policies, monetary conditions, and international trade arrangements can help to solve problems or they can make matters worse. We have tried to show why we believe that they did the former after the Second World War, the latter after the First.

10.2 Convergence to a common productivity standard

In discussing the features of the golden age which followed the Second World War the focus has been on the exceptional growth of output and trade achieved by the developed capitalist countries in the years 1948–73. There is one further feature of this period which is also extremely important and relevant to the themes of this book. When the war ended, the disparity in productivity levels between the various countries was remarkably large, larger even than it had been in 1913. This is partly a reflection of their different starting-points and the divergence in their economic fortunes in the period from the First World War to 1938 covered in earlier chapters, but is mainly the result of their very different experience during the Second World War.

A broad indication of the relative economic efficiency of twelve European capitalist countries in 1913, 1950, 1973, and 1992 is shown in the upper block of Table 10.2, with labour productivity (GDP per hour worked) taken as the measure of economic performance. At each date the level of productivity in the most advanced nation, the United States of America, is set at 100, and the level in the individual European countries is compared with that. The countries are listed according to their rank in 1950. At that date the performance gap between the United States and almost all European countries had widened considerably compared to the position in 1913. Productivity in the four countries most adversely affected by the war, Germany, Italy, Finland, and Austria, was barely one-third of the level in the United States; Switzerland was the only country which came within two-thirds of that level.

By 1973 the position had been totally transformed. The lowest of the twelve European countries at that date, Finland, had reached 57 per cent of the US level, and six other countries were within 70 per cent of that. In the course of this convergence the dispersion within this group of European nations had thus narrowed substantially. The process of catch-up continued in the subsequent phase, though more slowly. By 1992 productivity in all twelve countries was

Table 10.2. GDP per hour worked relative to the United States: European countries and regions, 1913, 1950, 1973, and 1992 (level in the USA = 100)

	1913	1950	1973	1992
12 western European countries				
Switzerland	63	69	78	87
United Kingdom	86	62	68	82
Sweden	50	56	77	79
Netherlands	78	51	81	99
Belgium	70	48	70	98
Denmark	66	46	68	75
France	56	45	76	102
Norway	43	43	60	88
Germany	68	35	71	95
Italy	41	34	66	85
Finland	35	32	57	70
Austria	57	32	65	83
European regions[a]				
Western Europe	60	46	70	87
Southern Europe	33[b]	23	44	62
Central and eastern Europe	—	19	26	23[c]

[a] Arithmetic averages: for western Europe of the estimates for the 12 countries listed above; for southern Europe for Greece, Ireland, Portugal, and Spain; and for central and eastern Europe for Bulgaria, Czechoslovakia, Hungary, Poland, Romania, and the USSR.

[b] This is a very rough approximation.

[c] A rough estimate of the Figure for 1989, the last year before the collapse of central planning, is 27.

Source: Maddison (1995: 249).

within 70 per cent of the United States level, and in seven it was at least 85 per cent. The evidence of Table 10.2 thus suggests that when the overall economic environment is appropriate—as it was after 1945 but not after 1918—all these western European economies can converge towards the highest levels of economic performance. Their achievement in the four decades following the Second World War thus vividly underlines the heavy costs of the turmoil and policy errors between the wars.

Several factors contributed to this process of convergence. All the countries in the upper block of Table 10.2 possessed the necessary pre-conditions for economic growth, including a well-educated labour force, efficient government, competent managers, entrepreneurs willing to innovate and take risks, and suitable financial and legal systems. In the countries which had suffered most severely from the Second World War the determination at all levels of society to improve their economic conditions, and a willingness to accept the sacrifices and changes required for this (for example in forgoing consumption to raise investment), was a powerful force.

However, the most significant explanatory factor was the ability of the relatively backward countries to borrow from those ahead of them, particularly the United States of America. The latecomers did not have to generate their own technical progress. They could learn from the experience of those who had gone first, study the sources of high levels of productivity in the leading economies, apply and adapt these to their own conditions. This applied not only to all forms of modern technology, such as machinery or electronic equipment, but also to a wide range of economic and social best-practice features; for example, in corporate organization, management, financial systems, property relations, and government supply-side policies. Changes in economic structure, notably the transfer of labour from agriculture to industry and services, were also important both as a direct contribution to higher productivity and, indirectly, as a source of labour permitting the expanding sectors to grow without being constrained by a tight labour market.

The countries of southern Europe also participated in this process, and have indeed converged on the United States more rapidly than those in western Europe, thus narrowing the gap between them and their European neighbours. However, they started from a much lower base and are still a considerable way behind. As can be seen in the lower block of Table 10.2, the average GDP per hour worked of four countries in this region was only 23 per cent of the United States level in 1950; by 1973 it had risen to 44 per cent and by 1992 to 62 per cent. The process of catch-up in these countries has been considerably assisted by their membership of the European Union, and there is every prospect that they will continue to move closer to the productivity levels of the leading group.

The position in central and eastern Europe (including the former USSR) is much less promising. In the years following the Second World War, the then Communist economies also enjoyed a rapid growth spurt, but the rate of advance in labour productivity was slower than in other European countries and it was not sustained. Once the possibilities of extensive growth had been exhausted, systemic weaknesses, most notably in respect of technical progress, became increasingly evident. The position of these countries relative to the United States improved slightly, but only from 19 per cent in 1950 to 26 per cent in 1973, and then levelled off. By 1989 they were probably no nearer than they had been in 1913. Since then their relative position has deteriorated sharply, with output and income declining after the collapse of their planned economies. The massive problems of the transition in these former socialist econo-mies of Europe brings us to our final theme.

10.3 The European economy in the 1990s

Are there any further lessons which might be learned from the historical developments studied in this book? We suggest in closing that it may be peculiarly important to explore this question at the present time. The end of the cold war has produced a shock that is in some respects comparable with that delivered by the two world wars. The problems arise first from the reduction in military ex-penditure from the levels thought necessary on both sides during the cold war; and secondly from the fundamental economic restruc-turing which is required in the former socialist countries. The new structures and patterns of production emerging in those countries have major implications both for them and for the international system of trade and finance.

There are also more subtle factors in the present situation which could have a significant influence on the way in which the world economy responds to this dual shock. The threat of war was a powerful force binding the western allies together and encouraging unity and co-operation for many purposes. With the removal of that pressure divisions are beginning to appear in relation to a variety of economic and political issues. This tendency is reinforced by a further factor. It is now more than sixty years since the Great Depression. The disasters of the 1930s were cogent arguments in support of the radically different policies adopted with such success in the period after 1945. But those events are no longer fresh in the memory of the present generation. Policies which would have been briskly rejected in the 1940s are given a respectful hearing in the 1990s. The case for flexibility in the international monetary system, for free trade, and for a willingness to put interna-tional co-operation and policy co-ordination ahead of the pursuit of narrowly conceived national interests can no longer be taken for granted.

The dual shock

The countries of the former USSR and the other centrally planned economies of central and eastern Europe have embarked with varying degrees of enthusiasm on a process of transformation towards the market economy. Some, notably Poland, Hungary, and the Czech Republic, have made excellent progress; others have barely begun. If the transition is to succeed it will require large shifts in the structure of production and a massive reallocation of resources. First, alternative employment must now be found for the large share of their resources previously absorbed by military outlays. Secondly, there is a very substantial mismatch between the output which resulted from the preferences of the planners who previously determined what should be produced, and the supply of goods and services which is required today for sale in a free market to domestic consumers and foreign buyers.

The problems of reconstruction are exacerbated by territorial changes involving the breakup of the former Soviet Union, of Czechoslovakia, and of Yugoslavia. In their place new states have been formed, with divergent economic strategies and interests. Supplies of raw materials and sales of finished goods, previously organized in a framework of internal trade, have now to be negotiated across national boundaries, with attendant complications of currencies and tariffs. There are obvious analogies with the problems caused after the First World War by the breakup of the Habsburg and tsarist empires. As then, so now in the 1990s, the region is beset by ethnic and national conflicts which are highly detrimental to trade and economic co-operation.

The end of the cold war has also had an impact on the capitalist economies. As the threat of global war has receded, the demand for arms has declined. NATO expenditures for major military weapons fell by one-quarter from 1989 to 1992. However, total military spending in the NATO countries has not declined rapidly as a share of the national product. It has been hard to reduce military personnel during a period of high unemployment, and military establishments in these countries have been supported in the same way uneconomic (at world prices) production has been supported in the former centrally planned economies. The full force of the economic shock has yet to be felt in the West.

We know from the preceding comparison of the experience following the First and Second World Wars that the existence of a major economic shock does not mean that there will necessarily be a crisis. What is critical is the form of the response, and the economic and political settlement that is established to deal with the new conditions. At present there are grounds for thinking that the response to the shock arising from the collapse of the Communist economies and the end of the cold war has some disturbing parallels with the period after the First World War. The most important of these are the trade barriers erected in order to regulate excess supplies of agricultural products, and the weaknesses in the international payments system. We do not want to stretch this parallel too far, only to suggest that there may be lessons for the present in our account of the past.

Agricultural markets

In each world war, non-European countries increased their supply of agricultural goods, creating the conditions for a post-war excess supply as the soldiers in former belligerent countries left the sword for the plough. The dislocation after the First World War was described in Chapter 4.3. More data are shown in Table 10.3. Western European imports of five grains increased only slightly across each of the two world wars, but exports from the western hemisphere increased dramatically in each case. They more than offset

Table 10.3. World trade in five grains, 1909–1913 to 1948/1949 (millions of tons)

	1909–13	1925–29	1934–38	1948/9
European net imports				
Western continental Europe	16.4	17.7	10.5	13.5
United Kingdom and Ireland	9.9	9.1	10.4	8.5
Total	26.3	26.8	20.9	22.0
Main exporting areas, net exports				
Eastern continental Europe	2.7	0.6	2.0	—
Russia/USSR	10.5	0.8	1.2	—
United States and Canada	6.4	15.1	5.4	23.8
Southern hemisphere	7.5	13.6	13.9	9.7
Total	27.1	30.1	22.5	33.5

Note: The five grains are wheat, rye, barley, oats, and maize.

Source: Svennilson (1954: table 19).

the decline in exports from eastern Europe and Russia after the First World War, and they greatly added to world supplies after the Second World War.

The post-war shock was twofold. In the Americas, the price fell back sharply from the wartime peaks that had induced the expansion of production. In western Europe, the increase in supply threatened to drown domestic agriculture in a flood of imports. This had happened once before, in the 1880s. After each world war, continental European countries responded as they had done to falling freight rates in the 1890s: they protected their farmers by restricting agricultural imports. They acted individually after the First World War; they adopted the Common Agricultural Policy after the second. The closed European markets then intensified the shock to the producing regions in the rest of the world.

The end of the cold war poses a similar allocative problem. The countries of eastern Europe are returning to the world economy after a prolonged absence. Their industrialization in the intervening period was based on a set of prices very different from those in the western economy. They consequently find themselves in a position similar to that of the southern hemisphere after the two world wars. They need revenue from exports to finance the reconstruction of their industrial base. Agricultural products represent one area where they can compete on world markets at their new exchange rates. But the Common Agricultural Policy bars them from their natural markets.

The current protectionist stance of the European Union in agriculture points perilously in the direction of a similarity with the 1920s and 1930s. Indeed, western Europe has put itself in the untenable position of simultaneously asking the countries of eastern Europe to open up their economies while maintaining trade barriers against their exports. This results in a crippling of eastern European growth, and also in great loss of credibility at a time when leadership is not only needed but sought after.

The current international payments system

The current international payments system, while not totally dysfunctional, is also not in robust health. The Bretton Woods system was abandoned at the end of the long post-war boom, essentially because the economic revival of Europe and Japan had fundamentally changed their relationship with the United States. Parities and policies appropriate in the 1940s were no longer suitable in the 1970s. While the aftermath of Bretton Woods has not been as inimical as the trading blocs of the Great Depression, trade has suffered both from persistent barriers and from wild exchange rate fluctuations, particularly for the dollar and the yen. The countries of the European Union reacted to the end of the Bretton Woods era by attempting to establish a system linking their currencies within narrow bands, and are now planning to move towards a single currency.

The end of the cold war has made its main impact in this sphere as a consequence of the problems created by the reunification of Germany. From a macro-economic point of view the best policy would have been a temporary increase in German taxes in order to finance the investment required in the former eastern territories. Chancellor Kohl chose instead to finance the investment by borrowing. Germany's macro-economic stance was thus composed of a very expansive fiscal policy countered by a very tight monetary policy. This policy configuration represented a large shock to the European economy and the European Monetary System (EMS).

The EMS prevented the mark from rising relative to other European currencies. The result was great strain in Germany's trading partners as they raised interest rates in an attempt to protect their currencies. As in the early 1930s, a commitment to fixed exchange rates threatened to transmit a macro-economic shock around Europe (Chapter 6.2). On this occasion, however, Britain, Italy, and Finland were willing to abandon the EMS at that point before it could do lasting damage to their economies.

Despite these and other strains, monetary prospects within the European Union continue to be dominated by the project to establish a single currency by 1999. The driving force behind this proposal is the political determination of France and Germany to cement the political unity which both countries for different reasons see as essential to the future peace and security of Europe. Unfortunately such political motives, however worthy, may not be the best guide to economic policy. The attempt to bring budget deficits within the range prescribed by the Maastricht Treaty is forcing countries to impose severe deflationary pressure at a time when unemployment still remains at very high levels in Europe. This inevitably provokes a hostile response and increases political instability.

Perhaps more seriously, the introduction of a single currency will deprive the countries concerned of a significant element of flexibility in adjusting to changing economic circumstances. If changes in exchange rate parities are no longer possible, deflation is effectively the only option left for a country which develops a persistent balance-of-payments deficit. It is by no means clear that the benefits of the policy will outweigh these disadvantages. It is notable that it is the leaders of the former gold bloc countries who are today most strongly committed to the EMS and the single currency. Only time will tell if they are condemning their people to relive the painful contractions of the mid-1930s.

The need for international leadership and co-operation

The issues outlined above would by themselves be sufficient grounds for unease about the ability of the world economy to cope successfully with the problems posed by the end of the cold war. Our analysis of the past suggests two further factors which may add to the difficulties. In the inter-war years the problems of managing the gold standard were aggravated by the absence of adequate international leadership and co-operation. Here too there are overtones of the 1920s in the current situation.

In discussing possible explanations for the Great Depression we noted what has come to be known as the hegemonic theory. Britain was the hegemon before the First World War, the United States after the Second. In the middle there was a void: no longer London, not yet New York. The lack of clear leadership, in this story, led to poor policies which led in turn to depression. After 1929 each country tried to deal with the fall in demand in its own way; there was no effective lender of last resort for banks or currencies in distress.

The United States is the only candidate for hegemonic status today. But there is a tendency in the United States to turn away from external responsibilities, much as there was in the 1920s. Just as Congress then refused to support the League of Nations, so Congress today wants to cripple the United Nations. There are signs of a popular impatience with the burdens of world leadership, a growing belief that the United States should concentrate on solving its internal problems. More importantly, the United States is currently an importer of capital on a large scale. Britain's leadership before 1914, and America's after 1945, were based on capital exports. It is hard to see how the United States can exert the kind of economic leadership that is needed today, given its current balance-of-payments problems.

We also referred to an alternative view of the inter-war period: that it was the absence of international co-operation which led to the policy mistakes that caused the Great Depression. The most powerful factor inhibiting the necessary co-operation was the move to more representative governments in the aftermath of the First World War. The rise of organized labour and of the political parties (see Chapter 2.3) reduced the autonomy of all central bankers in charge of maintaining the gold standard. It was increasingly difficult to give priority to external balance if achieving this required continuous deflationary measures and higher unemployment at home.

How does this affect the present time? If international leadership is lacking today, can international co-operation substitute for it? The signs are not encouraging. The end of the cold war has loosened the ties that bound the western community. International political disarray is evident in divergent policies toward the former Yugoslavia and in the conflicts over trade with Cuba, Libya, and Iran. International economic disunity is shown in the disagreements within Europe over the European Monetary System and the single currency, and between Europe and the United States over the GATT negotiations and other issues of trade and investment. There is also the intense rivalry between the United States and Japan, and disagreements among the leading countries over the IMF policy towards the developing countries.

History never repeats itself, and we are aware of both the analogies and the enormous differences with the situation after 1918 and after 1945. However, one of the principal lessons to be learned from our study of the economic history of twentieth-century Europe is that growth and prosperity were achieved in periods when there was an environment of multilateral trade, regulated exchange rate flexibility, and international financial co-operation, not in periods of tariff barriers, trade wars, financial rigidity, and conflicting monetary areas. Is that elementary lesson in danger of being forgotten?

Guide to Further Reading

T HERE is a huge literature dealing with various features of the economic history of Europe in the inter-war period, and with the related political disputes. The following survey is confined to published work in English, and is intended as a brief guide to books and articles most relevant for further study of the topics discussed in this book.

Major themes

General works

Munting and Holderness (1991) is the most recent general introduction to the economic history of the period and is very concise and well-organized. Ambrosius and Hubbard (1989) cover many of the related aspects of the social history of the period. There is much useful information and an excellent analysis of the period from 1914 to 1945 in a related four-volume series: the First World War by Hardach (1977); the 1920s by Aldcroft (1977); the 1930s by Kindleberger (1973); and the Second World War by Milward (1977). Moggridge (1989) gives a very clear and thorough assessment of inter-war financial and exchange rate policies, as does Kindleberger (1989) for commercial policy.

There is an illuminating analysis of the post-war political conflicts which played such an important role in the subsequent economic developments in Maier (1975); other important studies of these issues are Schuker (1976), Silverman (1982), Boyce (1987), and Orde (1990). The vexed topic of reparations continues to attract attention from scholars, and has been debated by Felix (1971), Marks (1978), Trachtenberg (1980), Silverman (1982), and Schuker (1988).

The Great Depression

The most important modern studies of the fundamental macro-economic issues are Temin (1989) and Eichengreen (1990, 1992*a*).

Fearon (1979) and Eichengreen (1992b) provide a clear and concise introduction to recent views on the causes of the Great Depression. Foreman-Peck *et al.* (1996) make an ambitious attempt to construct a comprehensive econometric model to test a number of propositions about the policies which might have averted the depression. There are also important insights to be gained from earlier accounts, including the classic report written for the League of Nations by Ohlin (1931) and interpretations of the crisis by Robbins (1934), Hodson (1938), and Lewis (1949).

For readers who want more information about the closely related events in the United States, Fearon (1987) is a very good introduction to the economic history of the inter-war period, and Bernstein (1987) provides a perceptive recent discussion of developments from 1929. A graphic account of the Wall Street stock exchange collapse is given by Galbraith (1955).

The recovery and the 1930s

The policies adopted to promote economic recovery in the 1930s are discussed in Eichengreen and Sachs (1985) and in Temin (1989). Significant contemporary studies include Hodson (1938), Arndt (1944), and Lewis (1949). Landes (1969) also has a useful chapter on this decade. The best modern accounts of the recovery in individual countries are Richardson (1967) on Britain and Overy (1994, 1996) on Germany.

For other aspects of economic policy in this decade see Kaiser (1980) on international economic relations; Clarke (1977) and Drummond (1979) on the Tripartite Agreement between Britain, France, and the United States; Drummond (1972, 1981) on Commonwealth economic policy and on sterling and the sterling area; Jones (1934) on the tariff wars; Ellis (1941) on the detailed operation of exchange controls; and Neal (1979) and Kitson (1992) on Nazi clearing agreements and trade policy.

Banking, finance, and the gold standard

Drummond (1987) is a good explanation of the basic concepts of the gold standard, and an influential contemporary view of how it worked is given in Hawtrey (1939). Eichengreen (1990, 1992a) examines many aspects of its operation in the inter-war period; and interesting earlier research is reported in Jack (1927), Brown (1940), Nurkse (1944), and Bloomfield (1959).

The way in which the return to gold contributed to the exceptional international scope of the Great Depression, as well as to its severity and duration, is analysed in Temin (1989) and Eichengreen (1992a). Bernanke and James (1991) is an important study of the relationship between the gold standard and the banking crises, but assumes a more advanced knowledge of economics.

Feinstein (1995) has several comparative studies of exchange rate policy, as well as detailed histories of inter-war banking policies in each of the main countries. The role of the banks in individual countries is also examined in James *et al.* (1991) and in a special supplement to the *Journal of European Economic History* (1984).

Trade, production, and unemployment

Svennilson (1954) is an exceptionally informative and comprehensive analysis of developments in industry and trade in inter-war Europe, and of the related technological advances; and the relevant chapters in Landes (1969) should also be consulted on these topics. Caron *et al.* (1995) contains several stimulating studies of European innovation and technical change. Maizels (1965) is a superb analysis of the changes in the composition and direction of international trade; and the study undertaken by Hilgerdt for the League of Nations (1941) is still a useful source of information on European trade.

Tracy (1964) is a good starting-point for an account of the developments in agriculture. League of Nations (1931) and Royal Institute of International Affairs (1932) are interesting as an indication of how the problem was seen by contemporaries. Malenbaum (1953) and Timoshenko (1953) are both substantial investigations of this important sector.

The introduction to Eichengreen and Hatton (1988) is the best guide to the movements in unemployment, with information about individual countries in the other chapters. Other useful studies include Garside (1990) on the situation in Britain and Stachura (1986) on Germany.

The period after the Second World War

Until recently it was left mainly to the applied economists to study post-war developments, but economic historians are beginning to enter the field and can bring to the task the advantage of a longer perspective. Crafts and Toniolo (1996) is an excellent example and a very good starting-point for further reading on this period. Milward (1984, 1992) provides an authoritative study of post-war reconstruction and of the moves towards a common economic community; and there is an excellent retrospective assessment of Bretton Woods in Bordo and Eichengreen (1993). The best introductions to the process of convergence are Abramovitz (1990) and Maddison (1991, 1995). Dornbusch et al. (1993) examine the theme of reconstruction after the Second World War and the lessons this might have for the transition in process in eastern Europe.

National studies

The economic problems of inter-war Germany have generated a large literature in English, but the material available on the other Continental economies is relatively limited. However, there are good chapters on individual countries in Cipolla (1976), and in a number of the collective studies which report on recent research; for example, Cottrell and Teichova (1983), James et al. (1991), Cottrell et al. (1992), Garside (1993), Feinstein (1995), and Crafts and Toniolo (1996).

The series of reprinted studies recently published under the general title of The Economic Development of Modern Europe since 1870 also has a number of relevant articles and chapters on the inter-war period, many of which are not easily accessible elsewhere. The series includes volumes on Austria (Matis 1994), Belgium (van der Wee and Blomme 1997), Denmark (Persson 1993), France (Crouzet 1993), Germany (Fischer 1997), Ireland (Ó Gráda 1994), Italy (Federico 1994), the Netherlands (van Zanden 1996), Sweden (Jonung and Ohlsson 1997), and Spain (Martin-Aceña and Simpson 1995).

Britain

Pollard (1992) and Floud and McCloskey (1994: vol. 2) are the most complete and up-to-date general economic histories of modern Britain, and will also serve as comprehensive guides to the huge literature which is available on inter-war Britain and cannot be fully reviewed in this brief survey. Aldcroft (1970) is a good survey and covers the period in considerable detail, but some parts have been superseded by later work. Matthews *et al.* (1982) explore many aspects of the overall economic growth of the economy, placing the inter-war period in a longer historical perspective.

The outstanding account of the return to gold is Moggridge (1972), and a useful collection of representative articles on the subject is reprinted in Pollard (1970). There is a judicious account of financial policy in the history of the Bank of England by Sayers (1976); and although Nevin (1955) is now somewhat dated it is still informative on the collapse of the gold standard and the introduction of cheap money. The 1931 devaluation is analysed and set in context with later devaluations in Cairncross and Eichengreen (1983). Clarke (1988) is an illuminating history of the evolution of Keynes's theory of macro-economic policy, and the slow evolution of actual policy in response to these advances in economic theory can be studied in Middleton (1985), Booth (1989), and Tomlinson (1990).

Aldcroft and Richardson (1969) brings together articles by these two authors which stimulated much of the modern discussion of British policy and performance. The recovery is analysed in more detail in Richardson (1967) and there are useful studies of individual industries in Buxton and Aldcroft (1979). A rather different perspective is given by the editors and other contributors to Elbaum and Lazonick (1986). Von Tunzelmann (1982) is an innovative study of the impact of technical progess on the structure of the economy. The contribution of the introduction of tariff protection to the recovery is examined in Kitson and Solomou (1990).

Two interesting but highly technical studies of the inter-war labour market are Dimsdale *et al.* (1989) and Beenstock and Warburton (1991); the latter gives more weight to supply-side factors in accounting for the rise in unemployment.

France, Belgium, Italy, and the Netherlands

The best modern economic history of Italy is Zamagni (1993). Comparable up-to-date accounts of other countries are lacking, though Kemp (1972) presents an interesting if rather critical view of developments in France. Mouré (1991) is the most valuable modern study of exchange rate policy in France, and other aspects are discussed in Wolfe (1957), Eichengreen (1990), and Eichengreen and Wyplosz (1990). The revaluation of the Italian lira is examined in Cohen (1972); and there are comparative studies of France and Italy by Asselain and Plessis (1995), and of France and Belgium by Cassiers (1995). The economic policies of Italian Fascism are analysed in Welk (1939), Toniolo (1980), and Cohen (1988). For the gold bloc countries, some aspects of the experience of the Netherlands in the 1930s can be studied in Griffiths (1988), and of France in Jackson (1985, 1988).

Germany

Hardach (1980) and Braun (1990) provide general economic histories of the period. The many studies of the early post-war years and the extraordinary hyper-inflation include Bresciani-Turroni (1937), Laursen and Pedersen (1964), Feldman *et al.* (1982), Holtfrerich (1986), Webb (1989), Feldman (1993), and Ferguson (1995). McNeil (1986) is a modern history of American capital flows to Weimar Germany.

James (1986) is the best introduction to subsequent macro-economic policies and the descent into the Depression; and he has also made a very full study of the policy of the Reichsbank and other financial aspects (James 1985). There is also a very detailed treatment of these issues, based on extensive original research, in Balderston (1993, 1995). The diplomatic aspects of the crisis are covered by Bennett (1962).

Borchardt (1991) is a welcome English translation of several penetrating and original studies of German economic policy and performance; and there is a good summary of the debate stimulated by his view that high wages were a crucial cause of economic collapse in von Kruedener (1990). The most recent contribution to this topic is Voth (1995).

There are a number of excellent studies of the economic recovery in Germany and of the Nazi war economy. The first detailed analyses were made by Guillebaud (1939) and Poole (1939); subsequent studies include Klein (1959), Milward (1965), James (1986), and Temin (1991). Overy (1994, 1996) are the latest and most comprehensive examinations of the issue.

Eastern and central Europe

There are a few general economic histories, including Berend and Ranki (1974*a*) and Teichova (1989) on the area as a whole, Berend and Ranki (1974*b*) on Hungary, Lampe and Jackson (1982) on the Balkan states, Teichova (1988) on Czechoslovakia, and Landau and Tomaszewski (1988) on Poland. Kaser and Radice (1985, 1986) report the results of much original research on the countries in this region.

Specialist studies are harder to find. The Austrian crisis of the early 1920s is covered in Walré de Bordes (1924), and Schubert (1991) has recently published a full account of the famous crisis of the Credit-Anstalt bank, which many see as the trigger for the crisis of 1931. Teichova (1985) is a detailed examination of the extent and effect of foreign investment in inter-war Czechoslovakia.

Other European countries

For the Scandinavian and southern European countries the material available in English is very limited. The few general economic histories include Hodne (1983) on Norway, Johansen (1987) on Denmark, and Harrison (1985) and Sanchez-Albornoz (1987) on Spain. Lester (1939) gives a very full account of the exchange rate policies adopted by Denmark and Norway in the 1920s, and there is a study of the contrasting policies of Sweden and Finland in Haavisto and Jonung (1995).

Jonung (1981) examines the depression in Sweden, and there is an older study by Montgomery (1938). Dahmén (1970) covers many of the advances in Swedish industry. For Greece, Mazower (1991) is an important study of the Great Depression. There are also several excellent articles on the Scandinavian countries and on Spain, Greece, and Portugal in the various collective works mentioned earlier.

References

ABRAMOVITZ, MOSES (1990), 'The Catch-Up Factor in Post-War Economic Growth', *Economic Inquiry* 38: 1–18.

ALDCROFT, DEREK H. (1970), *The Inter-War Economy: Britain 1919–1939* (London: Batsford).

——(1977), *From Versailles to Wall Street* (London: Allan Lane).

——and RICHARDSON, HARRY W. (1969), *The British Economy, 1870–1939* (London: Macmillan).

AMBROSIUS, GERLAD, and HUBBARD, William H. (1989), *A Social and Economic History of Twentieth-Century Europe* (Cambridge, Mass.: Harvard University Press).

ARNDT, H. W. (1944), *The Economic Lessons of the Nineteen-Thirties* (London: Oxford University Press).

ASSELAIN, JEAN-CHARLES, and PLESSIS, ALLAIN (1995), 'Exchange-Rate Policy and Macro-Economic Performance: A Comparison of French and Italian Experience Between the Wars', in Feinstein (1995), 187–213.

BAGEHOT, WALTER (1873), *Lombard Street: A Description of the Money Market* (London: Kegan Paul and Trench).

BAIROCH, PAUL *et al.* (1968), *The Growth of Population and its Structure* (Brussels: Université Libre de Bruxelles).

BAKKE, E. WIGHT (1993), *The Unemployed Man: A Social Study* (London: Nisbet).

BALDERSTON, THEODORE (1982), 'The Origins of Economic Instability in Germany, 1924–1930: Market Forces versus Economic Policy', *Vierteljahrschrift für Sozial und Wirtschaftsgeschichte* 69: 488–514.

——(1983), 'The Beginning of the Depression in Germany, 1927–30: Investment and the Capital Market', *Economic History Review* 36: 395–415.

——(1993), *The Origins and Course of the German Economic Crisis, 1923–1932* (Berlin: Haude and Spener).

——(1995), 'German and British Monetary Policy, 1919–1932', in Feinstein (1995), 151–86.

BEENSTOCK, MICHAEL, and WARBURTON, PETER (1991), 'The Market for Labour in Inter-War Britain', *Explorations in Economic History* 28: 287–308.

BENJAMIN, D. K., and KOCHIN, L. A. (1979), 'Searching for an Explanation for Unemployment in Inter-War Britain', *Journal of Political Economy* 87: 441–78.

BENNETT, EDWARD W. (1962), *Germany and the Diplomacy of the Financial Crisis* (Cambridge, Mass.: Harvard University Press).

BEREND, IVAN T., and RANKI, GYORGY (1974a), *Hungary, A Century of Economic Development* (Newton Abbot: David and Charles).

———— (1974b), *Economic Development in East-Central Europe in the 19th and 20th Centuries* (New York: Columbia University Press).

BERGSON, ABRAM (1961), *The Real National Income of Soviet Russia since 1928* (Cambridge, Mass.: Harvard University Press).

BERNANKE, BEN (1993), 'The World on a Cross of Gold', *Journal of Monetary Economics* 31: 251–67.

—— and JAMES, HAROLD (1991), 'The Gold Standard, Deflation and Financial Crisis in the Great Depression: An International Comparison', in R. Glen Hubbard (ed.), *Financial Markets and Financial Crises* (Chicago: National Bureau of Economic Research), 33–68.

BERNSTEIN, MICHAEL A. (1987), *The Great Depression: Delayed Recovery and Economic Change in America, 1929–1939* (Cambridge: Cambridge University Press).

BEVERIDGE, SIR WILLIAM (1937), 'An Analysis of Unemployment, II', *Economica* 4: 1–17.

BLANCHARD, OLIVIER JEAN (1987), 'Reaganomics', *Economic Policy* (Oct.), 17–56.

BLOOMFIELD, ARTHUR I. (1950), *Capital Imports and the American Balance of Payments* (Chicago: Chicago University Press).

—— (1959), *Monetary Policy under the International Gold Standard, 1880–1914* (New York: Federal Reserve Bank of New York).

BOARD OF TRADE (1940), *83rd Statistical Abstract for the United Kingdom 1924–1938* (London: HMSO).

BOOTH, ALAN (1989), *British Economic Policy, 1931–1949: Was There a Keynesian Revolution?* (London: Harvester Wheatsheaf).

BORCHARDT, KNUT (1979, Eng. tr. 1991), 'Constraints and Room for Manoeuvre in the Great Depression of the Early Thirties: Towards a Revision of the Received Historical Picture', in Borchardt (1991), 143–60.

—— (1984), 'Could and Should Germany Have Followed Great Britain in Leaving the Gold Standard?', *Journal of European Economic History* 13: 471–98.

—— (1991), *Perspectives on Modern German Economic History and Policy* (Cambridge: Cambridge University Press).

BORDO, MICHAEL D., and EICHENGREEN, BARRY (eds.) (1993), *A Retrospective on the Bretton Woods System* (Chicago: University of Chicago Press).

BOYCE, ROBERT W. D. (1987), *British Capitalism at the Crossroads, 1919–1932* (Cambridge: Cambridge University Press).

BRAUN, H.-J. (1990), *The German Economy in the Twentieth Century: The German Reich and the Federal Republic* (London: Routledge).

BRESCIANI-TURRONI, C. (1937), *The Economics of Inflation* (London: Allen and Unwin).

BROADBERRY, STEVE N. (1993), 'Manufacturing and the Convergence Hypothesis: What the Long-Run Data Show', *Journal of Economic History* 53: 772–95.

BROWN, WILLIAM ADAMS (1940), *The International Gold Standard Reinterpreted, 1914–1934*, 2 vols. (New York: National Bureau of Economic Research).

BUXTON, NEIL K., and ALDCROFT, DEREK H. (1979), *British Industry Between the Wars: Instability and Industrial Development* (London: Scolar Press).

CAIRNCROSS, ALEC, and EICHENGREEN, BARRY (1983), *Sterling in Decline: The Devaluations of 1931, 1949 and 1967* (Oxford: Blackwell).

CARBONNELLE, C. (1959), 'Recherches sur l'évolution de la production en Belgique de 1900 à 1957', *Cahiers Économiques de Bruxelles* 3: 353–77.

CARON, FRANÇOIS, ERKER, PAUL, and FISCHER, WOLFRAM (1995), *Innovations in the European Economy Between the Wars* (Berlin: Walter de Gruyter).

CASSIERS, ISABELLE (1995), 'Managing the Franc in Belgium and France: The Economic Consequences of Exchange-Rate Policies, 1925–1936', in Feinstein (1995), 214–36.

CHANDLER, ALFRED D. JR. (1990), *Scale and Scope: The Dynamics of Industrial Capitalism* (Cambridge, Mass: Harvard University Press).

CHILDERS, THOMAS (1983), *The Nazi Voter: The Social Foundations of Fascism in Germany, 1919–1933* (Chapel Hill, NC: University of North Carolina Press).

CHOUDHRI, EHSAN U., and KOCHIN, LEVIS A. (1980), 'The Exchange Rate and the International Transmission of Business Cycle Disturbances', *Journal of Money, Credit and Banking* 12: 565–74.

CIPOLLA, CARLO M. (1976), *The Fontana Economic History of Europe*, vol. 5 (London: Fontana).

CLARKE, PETER (1988), *The Keynesian Revolution in the Making* (Oxford: Oxford University Press).

CLARKE, STEPHEN V. O. (1967), *Central Bank Cooperation, 1924–31* (New York: Federal Reserve Bank of New York).

—— (1977), *Exchange-Rate Stabilization in the Mid-1930s: Negotiating the Tripartite Agreement*, Princeton Studies in International Finance, no. 41 (Princeton: International Finance Section).

COHEN, JON S. (1972), 'The 1927 Revaluation of the Lira: A Study in Political Economy', *Economic History Review* 25: 642–54.

—— (1988), 'Was Italian Fascism a Developmental Dictatorship? Some Evidence to the Contrary', *Economic History Review* 41: 95–113.

COTTRELL, PHILIP L., and TEICHOVA, ALICE (1983), *International Business and Central Europe, 1918–1939* (Leicester: Leicester University Press).

—— LINDGREN, HÅKAN, and TEICHOVA, ALICE (eds.) (1992), *European Industry and Banking Between the Wars* (Leicester: Leicester University Press).

CRAFTS, NICHOLAS F. R. (1987), 'Long Term Unemployment in Britain in the 1930s', *Economic History Review* 40: 418–32.

—— and TONIOLO, GIANNI (1996), 'Post-War Growth: An Overview', in N. Crafts and G. Toniolo (eds.), *Europe's Economic Performance, 1945–1993* (Cambridge: Cambridge University Press), 1–37.

CROUZET, FRANÇOIS (ed.) (1993), *The Economic Development of France since 1870* (Aldershot: Edward Elgar).

DAHMÉN, ERIK (1970), *Entrepreneurial Activity and the Development of Swedish Industry* (Homewood, Ill.: Irwin).

DIMSDALE, NICHOLAS H., NICKELL, S. J., and HORSEWOOD, N. (1989), 'Real Wages and Unemployment in Britain during the 1930s', *Economic Journal* 99: 271–92.

DORNBUSCH, RUDIGER, NOLLING, WILHELM, and LAYARD, RICHARD (eds.) (1993), *Post-War Reconstruction and Lessons for the East Today* (Cambridge, Mass.: MIT Press).

DRUMMOND, IAN M. (1972), *British Economic Policy and the Empire, 1919–1939* (London: Allen and Unwin).

—— (1979), *London, Washington, and the Management of the Franc, 1936–39*, Princeton Studies in International Finance, no. 45 (Princeton: International Finance Section).

—— (1981), *The Floating Pound and the Sterling Area, 1931–1939* (Cambridge: Cambridge University Press).

—— (1987), *The Gold Standard and the International Monetary System, 1900–1939* (London: Macmillan).

ECKSTEIN, ALEXANDER (1955), 'National Income and Capital Formation in Hungary, 1900–1950', in S. Kuznets (ed.), *Income and Wealth*, V (London: Bowes and Bowes), 152–223.

EICHENGREEN, BARRY (1985), 'International Policy Coordination in Historical Perspective: A View from the Inter-War Years', in Willem Buiter and Richard Marston (eds.), *International Economic Policy Coordination* (Cambridge: Cambridge University Press), 139–78.

—— (1986), 'The Bank of France and the Sterilization of Gold, 1926–32', *Explorations in Economic History* 23: 56–84.

—— (1987), 'Unemployment in Inter-War Britain: Dole or Doldrums?', *Oxford Economic Papers* 39: 597–623.

——(1990), *Elusive Stability: Essays in the History of International Finance, 1919–1939* (Cambridge: Cambridge University Press).

——(1992a), *Golden Fetters: The Gold Standard and the Great Depression, 1919–1939* (Oxford: Oxford University Press).

——(1992b), 'The Origins and Nature of the Great Slump Revisited', *Economic History Review* 45: 213–39.

——(1994), 'Perspectives on the Borchardt Debate', in Christoph Buchheim, Michael Hutter, and Harold James (eds.), *Zerrissene Zwischenkriegszeit* (Baden-Baden: Nomos Verl.-Ges.), 177–203.

——and HATTON, TIMOTHY J. (1988), 'Inter-War Unemployment in International Perspective: An Overview', in Barry Eichengreen and Timothy J. Hatton (eds.), *Inter-War Unemployment in International Perspective* (Dordrecht: Kluwer Academic Publishers), 1–59.

——and SACHS, JEFFREY (1985), 'Exchange Rates and Economic Recovery in the 1930s', *Journal of Economic History* 45: 925–46.

——and WYPLOSZ, CHARLES (1990), 'The Economic Consequences of the Franc Poincaré', in Eichengreen (1990), 153–79.

ELBAUM, BERNARD, and LAZONICK, WILLIAM (1986), *The Decline of the British Economy* (Oxford: Oxford University Press).

ELLIS, HOWARD S. (1941), *Exchange Control in Central Europe* (Cambridge, Mass.: Harvard University Press).

FALKUS, MALCOLM E. (1975), 'The German Business Cycle in the 1920s', *Economic History Review* 28: 451–65.

FALTER, JURGEN (1986), 'Unemployment and the Radicalisation of the German Electorate 1928–1933: An Aggregate Data Analysis with Special Emphasis on the Rise of National Socialism', in Stachura (1986), 187–208.

FEARON, PETER (1979), *The Origins and Nature of the Great Slump, 1929–1932* (London: Macmillan).

——(1987), *War, Prosperity and Depression: The US Economy 1917–1945* (Deddington, Oxon.: Philip Allan).

FEDERICO, GIOVANNI (ed.) (1994), *The Economic Development of Italy since 1870* (Aldershot: Edward Elgar).

FEINSTEIN, CHARLES H. (1972), *National Income, Expenditure and Output of the United Kingdom* (Cambridge: Cambridge University Press).

——(ed.) (1995), *Banking, Currency, and Finance in Europe Between the Wars* (Oxford: Oxford University Press).

——and WATSON, KATHERINE (1995), 'Private International Capital Flows in the Inter-War Period', in Feinstein (1995), 94–130.

FEIS, HERBERT (1966), *1933: Characters in Crisis* (Boston: Little, Brown and Co.).

FELDMAN, GERALD D. (1993), *The Great Disorder: Politics, Economics and Society in the German Inflation, 1914–1924* (Oxford: Oxford University Press).

——HOLTFRERICH, CARL-LUDWIG, RITTER, GERALD A., and WITT, PETER-CHRISTIAN (eds.) (1982), *The German Inflation Reconsidered: A Preliminary Balance* (Berlin and New York: Walter de Gruyter).

FELIX, DAVID (1971), 'Reparations Reconsidered with a Vengeance', *Central European History* 4: 171–9.

FERGUSON, NIALL (1995), *Paper and Iron: Hamburg Business and German Politics in the Era of Inflation, 1897–1927* (Cambridge: Cambridge University Press).

FISCHER, WOLFRAM (ed.) (1997), *The Economic Development of Germany since 1870* (Aldershot: Edward Elgar).

FLEISIG, HEYWOOD (1972), 'The United States and the Non-European Periphery during the Early Years of the Great Depression', in Herman van der Wee (ed.), *The Great Depression Revisited* (The Hague: Martinus Nijhoff), 145–81.

FLOUD, RODERICK, and McCLOSKEY, DONALD (1994), *The Economic History of Britain since 1700*, 2nd edn. (Cambridge: Cambridge University Press).

FOREMAN-PECK, JAMES (1995), *A History of the World Economy: International Economic Relations since 1850*, 2nd edn. (London: Harvester-Wheatsheaf).

——HUGHES HALLETT, A., and MA, Y. (1996), 'Optimum International Policies for the World Depression, 1929–1933', *Économies et Sociétiés* 22: 219–42.

FRIEDMAN, MILTON, and SCHWARTZ, ANNA J. (1963), *A Monetary History of the United States* (Princeton: Princeton University Press).

GALBRAITH, JOHN KENNETH (1955), *The Great Crash, 1929* (London: Hamish Hamilton).

GALENSON, WALTER, and ZELLNER, ARNOLD (1957), 'International Comparison of Unemployment Rates', in National Bureau of Economic Research, *The Measurement and Behavior of Unemployment* (Princeton: Princeton University Press), 439–580.

GARSIDE, WILLIAM R. (1990), *British Unemployment, 1919–1939: A Study in Public Policy* (Cambridge: Cambridge University Press).

——(ed.) (1993), *Capital in Crisis: International Responses to the Great Depression* (London: Pinter).

GOOD, DAVID F. (1994), 'The Economic Lag of Central and Eastern Europe: Income Estimates for the Habsburg Successor States', *Journal of Economic History* 54: 869–91.

GRAHAM, FRANK D. (1930), *Exchange, Prices and Production in Hyperinflation in Germany, 1920–1923* (Princeton: Princeton University Press).

GRIFFITHS, RICHARD T. (ed.) (1988), *The Netherlands and the Gold Standard, 1931–1936* (Amsterdam: NEHA).

GUILLEBAUD, CLAUDE W. (1939), *The Economic Recovery of Germany* (Cambridge: Cambridge University Press).

HAAVISTO, TAARMO, and JONUNG, LARS (1995), 'Off Gold and Back Again: Finnish and Swedish Monetary Policies, 1914–1925', in Feinstein (1995), 237–66.

HAMILTON, RICHARD (1982), *Who Voted for Hitler?* (Princeton: Princeton University Press).

HARDACH, GERD (1977), *The First World War 1914–1918* (London: Allen Lane).

HARDACH, KARL (1980), *The Political Economy of Germany in the Twentieth Century* (Berkeley: University of California Press).

HARRISON, JOSEPH (1985), *The Economic History of Spain in the Twentieth Century* (Manchester: Manchester University Press).

HARRISON, MARK (1988), 'Resource Mobilization for World War II: The U.S., U.K., U.S.S.R., and Germany, 1938–1945', *Economic History Review* 41: 171–92.

HATTON, TIMOTHY J. (1987), 'The Outlines of a Keynesian Solution', in Alan Booth and Sean Glynn (eds.), *The Road to Full Employment* (London: Allen and Unwin), 82–94.

HAWLEY, ELLIS (1966), *The New Deal and the Problem of Monopolies: A Study in Economic Ambivalence* (Princeton: Princeton University Press).

HAWTREY, RALPH G. (1925), 'Public Expenditure and the Demand for Labour', *Economica* 5: 38–48.

—— (1939), *The Gold Standard in Theory and Practice*, 4th edn. (London: Longmans).

HAYES, PETER (1987), *Industry and Ideology: IG Farben in the Nazi Era* (Cambridge: Cambridge University Press).

HJERPPE, RITA (1996), *Finland's Historical National Accounts, 1860–1994* (Jvyäskylä: Jvyäskylän Yliopisto Historian Laitos).

HODNE, FRITZ (1983), *The Norwegian Economy in the Twentieth Century* (London Routledge).

HODSON, H. V. (1938), *Slump and Recovery, 1929–1937* (Oxford: Oxford University Press).

HOLTFRERICH, CARL-LUDWIG (1986), *The German Inflation, 1914–1923: Causes and Effects in International Perspective* (Berlin and New York: Walter de Gruyter).

HOWSON, SUSAN (1975), *Domestic Monetary Management in Britain, 1919–1938* (Cambridge: Cambridge University Press).

Jack, D. T. (1927), *The Restoration of European Currencies* (London: P. S. King).

Jackson, Julian (1985), *The Politics of Depression in France, 1932–1936* (Cambridge: Cambridge University Press).

——(1988), *The Popular Front in France: Defending Democracy, 1934–1938* (Cambridge: Cambridge University Press).

Jahoda, Marie, Lazarsfeld, Paul F., and Zeisel, Hans (1971 edn.), *Marienthal: The Sociography of an Unemployed Community* (New York: Aldine Atherton).

James, Harold (1985), *The Reichsbank and Public Finance in Germany, 1924–1933* (Frankfurt am Main: Fritz Knapp Verlag).

——(1986), *The German Slump: Politics and Economics, 1924–1933* (Oxford: Clarendon Press).

——Lindgren, Hakan, and Teichova, Alice (eds.) (1991), *The Role of Banks in the Inter-War Economy* (Cambridge: Cambridge University Press).

Johansen, H. (1987), *The Danish Economy in the Twentieth Century* (London: Routledge).

Jones, Joseph M. (1934), *Tariff Retaliation* (Philadelphia: University of Pennsylvania Press).

Jonung, Lars (1981), 'The Depression in Sweden and the US: A Comparison of Causes and Policies', in Karl Brunner (ed.), *The Great Depression Revisited* (The Hague: Martin Nijhoff), 286–315.

——and Ohlsson, Rolf (eds.) (1997), *The Economic Development of Sweden since 1870* (Aldershot: Edward Elgar).

Journal of European Economic History (1984), spec. suppl. to vol. 13.

Kahn, Alfred E. (1946), *Great Britain in the World Economy* (London: Pitman).

Kaiser, D. E. (1980), *Economic Diplomacy and the Origins of the Second World War: Germany, Britain and Eastern Europe, 1930–39* (Princeton: Princeton University Press).

Kaser, Michael C., and Radice, E. A. (eds.) (1985), *The Economic History of Eastern Europe, 1919–1975. I: Economic Structure and Performance Between the Two Wars* (Oxford: Oxford University Press).

————(eds.) (1986), *The Economic History of Eastern Europe, 1919–1975. II: Inter-War Policy, the War and Reconstruction* (Oxford: Oxford University Press).

Kemp, Tom (1972), *The French Economy 1913–1939: The History of a Decline* (London: Longman).

Keynes, John Maynard (1919), *The Economic Consequences of the Peace* (London: Macmillan), repr. as vol. 2 of Keynes (1971–89).

KEYNES, JOHN MAYNARD (1932), *The World's Economic Crisis and the Way of Escape*, Halley Stewart Lecture 1931 (London: Allen and Unwin), 71–88, repr. in Keynes (1971–89: vol. 21, pp. 51–62).

——(1971–89), *Collected Works*, ed. Donald. E. Moggridge, 30 vols. (London: Macmillan).

KINDLEBERGER, CHARLES P. (1973, 2nd edn. 1986), *The World in Depression, 1919–1939* (London: Allen Lane).

——(1989) 'Commercial Policy Between the Wars', in Mathias and Pollard (1989), 161–96.

KITSON, MICHAEL (1992), 'The Move to Autarky: The Political Economy of Nazi Trade Policy', DAE, University of Cambridge, Working Paper no. 9201.

——and SOLOMOU, SOLOMOS (1990), *Protection and Revival: the British Inter-War Economy* (Cambridge: Cambridge University Press).

KLEIN, BURTON H. (1959), *Germany's Economic Preparations for War* (Cambridge, Mass.: Harvard University Press).

KUZNETS, SIMON (1966), *Modern Economic Growth: Rate, Structure, and Spread* (New Haven: Yale University Press).

LAMPE, JOHN R., and JACKSON, MARTIN R. (1982), *Balkan Economic History, 1550–1950: From Imperial Borderlands to Developed Nations* (Bloomington, Ind.: Indiana University Press).

LANDAU, ZBIGNIEW, and TOMASZEWSKI, JERZY (1988), *The Polish Economy in the Twentieth Century* (London: Routledge).

LANDES, DAVID (1969), *The Unbound Prometheus: Technological Change and Industrial Development in Western Europe from 1750 to the Present* (Cambridge: Cambridge University Press).

LARY, HAL B. (1943), *The United States in the World Economy* (Washington, DC: US Department of Commerce).

LAURSEN, KARSTEN, and PEDERSEN, JORGEN (1964), *The German Inflation, 1918–1923* (Amsterdam: North Holland).

LEAGUE OF NATIONS (1927), *Report and Proceedings of the World Economic Conference, held at Geneva 4–23 May 1927*, vol. 1 (Geneva: League of Nations).

——(1931), *The Agricultural Crisis* (Geneva: League of Nations).

——(1932), *International Trade Statistics, 1930* (Geneva: League of Nations).

——(1933), *World Economic Survey 1932/33* (Geneva: League of Nations).

——(1937), *Monthly Bulletin of Statistics* 18 (Geneva: League of Nations).

——(1939a), *Review of World Trade, 1938* (Geneva: League of Nations).

——(1939b), *International Trade Statistics, 1938* (Geneva: League of Nations).

——(1941), *Europe's Trade* (Geneva: League of Nations).

—— (1945), *Industrialisation and Foreign Trade* (Geneva: League of Nations).

LEE, BRADFORD A. (1982), 'The New Deal Reconsidered', *Wilson Quarterly* 6: 62–76.

LESTER, RICHARD A. (1939), *Monetary Experiments, Early American and Recent Scandinavian* (Princeton: Princeton University Press).

LEWCHUK, WAYNE (1987), *American Technology and the British Vehicle Industry* (Cambridge: Cambridge University Press).

LEWIS, W. ARTHUR (1949), *Economic Survey, 1919–1939* (London: Allen and Unwin).

MCNEIL, WILLIAM C. (1986), *American Money and the Weimar Republic* (New York: Columbia University Press).

MADDISON, ANGUS (1982), *Phases of Capitalist Development* (Oxford: Oxford University Press).

—— (1991), *Dynamic Forces in Capitalist Development: A Long-Run Comparative View* (Oxford: Oxford University Press).

—— (1995), *Monitoring the World Economy 1820–1992* (Paris: OECD).

MAIER, CHARLES S. (1975), *Recasting Bourgeois Europe: Stabilization in France, Germany and Italy in the Decade after World War I* (Princeton: Princeton University Press).

—— (1987), *In Search of Stability: Explanations in Historical Political Economy* (Cambridge: Cambridge University Press).

MAIZELS, ALFRED (1965), *Industrial Growth and World Trade* (Cambridge: Cambridge University Press).

MALENBAUM, WILFRID (1953), *The World Wheat Economy, 1885–1939* (Cambridge, Mass.: Harvard University Press).

MANTOUX, ÉTIENNE (1946), *The Carthaginian Peace—or the Economic Consequences of Mr. Keynes* (Oxford: Oxford University Press).

MARKS, SALLY (1978), 'The Myths of Reparations', *Central European History* 3: 231–55.

MARTÍN-ACEÑA, PABLO (1995), 'Spanish Banking in the Inter-War Period', in Feinstein (1995), 502–27.

—— and SIMPSON, JAMES (eds.) (1995), *The Economic Development of Spain since 1870* (Aldershot: Edward Elgar).

MATHIAS, PETER, and POLLARD, SIDNEY (eds.) (1989), *The Cambridge Economic History of Europe: The Industrial Economies. VIII: The Development of Economic and Social Policies* (Cambridge: Cambridge University Press).

MATIS, HERBERT (ed.) (1994), *The Economic Development of Austria since 1870* (Aldershot: Edward Elgar).

MATTHEWS, ROBERT C. O., FEINSTEIN, CHARLES H., and ODLING-SMEE, JOHN C. (1982), *British Economic Growth, 1856–1973* (Oxford: Oxford University Press).

MAZOWER, MARK (1991), *Greece and the Inter-War Economic Crisis* (Oxford: Oxford University Press).

MIDDLETON, ROGER (1985), *Towards the Managed Economy: Keynes, the Treasury and the Fiscal Policy Debate of the 1930s* (London: Methuen).

MILWARD, ALAN S. (1965), *The German Economy at War* (London: Athlone).

——(1977), *War, Economy and Society, 1939–1945* (London: Allen Lane).

——(1984), *The Reconstruction of Western Europe, 1945–51* (London: Methuen).

——(1992), *The European Rescue of the Nation State* (Berkeley: University of California Press).

MITCHELL, BRIAN R. (1978), *European Historical Statistics, 1750–1975*, 2nd edn. (London: Macmillan).

MOGGRIDGE, DONALD E. (1972), *British Monetary Policy, 1924–1931: The Norman Conquest of $4.86* (Cambridge: Cambridge University Press).

——(1989), 'The Gold Standard and National Financial Policies, 1913–1939', in Mathias and Pollard (1989), 250–314.

MONTGOMERY, ARTHUR (1938), *How Sweden Overcame the Depression, 1930–1933* (Stockholm: Alb. Bonniers Boktryckeri).

MORGAN, E. VICTOR (1952), *Studies in British Financial Policy, 1914–1925* (London: Macmillan).

MOURÉ, KENNETH (1991), *Managing the Franc Poincaré: Economic Understanding and Political Constraint in French Monetary Policy, 1928–1936* (Cambridge: Cambridge University Press).

MOWAT, CHARLES LOCH (1955), *Britain Between the Wars, 1918–1940* (London: Methuen).

MUNTING, ROGER, and HOLDERNESS, B. A. (1991), *Crisis, Recovery, and War: An Economic History of Continental Europe, 1918–1945* (London: Philip Allan).

NEAL, LARRY (1979), 'The Economics and Finance of Bilateral Clearing Agreements in Germany, 1934–8', *Economic History Review* 32: 391–404.

NEVIN, EDWARD (1955), *The Mechanism of Cheap Money* (Cardiff: University of Wales Press).

NIXON, EDGAR B. (ed.) (1969), *Franklin D. Roosevelt and Foreign Affairs, January 1933–February 1934*, vol. 1 (Cambridge, Mass.: Harvard University Press).

NÖTEL, RUDOLF (1986), 'International Credit and Finance', in Kaser and Radice (1986), 170–295.

NURKSE, RAGNAR (1944), *International Currency Experience: Lessons of the Inter-War Period* (Geneva: League of Nations).

Ó GRÁDA, CORMAC (ed.) (1994), *The Economic Development of Ireland since 1870* (Aldershot: Edward Elgar).

OHKAWA, KAZUSHI, and SHINOHARA, MIYOHEI (1979), *Patterns of Japanese Economic Development* (Berkeley: University of California Press).

OHLIN, BERTIL (1931), *The Course and Phases of the World Economic Depression* (Geneva: League of Nations).

ORDE, ANNE (1990), *British Policy and European Reconstruction after the First World War* (Cambridge: Cambridge University Press).

ORWELL, GEORGE (1937), *The Road to Wigan Pier* (London: Gollancz).

OVERY, RICHARD JAMES (1994), *War and Economy in the Third Reich* (Oxford: Oxford University Press).

——(1996), *The Nazi Economic Recovery*, 2nd edn. (Cambridge: Cambridge University Press).

PERSSON, GUNNAR (ed.) (1993), *The Economic Development of Denmark since 1870* (Aldershot: Edward Elgar).

POLLARD, SIDNEY (ed.) (1970), *The Gold Standard and Employment Policy Between the Wars* (London: Methuen).

——(1992), *The Development of the British Economy, 1914–1990* (London: Arnold).

POOLE, KENYON E. (1939), *German Financial Policies 1932–1939* (Cambridge, Mass.: Harvard University Press).

PRADOS DE LA ESCOSURA, LEANDRO (1995), *Spain's Gross Domestic Product, 1850–1993: Quantitative Conjectures* (Madrid: Universidad Carlos III de Madrid).

PRYOR, F. L., PRYOR, Z. P., STÁDNÍK, M., and STALLER, G. (1971), 'Czechoslovak Aggregate Production in the Inter-War Period', *Review of Income and Wealth* 17: 35–59.

RADICE, E. A. (1985), 'General Characteristics of the Region Between the Wars', in Kaser and Radice (1985), 23–65.

RICHARDSON, HARRY W. (1967), *Economic Recovery in Britain, 1932–39* (London: Weidenfeld and Nicolson).

ROBBINS, LIONEL (1934), *The Great Depression* (London: Macmillan).

ROSSI, N., and TONIOLO, GIANNI (1993), 'Un secolo di sviluppo economico italiano: Permanenze e discontinuità', *Rivista di storia economica* NS 10: 145–75.

ROYAL INSTITUTE OF INTERNATIONAL AFFAIRS (1932), *World Agriculture: An International Survey* (London: Humphrey Milford).

——(1935), *Unemployment, An International Problem. A Report by a Study Group of Members of the Royal Institute of International Affairs* (Oxford: Oxford University Press).

——(1937), *The Problem of International Investment* (London: Oxford University Press).

SANCHEZ-ALBORNOZ, NICOLAS (1987), *The Economic Modernization of Spain,*

1836–1930 (New York: New York University Press).

SARGENT, THOMAS J. (1983), 'The Ends of Four Big Inflations', in Thomas Sargent (ed.), *Rational Expectations and Inflation* (New York: Harper and Row), 40–109.

SAYERS, RICHARD S. (1976), *The Bank of England, 1891–1944* (Cambridge: Cambridge University Press).

SCHUBERT, AUREL (1991), *The Credit-Anstalt Crisis of 1931* (Cambridge: Cambridge University Press).

SCHUKER, STEPHEN A. (1976), *The End of French Predominance in Europe: The Financial Crisis of 1924 and the Adoption of the Dawes Plan* (Chapel Hill, NC: University of North Carolina Press).

——(1988), *American 'Reparations' to Germany, 1919–33: Implications for the Third World Debt Crisis*, Princeton Studies in International Finance, no. 61 (Princeton: International Finance Section).

SILVERMAN, D. P. (1982), *Reconstructing Europe after the Great War* (Cambridge, Mass.: Harvard University Press).

SOMMARIVA, ANDREA, and TULLIO, GIUSEPPE (1987), *German Macroeconomic History, 1880–1979* (London: Macmillan).

STACHURA, PETER D. (ed.) (1986), *Unemployment and the Great Depression in Weimar Germany* (New York: St. Martin's Press).

STOLPER, GUSTAV, HAUSER, KARL, and BORCHARDT, KNUT (1967), *The German Economy, 1870 to the Present*, 2nd edn. (London: Weidenfeld and Nicolson).

SVENNILSON, I. (1954), *Growth and Stagnation in the European Economy* (Geneva: United Nations Economic Commission for Europe).

TEICHOVA, ALICE (1985), *An Economic Background to Munich: International Business and Czechoslovakia, 1918–38* (Cambridge: Cambridge University Press).

——(1988), *The Czechoslovak Economy, 1918–1980* (London: Routledge).

——(1989), 'East-Central and South-East Europe 1913–1939', in Mathias and Pollard (1989), 887–983.

TEMIN, PETER (1971), 'The Beginning of the Depression in Germany', *Economic History Review* 24: 240–8.

——(1989), *Lessons from the Great Depression* (Cambridge, Mass.: MIT Press).

——(1991), 'Soviet and Nazi Economic Planning in the 1930s', *Economic History Review* 44: 573–93.

——and WIGMORE, BARRIE A. (1990), 'The End of One Big Deflation', *Explorations in Economic History* 27: 483–502.

THOMAS, MARK (1988), 'Labour Market Structure and the Nature of Unemployment in Inter-War Britain', in Barry Eichengreen and Timothy J.

Hatton (eds.), *Inter-War Unemployment in International Perspective* (Dordrecht: Kluwer Academic Publishers), 97–148.

THOMAS, TERRY (1981), 'Aggregate Demand in the United Kingdom, 1918–1945', in Roderick Floud and Donald McCloskey (ed.), *The Economic History of Britain since 1700*, 1st edn., vol. 2 (Cambridge: Cambridge University Press), 332–406.

THOMSON, DAVID (1966), *Europe since Napoleon* (Harmondsworth: Penguin).

TIMOSHENKO, VLADIMIR P. (1953), *World Agriculture and the Depression* (Ann Arbor: University of Michigan).

TOMLINSON, JIM (1990), *Public Policy and the Economy since 1900* (Oxford: Oxford University Press).

TONIOLO, GIANNI (1980), *L'economia dell'Italia Fascista* (Rome: Bari Laterza).

TRACHTENBERG, M. (1980), *Reparations in World Politics: France and European Economic Diplomacy, 1916–1923* (New York: Columia University Press).

TRACY, MICHAEL (1964), *Agriculture in Western Europe: Crisis and Adaptation since 1880* (London: Jonathan Cape).

UNITED NATIONS (1949), *International Capital Movements during the Inter-War Period* (Lake Success, NY: United Nations).

US DEPARTMENT OF COMMERCE (1975), *Historical Statistics of the United States, Colonial Times to 1970* (Washington, DC: Government Printing Office).

VAN DER WEE, HERMAN, and BLOMME, JAN (eds.) (1997), *The Economic Development of Belgium since 1870* (Aldershot: Edward Elgar).

VAN ZANDEN, JAN LUITEN, (ed.) (1996), *The Economic Development of Netherlands since 1870* (Aldershot: Edward Elgar).

VON KRUEDENER, JURGEN BARON (ed.) (1990), *Economic Crisis and Political Collapse: The Weimar Republic, 1924–1933* (New York: Berg).

VON TUNZELMANN, G. NICHOLAS (1982), 'Structural Change and Leading Sectors in British Manufacturing, 1907–68', in C. P. Kindleberger and G. di Tella (eds.), *Economics in the Long View*, vol. 3 (London: Macmillan).

VOTH, HANS-JOACHIM (1995), 'Did High Wages or High Interest Rates Bring Down the Weimar Republic? A Cointegration Model of Investment in Germany, 1925–1930', *Journal of Economic History* 55: 801–21.

WAIGHT, L. (1939), *The History and Mechanism of the Exchange Equalisation Account* (Cambridge: Cambridge University Press).

WALRÉ DE BORDES, J. (1924), *The Austrian Crown* (London: P. S. King).

WEBB, STEVEN B. (1989), *Hyperinflation and Stabilization in Weimar Germany: Policies, Politics, and Market Reactions* (Oxford: Oxford University Press).

WELK, WILLIAM (1939), *Fascist Economic Policy* (Cambridge, Mass.: Harvard University Press).

WHEELER-BENNETT, JOHN W. (1933), *The Wreck of Reparations* (London: Allen and Unwin).

WILLIAMS, JOHN H. (1922), 'German Foreign Trade and Reparations Payments', *Quarterly Journal of Economics* 36: 482–503.

WOLFE, MARTIN (1957), *The French Franc Between the Wars, 1919–1939* (New York: Columbia University Press).

WOYTINSKY, W. S., and WOYTINSKY E. S. (1955), *World Commerce and Government* (New York: Twentieth Century Fund).

ZAMAGNI, VERA (1993), *The Economic History of Italy, 1860–1990* (Oxford: Oxford University Press).

Index